Broken Record

SUNY series in Feminist Criticism and Theory

Michelle A. Massé, editor

Broken Record

Gendered Abuse in Academia

Edited by

Mary K. Holland, Carrie Rohman,
and Carlyn Ena Ferrari

Afterword by

Sara Ahmed

SUNY PRESS

Published by State University of New York Press, Albany

© 2025 State University of New York

All rights reserved

Printed in the United States of America

EU GPSR Authorised Representative:
Logos Europe, 9 rue Nicolas Poussin, 17000, La Rochelle, France
contact@logoseurope.eu

For information, contact State University of New York Press, Albany, NY
www.sunypress.edu

Library of Congress Cataloging-in-Publication Data

Names: Holland, Mary, 1970– editor. | Rohman, Carrie, editor. | Ferrari,
   Carlyn Ena, 1984– editor.
Title: Broken record : gendered abuse in academia / edited by Mary K.
   Holland, Carrie Rohman, and Carlyn Ena Ferrari.
Description: Albany : State University of New York Press, [2025] | Series:
   SUNY series in feminist criticism and theory | Includes bibliographical
   references and index.
Identifiers: LCCN 2024042812 | ISBN 9798855801965 (hardcover : alk. paper) |
   ISBN 9798855801989 (ebook) | ISBN 9798855801972 (pbk. : alk. paper)
Subjects: LCSH: Sexual harassment in universities and colleges—United
   States. | Sex discrimination in higher education—United States. | Women
   in higher education—United States—Social conditions.
Classification: LCC LC212.862 .B76 2025 | DDC 305.43/378—dc23/eng/20241214
LC record available at https://lccn.loc.gov/2024042812

For all who have suffered abuse in academia,
especially those whose stories remain untold

Contents

**Part Two
Resistance and Consequences**

Part Three
Theorizing and Enacting Change
as Individuals and Collectives

Introduction

"A Fragile Archive"

MARY K. HOLLAND, CARRIE ROHMAN,
AND CARLYN ENA FERRARI

What are the words you do not yet have? What do you need to say?
What are the tyrannies you swallow day by day and attempt to make
your own until you will sicken and die of them, still in silence?

—Audre Lorde, *Sister Outsider*[1]

The ubiquity and diversity of gendered abuse in academia is no secret.
For over twenty years, scholars across fields have been researching and
reporting on the multitude of ways in which women[2] in academia, particularly women of color, are routinely harassed, disadvantaged, impeded,
belittled, bullied, discounted, threatened, and sexually assaulted, and on
the oppressive systems that enable such abuse.[3] Sara Ahmed's monumen-
tal *Complaint!* (2021) has recently provided a grisly interior view of how
these systems also justify, erase, or cover up gender-based violence against
women, turning complaint procedures into vehicles for punishing those who
complain. Ultimately it illustrates the inherent futility of most attempts to
bring sweeping change or public justice against individual actors through
official means, including the efforts of the complaint collective to which
Ahmed belongs and around whose experience the book is organized. Yet
Complaint! also delivers a powerful message about possibilities for future
activism: the act of complaining, however institutionally unsuccessful, *does*

1

lead to meaningful change, and never more so than when others are part of and privy to the complaint.

That is, women in academia need to complain more, not less. But we need to do it not only or perhaps not even primarily through the choking channels dubiously offered by self-interested institutions. And we need to do it together. Elsewhere, Ahmed refers to the classic texts and encounters that attest to the struggles and resistances of "living a feminist life" as "a fragile archive, a body assembled from shattering, from splattering, an archive whose fragility gives us responsibility: to take care" (17). Together, we three editors created *Broken Record* as a contribution to that archive, an invitation to assemble, a way of taking care.

Academia is a world freighted with white-male history and structured according to masculine power and privilege. It is an institutional system created by and for white, cis men, where male academics continue to set the cultural standard and typically succeed at much higher rates than do women, especially women of color.[4] And yet, perhaps because of its associations with "progressive" and idealized discourses of curiosity, academic freedom, agency, and intellectual autonomy, the academy is still aligned with "equality" and "equity" in our cultural imaginary. Academics themselves have a difficult time confronting the gendered abuse that is endemic in our profession, because many of us think of academia as a world apart, as a "special" and idyllic place, that is ennobled and therefore immune to unenlightened cruelties. And so, a significant disjunction exists between the profession we tend to idealize and the one we inhabit.[5]

In her 1938 musings in *Three Guineas*, Virginia Woolf asked us to consider what it would mean for women to follow their educated brothers into the professions. She provided a blistering account of the violences of colleges and universities and repeatedly imagined burning them and their hypocrisies to the ground. "It is true that for the past twenty years we have been admitted to the Civil Service and to the Bar," she wrote, "but our position there is still very precarious and our authority of the slightest" (12). Nearly a hundred years later, this sentiment still resonates. Woolf was more than prescient in warning women about what we would face as we joined the ranks of patriarchal institutions. Our contemporary failures to confront the institutional harms that continue to be reproduced within our profession—that continue to be *central to* our profession—exacerbate her prophecies all the more.[6]

The 2014 book, *Women Who Make a Fuss: The Unfaithful Daughters of Virginia Woolf*, examines in greater detail why women do not flourish in academia today. Written by two Belgian philosophers, Isabelle Stengers and Vinciane Despret, and a collective of academic women, the project asks if women in academia have changed the forms of thought in their respective fields. While the primary authors make it clear that experiences of gendered "discrimination" are not the centerpiece of their project, the disillusioning realities of being a woman academic inevitably seep into their powerful volume. Stengers and Despret highlight the entrapments of academic life, explaining how "seeking to make a career in the university, is to be captured by it (for both young men and women)." But primarily for women, as their incorporation of multiple female voices attests, "*once you are inside, they will look for ways to devitalize you*" (Sironi qtd. in Stengers and Despret 103, original emphasis). "Once you are inside": this phrase constitutes a powerful nod, first to the extraordinary labor required to make it "in" at all, and second to the desperation of the current climate, in which any sort of security in academia seems increasingly out of reach, particularly for emerging teacher-scholars. Most women academics, especially those in the precarious humanities, are always aware of their disposability, and so can feel extra "grateful" to have and hold onto a position in an abusive profession.

Another piquing phrase from Sironi should get our attention: "they will look for ways." One of the great ironies of working in academia is the extraordinary disjunction between what people in power profess, research, and teach in a public-facing manner, and the ways they actively abuse their women colleagues in deliberate and calculated ways, ways that often give the lie to their outward commitments to critiques of power. "Academic mobbing," a kind of coordinated bullying designed to control access to power, opportunities, and all kinds of support in academic careers, is common in practice but rarely researched, and has been shown to typically target highly competent, high-achieving, and "outspoken" women faculty members.[7] Such bullying takes many forms and is often intersectional. In a 2022 piece in the *Chronicle of Higher Education*, Gillian Marshall describes her tenure denial as a racist and sexist form of bullying, motivated by her accomplishments: "They were bullying me to get out. They denied me tenure because I am a Black woman, and I am a successful Black woman." All forms of mobbing are alike, though, in making accomplished women feel unwelcome, out of place, *devitalized*, using socially and professionally acceptable behaviors that are actually polite and sophisticated forms of workplace abuse.

Academic systems and hierarchies encourage, sustain, and reward these and other kinds of gendered abuses. A common context for them is the "mentorship" relationship of teacher and student, grad professor and grad student, or "senior" and "junior" faculty member.[8] These power imbalances are the bread and butter of academic systems and yet, unlike most larger businesses, universities often have no formal mechanisms for keeping those with power in check and accountable.[9] Many colleges and universities even lack a neutral ombudsperson to receive and arbitrate reports of abuse. Moreover, at some institutions, any formal complaint one files will become part of their tenure file, effectively ensuring that no professor will file a formal grievance before earning tenure. Meanwhile, as two of our contributors detail, informal complaints and complaints that are officially rejected or dismissed—often without proper investigation—are not attached to perpetrators' files, allowing them to repeat their harassment on further targets.[10] And so, one abusive colleague or department head is replaced with the next one, and "senior" colleagues can continue to haze and bully their pretenure—or tenured but more "junior"—colleagues, ad infinitum.

These cycles of abuse are reproduced because they are endemic and, to some degree, accepted and even rewarded within academic systems. Abusive faculty members are often those who succeed the most at colleges and universities, receiving institutional awards, endowed or leadership positions, and other material and professional supports, while their harassment and bullying of women are ignored or known by only a small subset of faculty members. And as our contributors reveal, often the senior harassers are other women.[11] Annette Kolodny testified to this painful reality in "I Dreamed Again That I Was Drowning" (1989), where she states that the "corrosive *professionalization* of identity within patriarchal institutions . . . constrains women from bonding with one another" and so prevents them from supporting or protecting each other (178, original italics). Moreover, as Robillard catalogs, certain women academics can make themselves "untouchable" by labeling themselves as feminists (100), or simply by working in a gender-centered discipline.

Provosts and deans are rarely trained to intervene in abusive climates that are gendered, often chalking tensions up to "personality conflicts" as a way to euphemize and avoid addressing serious harassment and power abuse.[12] Some of the scant research on academic mobbing notes that the concept of "personality conflict" is prevalent in academia because it neutralizes real abuse, discrimination, and harassment, effectively diminishing and erasing what is often targeted, deliberate, and ongoing mistreatment of particular faculty members, especially high-achieving women (Khoo

2010). Academic institutions therefore replicate the kinds of gendered abuses that individuals experience in other forms of relationship, such as intimate partner abuse and abuse in marriage and family structures. Abuse of this kind is "covered over," socially accepted, or explained away by the systems in which it occurs. The failures of various therapeutic models in these analogous scenarios operate similarly in academia. For instance, marriage counseling regularly attributes problems in marriage to "communication differences," when in fact, one partner is abusing another.[13] "Personality conflicts" and "communication differences" trivialize, distort, and ultimately edit out serious and damaging mistreatment. In the case of higher education, the recurring motif of "personality conflicts" lets institutions and higher administration off the hook, because it suggests that "nothing can be done," since all of the conflict is "personal."

In the face of such rhetorical contortion and erasure we offer this book, a record of unjust and abusive acts, of professional punishment and personal suffering, as documented by the unduly harmed in fierce rejection of the gaslighting fantasies spun by those with systemic power and their obsequious allies. It is not a record of the broken, but an archive of unfairly broken records of deserved achievement, and a "feminist ear" (*Complaint!* 3) for the complaints that must repeat like broken records, disturbing the oppressive peace, demanding movement and change.[14]

A History of the Archive

Gendered abuse in academia goes far beyond sexual harassment and violence, so our approach needs to go beyond the work that has been and is being inspired by #MeToo. And yet that social movement has something to teach us about how we might make gender-based abuse in academia more visible and motivate more people to care about it. Activists and scholars had been theorizing forms, causes, and resistance to sexual violence for over a century,[15] but it took the deluge of personal narratives about sexual violence sparked by #MeToo in 2017, when Tarana Burke's "Me Too" movement from 2006 was appropriated and went viral,[16] to make the larger public pay attention and to begin to enact real change. Powerful men across industries lost their jobs; some went to prison. Women across the world pressed successfully for legal reforms. Popular culture increasingly began to investigate and educate people about consent, gaslighting, testimonial injustice, and the intricacies of misogyny.

Meanwhile, academia has done what it tends to do with energizing pop-culture phenomena: we converted the social-media movement into a new batch of academic studies. Over the past seven years, the goals and energy of #MeToo have registered across fields and disciplines—in scores of published articles and books about the influence and uses of #MeToo, changes in pedagogy and curricula, and robust use of #MeToo on Academic Twitter.[17] This movement might also partially explain the recent wave of scholarly books about rape and sexual violence in general and on campuses in particular.[18] Such incitements evidence newly awakened or reenergized academics doing what many of us consider the most crucial work of academia: using our research, writing, and teaching to cause crucial change in the world. But there is little evidence of any corresponding awakening in the institution of academia itself. It has not yet reckoned with the message and motivations of #MeToo, and #MeToo has done little to affect the *lives* of women academics. *Broken Record* aims to bring the transformative power of #MeToo to bear on the shapes of academic institutions by harnessing its keenest tool, the personal narrative.[19]

In doing so, we contribute to a type of academic feminist activism—broadcasting the voices of oppressed, harassed, and abused women—that did not start with but has been reenergized by the general public's hunger for and heeding of #MeToo stories. Memoirs about the effects of misogyny on the experiences of women academics go back at least to Kass Fleisher's *Talking out of School* (2008), which unflinchingly documents how patriarchal systems shape our interactions with students, mentors, and colleagues, how these systems intersect with racism, and how we can wind up participating in them for our own self-protection. Victoria Reyes's hybrid work of memoir, feminist of color critique, and sociological analysis, *Academic Outsider: Stories of Exclusion and Hope* (2022), exposes how the oppressions that academics study outside the academy are the same oppressions the academy perpetrates. Other recent memoirs have focused on specifically sexual offenses, as in Donna Freitas's *Consent* (2019) and Carolyn Chalmers's *They Don't Want Her There* (2022). Similarly, recent years have seen many collections, orchestrated by academics, of sexual-violence survivor stories.[20] One of these, edited by Laura Gray-Rosendale (2020), zeroes in on survivors in the academy. The writers in that volume, all women, use their own experience of sexual violence (experienced within and outside academia) to reflect on the effects of such violence on every facet of their work, including, as for Tanya Serisier, their own theorizing of rape and sexual violence. *Broken Record* aims to continue such work while extending its context, documenting how not only sexual violence but all forms of gendered abuse manifest, how it feels and causes suffering, and how it shapes women academics and their careers.

It also aims to join and amplify the voices of women who have begun collecting evidence of such abuses. One of these, J. Libarkin, hosts Academic-Sexual-Misconduct-Database.org, which collects publicly documented instances of resolved or ongoing cases of sexual harassment and abuse in academia in the US. The site has only been up since 2016, and yet lists over 1,200 incidents. Karen Kelskey began a crowdsourced survey of sexual harassment in the academy in 2017, and the site was so barraged that she ultimately shut it down to new posts. The original nearly 2,500 entries, dated 2017 to 2018, can still be viewed as a Google spreadsheet on her website, theprofessorisin.com. With descriptions of abuse categorized according to the institutional position of abuser and abused, type of institution, and department, the spreadsheet is horribly akin to a similar one called "Women Count USA," which Dawn Wilcox created in 2017 to capture the details of the overwhelming number of women murdered by men in the US every day. More recently, Hansen and Nilsson's *Critical Storytelling: Experiences of Power Abuse in Academia* (2022) has provided a useful and visible open-access collection of first-person narratives of power abuses in academia.

Still, as academics, we know that documentation and testimony are not enough. The power of academics' testimony lies in our ability to theorize resistance and change out of our own experience, fueled by it, which is what the contributors to this volume collectively do. In this way, our most salient predecessors are *Presumed Incompetent* (edited by Gutiérrez y Muhs, Niemann, González, & Harris, 2012) and *Presumed Incompetent II* (edited by Niemann, Gutiérrez y Muhs, & González, 2020), whose essays explore the harassment experienced by women faculty of color at the intersection of gender, race, and class disadvantage. These collections use personal stories to "bridge the epistemological gap that frequently appears between the lives of people with a particular privilege and those that lack that privilege" (*PI* 3), contextualized in and by analysis of academic systems, structures, and cultures to theorize mechanisms for change. While Dr. Shardé M. Davis's *Being Black in the Ivory: Truth-Telling about Racism in Higher Education* (2024) expands on the work begun by these volumes by using personal narrative to explore specifically anti-Black[21] racism and its consequences in academia, *Broken Record* builds on the collections' intersectional work and theorizing testimony by focusing more broadly on accounts of all kinds of gendered abuse in academia, enriched by the wisdom gained from Ahmed's discoveries about the institutional workings of complaint. In several cases, our contributors had formed their own complaint collectives before we found them; in others, they formed collectives as a response to this project's invitation. These collectives themselves signal the impact of Ahmed's "complaint"—her book itself, but also the institutional complaint that inspired it and the collective whose mutual work and support over many painful years enabled that institutional complaint.[22]

We hope that *Broken Record* will operate as its own complaint collective, by bringing together the complaints of a diverse group of people, and by providing a platform for the voices of these complaint collectives whose work had already begun. In so doing, we are responding to every facet of Ahmed's call for continued feminist activism around gendered academic abuse: to document the lived experiences of those who suffer; as consciousness-raising for those who remain unaware of such abuses; to form collectives and assert the collectivity of our experiences; to gather information about the nature of such experiences and their causes; to help others complain and keep complaints going, regardless of their measurable success in institutions; and to share in the enormous emotional labor of complaint. We address those who have suffered, offering empathy, support, and the opportunity to band together in resistance; and we address those who can't yet imagine what such abuses look and feel like, how common they are, how detrimental to all of us who value the efficacy of academic institutions. In conversation with this archive, we also aim to cultivate an emerging subfield in critical university studies focused on the roles played by gender in academic abuse. All our voices together contribute to the long, "slow activism" (*Complaint!* 285) that leads to real and lasting change.

Contributing to the Archive

No one book can represent every form or setting of abuse. Still, the twenty-three chapters we include here demonstrate that gendered abuse is ubiquitous in higher education worldwide. While the overwhelming similarities and patterns that emerge from these narratives make visible common structures of power and methods of wielding and maintaining it, they also illustrate how abuse manifests differently in particular academic cultures and fields and the specificity of each person's experience of it. Our contributors represent experiences of gendered abuse from across academic fields, disciplines, and schools—including humanities, STEM, and social sciences—as well as in university administration and libraries. They write about abuses experienced while working in higher-education institutions across the US and around the world, in Canada, India, Bangladesh, Tunisia, Brazil, Switzerland, South Africa, and the Philippines. Reminding us that abuse can happen anywhere, they describe demoralizing and harrowing encounters in classrooms, their own and others' offices, and library stacks, at conferences, during interviews, off campus, and while away on field research. They write of being sexually or verbally assaulted and demeaned as graduate students, early-to-late career professors, social workers, or administrators. Their abusers are teachers, mentors, students, colleagues, chairs, and administrators, and are male and female, white and of color. Sometimes their abusers are proponents or even institutional representatives of Title IX or Diversity, Equity, and Inclusion groups. What abusers have in common is not any particular privilege of gender or race, but the ability and desire to defend the institutional power structures that benefit them.[23] In Reyes's terminology, abusers consolidate their own "academic citizenship"—certain rights, responsibilities, and privileges, but also a sense of belonging and acceptance (42–43)—by excluding and marginalizing others.

The abused share in a constellation of identity aspects that locate them outside the white, cis, het patriarchy that dominates all social relations in and outside academia. Sarah Cheshire testifies to the years of career damage that can be caused by sexual exploitation of students, confirming Robillard's insights about men's "feelings of entitlement to women's bodies, to their affection and attention, and to their space" and men's ability to infiltrate the thoughts of women, as a senior male "colonizes the young professor's physical and mental space" in various ways (91). Cheshire and Souhir Zekri Masson also demonstrate the ways that English faculty members have a facility for language that enables particularly sophisticated and sinister kinds of abuse (Robillard 105). Aimee Parkison's account of being harassed by a male student, on the other hand, reminds us that for women in the classroom, the power of patriarchy can trump any authority we have as professors. When religious institutions combine with higher education, gender abuse gets woven into the fabric of campus practices and policies in particularly offensive ways, as we see from Rachel Noorda's account of patriarchal hiring practices at a Mormon institution in the US, and from Zekri Masson's description of suffering the confluence of patriarchal gender politics and conservative Islam at an institution in Tunisia.

These hegemonic structures of power also shape the contours of the relationships in which such abuse becomes possible and common, with multiple markers of systemic disadvantage multiplying vectors of abuse and subtracting potential allies. As a result, women of color are at risk of disparagement by men and women of any race and can struggle to find effective allyship in their institutions, as detailed by Carlyn Ferrari and Nicole Carr. While Ferrari considers the particular problem of white women demeaning and harassing Black women in academia, Carr confronts intraracial harassment between Black academics. Likewise, queer academics face obstacles and abuse from a variety of angles, with regional differences exacerbating this form of abuse: Nancy Pathak attests not only to the harassment she experienced because of her queer politics and body positivity performance, but also to her particular vulnerability in an academic system in Delhi whose antidiscrimination laws only protect cis-het women.

Abuse occurs in different ways and intensities across academic disciplines as well. Traditionally male-dominated STEM fields provide opportunities and spaces at every educational and career step for women to be preyed on by powerful men.[24] While one anonymous contributor details her account of a supervisor's predatory behavior in the very unsafe space of remote field research, Christina Gallup et al. examine the gendered abuse causing the toxic environment of one math and statistics department. Perhaps more surprisingly, the methodology of philosophy provides insidious opportunities for abuse, as Darlene Demandante and Raphaella Miranda illustrate in their account of being reprimanded as "irrational"—a cardinal sin for a philosopher—when they complained about gendered abuse at their university in the Philippines.

In every case, these abuses are enabled by academic institutions' enactment of the same systems that regulate larger society—white supremacy, patriarchy, heteronormativity, and binary gender primary among them. Carolyn Carpan details the ways in which the classic strategies of misogyny infiltrate academic libraries, making bullying, gaslighting, verbal and financial abuse, habitual disparagement, and physical threats as integral to her workspace as to all the other spaces in which men routinely oppress and belittle women. Ferrari also speaks to ways in which misogyny becomes misogynoir, adding hypersexualizing and other racist tropes to the oppressive strategies suffered by Black women in academia. Kudzaiishe Vanyoro recognizes the same racist roots of sexual harassment in the abuses he witnessed as an undergraduate student in South Africa where, he acknowledges, colonialism may be used by men as a "scapegoat" for excusing their misogynist treatment of women. Sexualizing women to undercut them is so common as to almost disappear from view in patriarchal cultures, but many additional contributors describe how insidious, toxic, and extensive this kind of abuse is in academia. Of course, academics are also harassed and disparaged because of other power structures not represented by these pages but often intersectional with the experiences documented in them, including ablism and ageism.

Some of our writers explicitly make these connections between patterns of gendered abuse in academia and other non-academic systems of gendered domination. (Karen) Irene Countryman-Roswurm, who experienced abuse while directing a center to combat human trafficking, compares the dynamics that enabled her abuse and protected her abusers with those of the human trafficking she was hired to fight. And of course the many faces of misogynistic abuse documented by Carpan are the same as those experienced by victims of domestic violence and abuse, and the misogynist assumptions behind them are the same ones that regulate the procedures and rulings of family court, where many victims of domestic violence are retraumatized and further harmed while attempting to seek protection for themselves and their children.[25]

Several contributors demonstrate the dangerous consequences of universities' ineffective or nonexistent policies for preventing or reporting gendered abuse. While Rifat Siddiqui conveys the challenges of supporting an attacked student at a Bangladeshi university with no policies that might have protected or supported that student, Zekri Masson illustrates how such abuses can remain invisible, even to those suffering them, when institutions have and express no understanding of them. Nancy Pathak, a queer academic in India, considers what is at stake when the committee assembled to hear her complaint is required to include women and representatives of "scheduled" or marginalized castes but allows no representation of the group with which she identifies, non–trans queer individuals.

An anonymous writer in another part of the world chronicles her long and only partially successful attempt to protect herself from harassment by an academic at a different institution, and in off-campus contexts such as conference proceedings. Her account, "Tracking Sexual Predators across Academic Institutions," illustrates that gendered abuse in academia is not neatly confined to individual institutions or sets of policies. Rather, it occurs across and is fostered by the complex interinstitutional networks comprising academia. Typically, and legally, sexual harassment policy primarily or solely protects an institution's employees from abuses that interfere with their ability to perform their jobs. But what is an institution's responsibility to protect off-campus academics from its own faculty members? How can victims report gendered abuse committed by an institutional employee, regardless of their relationship to the institution, so that patterns of abuse might be recognized and others who work with perpetrators, including students at the institution and fellow academics at other institutions and in academic associations, might be protected? How can cross-institutional academic organizations protect their members from gendered abuse in meetings, at conferences, and everywhere academia operates?

"Tracking Sexual Predators" also reveals how academic abuse is often not an isolated incident, but part of a pattern of chronic predation. While many of our chapters touch on this aspect of abuse, "To Make a Fuss" focuses on this dimension of the problem. Its anonymous author illustrates in vivid detail the dangers of turning a blind eye to chronic predators and recommends ways of transforming academic departments from predators' playgrounds into environments they will find "toxic," rather than enabling of their abusive behavior.

Even more insidious are the ways that the very antiharassment systems designed to protect vulnerable academics are often enlisted as mechanisms for abuse. While the anonymous author of "Tall Poppy" documents how Title IX policies and #MeToo energy were harnessed against her, Francine Banner et al. speak to the uncanny experience of finding themselves harassed while researching gender-based discrimination, by the very people whose job was to protect academics from abuse. Despite the precise nature of the abuse, outcomes in all these cases are eerily similar: stalled or aborted careers, loss of positions and opportunities, years of exhausting and futile resistance, devitalization in every professional and personal aspect, lifelong trauma, and of course, the painful experience of being disbelieved, discounted, and silenced.

Shannon Walsh writes eloquently about the power of storytelling to alleviate pain and lead to change, and the importance—for one's own sake and for the sake of all fellow and future sufferers—of remembering these abuses, rather than forgetting them. However different our experiences, all of us, editors and contributors alike, are united by this urgent desire to speak, and to heed each other. As Zekri Masson illustrates, some of us only recognize our own abuse by reading the stories of others. But speaking out is not without risks and consequences. As Soraya Chemaly reminds us in *Rage Becomes Her*, speaking out in anger for justice is necessary and healing, and also sure to spark retaliatory anger from our oppressors—as Cheshire's essay illustrates so well. Ferrari points out the particular risks of speaking out for women of color and weighs with ambivalence the opportunity to speak against the seeming mandate for Black women to repeatedly testify to their pain and abuse over generations and centuries—to "bleed on the page" in order to be acknowledged and treated with respect. Carr weighs the value of speaking out about how Black academics oppress each other against the risk of being considered "traitorous." Several of our contributors, out of concern for their safety and the risk to their careers, chose to speak anonymously. Alison Vogelaar illustrates how even this strategy can't always keep us safe, and how easily patriarchy marshaled a narrative to vilify her as "the poison pen."

Many of our contributors go beyond describing experiences of abuse and conceptualizing its causes, to theorizing strategies for resistance and change. Two writers, having spent years struggling through official (Countryman-Roswurm) and unofficial (Anonymous, in "Tracking Sexual Predators") complaint channels, suggest ways of changing complaint processes to make them more useful for and protective of victims and less enabling of perpetrators. Carr offers ways of encouraging productive mentorship for women academics of color, while Vanyoro explores ways in which Black men can be part of the solution in academic institutions, rather than simply part of the problem. Siddiqui, on the other hand, illustrates how to work outside institutional systems altogether, when she describes creating an "enclaved safe space" to support her students after realizing her institution offered no resources to protect them. Several of these essays advocate for changes not in how we respond to complaints and suffering but in how we do academic work and structure administrative systems themselves, in the hope of lessening the occurrence of gendered abuse. While Possas and Barbosa document the power of collective discussion, research, and publication efforts, and Banner et al. explore the promise of their work as "feminist secretaries," Gallup et al. propose restructuring administrative systems using models of "power-sharing" and "design-thinking" rather than traditional hierarchies.

We three editors were struck by how many people responded to our call for this volume as collectives, some of which had been working as such for a long time, suggesting both the prescience and influence of Ahmed's theorizing of the complaint collective. Demandante and Miranda band together to testify to the abuses experienced by faculty and students across their department in the Philippines, finding strength in numbers to be the first in their country to speak out about such abuses. Six woman faculty members at the University of Minnesota Duluth—Christina Gallup, Anne Hinderliter, Njoki Kamau, Arshia Khan, Lu Smith, and Elizabethada Wright—use the same collective strategy in a very different context: to point out the continued reentrenchment of systems of sexual harassment that persevere despite an over forty-year history of their university's supposed acknowledgment of and response to public accusations of abuse.

Other groups preexisted our call, and we are pleased to provide a space where their work can gain wider acknowledgment and influence. One of these is a research group turned complaint collective: six scholars from the University of Michigan–Dearborn—Francine Banner, Pamela Aronson, Kathleen Darcy, Maureen Linker, Jean-Carlos Lopez, and Lisa Martin—view themselves as examples of Ahmed's "feminist secretaries" who, having experienced the harassment their research was meant to document, are moved to publicly examine their experiences and data in search of understanding and strategies for change. In her 2017 *Chronicle of Higher Education* essay, "The Sexism that Permeates the Academy," Peggy O'Donnell acknowledged this tendency to perpetuate the sexism in academia that leads to gendered abuse by refusing to admit it exists.

> As academic institutions march down the largely well-meaning path toward total gender equality, it is worth remembering that believing gendered hierarchy should not exist in the world that we want does not mean that gendered hierarchy does not exist in the world that we have. And refusing to recognize the existence of a gendered power differential—denying that women are often more vulnerable in hierarchical institutions like academia or the military—means not only denying the sexism women in those institutions experience, but also perpetuating it.

This chapter by the collective at the University of Michigan is an urgent reminder to academic institutions that the types of systemic abuse that exist in college and university settings will not be solved by well-meaning diversity, equity, and inclusion (DEI) initiatives or neoliberal rhetoric that simply denounces sexism. On the contrary, several of the chapters in this volume illustrate how such initiatives mask or even worsen gendered abuse with their "pseudo-efforts," as Gallup et al. call them.[26]

A collective formed by the research group Laboratório Interdisciplinar de Estudos de Gênero, or Interdisciplinary Laboratory of Gender

Studies (LIEG) in Brazil also documents how it evolved from archive to complaint collective as theorized by Ahmed. Like the collective at the University of Michigan, the LIEG collective arose out of women academics' desire to document and understand instances of gendered abuse. But this collective, represented by Lídia Maria Vianna Possas and Emilia Barbosa, focuses on increased reports of sexual harassment since the beginning of the COVID-19 pandemic at São Paulo State University and at other Latin American and US higher-ed institutions. Finally, we end the book with a piece that speaks equally to the power and importance of collective complaint and of literature and art as sites for real social change: the six authors of "It Is Better to Speak"—Lori Wright, Neisha Wiley, Elizabeth VanWassenhove, Brandelyn Tosolt, Rachel Loftis, and Meg L. Hensley—use blackout poetry to simultaneously represent the devastation of systemic silencing and the power of speech, of storytelling, of poetry, of print. All of these collectives, and this book operating itself as a collective, remind us that we are always more powerful when speaking together.

Keeping and Using Our Tongues

All around the country, at universities far and wide, at workplaces of all sizes and types, at companies that boast of doing good and making the world a better place, there are file cabinets full of the bloody tongues of women.

—Donna Freitas, *Consent: A Memoir of Unwanted Attention* (13)

In her book *Sister Citizen* (2011), scholar and critic Melissa Harris-Perry writes, "When they confront race and gender stereotypes, black women are standing in a crooked room, and they have to figure out which way is up. Bombarded with warped images of their humanity, some black women tilt and bend themselves to fit the distortion. . . . It can be hard to stand up straight in a crooked room" (29).[27] Though Harris-Perry is specifically talking about Black women's experiences, *Broken Record* illustrates that academia, at times, is a crooked room, one that distorts reality and undermines one's humanity in ways that are *systemically abusive*. The contributors of this volume have grown tired of bending and tilting. By sharing these stories, we hope that academia can become an environment where individuals can "stand up straight" while fully embodying the intersections of their identities and lived experiences.

Just as #MeToo is not a trend, but rather builds on Burke's decades-long activism with sexual-violence survivors, we see this project as the continuation of a movement, not an endpoint. More stories need to be told, such as those of people whose gender expression, abilities, age, social history or class, or religion make them vulnerable in ways this volume does not consider. But the topic is personal and traumatic enough that seeking contributors to write about particular kinds of experience and knowledge is unthinkable. So this archive is necessarily incomplete.

We editors also recognize the inherent privilege of our identities as cis-het women in being able to organize such a collection. Perhaps most importantly, we acknowledge that it is not—and should not be—the sole obligation of marginalized and underrepresented individuals to educate those in more privileged positions, while recognizing that there is much to be learned from those who are willing to share their stories, insights, and words of wisdom.[28] Nor should marginalized individuals have to share their trauma for their experiences to be taken seriously. Thus, the voices and experiences represented in this collection signal both systemic abuse and inequalities in higher-education institutions and societies throughout the world, and also systemic silencing.[29]

Some women with important stories to tell found writing about them for this collection too difficult and decided not to contribute. Others were willing to speak to us about their experiences but not to write. Along the way, we lost many contributors to a wide range of stresses and fears, far more than is typical for an edited collection. Chapter 2 stands as a testament to those voices lost to the forces of patriarchy. Its author is "Anonymous" in solidarity with our contributors who could not safely name themselves in this volume and with a long history of silenced women. One of our lost contributors left academia altogether as a result of her experience of abuse. The (anonymous) author of this book's opening chapter, "Survival Analysis," made the same decision long ago, and reminds us how vast and invisible these losses are, as is the abuse that led to them.

Many other women who remain in academia while enduring acute and ongoing abuse, suffering "physically, emotionally, and intellectually" (Reyes 104), also endure the precarity of constantly wondering if and how they might leave. Reyes acknowledges that the emotional toll of academic abuse is particularly profound. Being targeted with repeated, long-term exclusion feels like a withholding of love and worthiness, which function as forms of capital in our profession (Reyes 22, 23). Being denied resources, recognition, affinity, rights, responsibilities; being denied a basic sense of value and belonging—especially when we have worked so indefatigably to gain a place in the academic system—does intense and ongoing damage, radically altering our lives, physical and mental health, and basic sense of self-worth, even as we stay.

In harnessing the power of the personal narrative to manifest this incomplete archive and testament to the ongoing suffering of those who leave and those who stay, we editors have made the considered decision *not* to resolve the multiplicity and differences of our contributors' diverse experiences into neat and reassuring resolution. Allowing essays to differ in approach, allowing writers to express contradictory experiences and ideas, and allowing readers to feel and react differently to different essays, are part of the ethics of this book. What these chapters taken together do perhaps most clearly is demonstrate not just the diversity of types and experiences of abuse but also the diversity of people's experiences in trying to document, report, resist, and heal from abuse. Some authors offer no bullet-pointed solutions because they have found none. Their experiences are still important and illuminating. Some authors' carefully bullet-pointed suggestions contradict those offered by others. All of their experiences and suggestions are still instructive. Strategies that work for one author fail for another, and vice versa.

The only generalizable "best practices" we might extrapolate, such as the importance of documenting one's experiences of abuse, are both evident in the book itself and demonstrably not guaranteed to be of any use whatsoever, even if one files a complaint. Thus, we end not with a reductive "how-to" manual for surviving and fighting academic abuse, but with the organizing wisdom of Sara Ahmed. As both *Complaint!* and *Broken Record* demonstrate, the best thing we can do at the moment is become aware of the nuances of abuse and the systems that enable it, and of how futile most formal resistance is at this point—and why that is so—while coming together in solidarity with others to continue to raise awareness and advocate for systemic change.

More than an archive of past abuse, *Broken Record* has been, for its contributors and editors, a powerful opportunity for witnessing such suffering and for "journeying alongside" each other, as one contributor put it in an email, as we find our voices and use our tongues. As such, it is also an archive of the enormous *labor* required to file complaints, to endure their repercussions, to support others in doing so, to educate ourselves and others in how to navigate and survive these things more productively, to learn what kinds of changes will help future precarious academics, to enact these changes. To keep our heads up, move forward, or move away, when no amount of change solves the problem. Alison Vogelaar calls all this effort the "shadow labor of complaint," which we have aimed to bring out of the shadows with this book. In that spirit, we want to acknowledge the particularly intense—and rewarding—labor that went into editing this collection. All of our contributors were writing about trauma. Responding to their drafts meant supporting them in remembering and representing that trauma, meant participating in part of their working-through. We brought our own related experiences and writing about those experiences to bear when helping them conceptualize and articulate their trauma: we revisited our own traumatic pasts to support them in understanding theirs. Their writing inevitably bore the typical signs of trauma: first drafts were often disorderly, making unexplained leaps of logic or chronology; chaotic, with shifting verb tenses and perspectives; sometimes enormously long. We helped writers clarify their experiences so they could carve out clear essays about them.

In doing so, we editors forged intensely felt connections with each other and with our intrepid contributors. We learned from each other's shared experiences and reflections and felt supported by them. Our sense of solidarity transcended the theoretical, reaching out across the country and the globe as our emails raced around it, connecting us into a collective that will outlive this moment, this publication. We grew fierce along the way, surprising ourselves with the newly emboldened ways in which we now "live our feminist lives," despite and alongside the suffering and doubt inherent to the experience of being women in academia.

As Tressie McMillan Cottom writes in her memoir *Thick*, personal essays have become an effective means for Black women to "claim legitimacy" in spaces that exclude them, noting that "In a modern society, who is allowed to speak with authority is a political act" (19). That is, personal narratives are not just about exposing one's vulnerability; they are radical acts of resistance that challenge both *who* has the right to speak and *what* can be said. In affirming the legitimacy of personal narratives, which are regularly dismissed in academic spaces as nonscholarly and anti-intellectual, we hope to not only amplify the voices and lived experiences of the contributors in this collection, but also create space for others to share their stories. Therefore, this archive is also an invitation—for those who feel able, safe, and supported—to others to contribute their stories on other platforms and in future projects. And it's the beginning of a guide for how to protect those who speak before they can be silenced, and to give once-silenced women a place where they can finally speak. As Donna Freitas reminds us, "Women's tongues are dangerous when they let us keep them" (14).[30]

And as Audre Lorde warns, having acknowledged the compelling reasons why so many women "sicken and die . . . in silence"—"[Their] silence will not protect [them]" (40).

Notes

1. Epigraph from *Sister Outsider: Essays and Speeches by Audre Lorde*, "The Transformation of Silence into Language and Action," © 1984 Crossing Press.

2. We recognize the complexity of gender identifications and expressions, and of attending language. Our uses of *woman, women,* and *female* include all individuals who identify as such.

3. See, for example, Turner, 2002; Settles, et al., 2006; Roos, 2008; Pittman, 2010; Wu and Jing, 2011; Gardner, 2013; Anderson, 2018; Feder, 2018; Anitha, et al., 2020; Young and Wiley, 2021; Reyes, 2022; Robillard, 2023; and a special issue of *Feminist Formations* on this topic, 2019. Our hearty thanks to Lizzy Sobiesk for her help in gathering research sources for this project.

4. See especially Reyes's chapters "Living in Precarity" and "Overlapping Shifts and COVID-19" (60–103).

5. For extensive discussion of and data supporting these assertions, see *Presumed Incompetent* pp. 1–3, and "Race/ethnicity of College Faculty" at the *National Center for Education Statistics* website (nces.ed.gov/fastfacts/display.asp?id=61). See also Robillard's Introduction on the profound hypocrisies of English departments, for instance, with their outward or performative commitments to diversity, equity, and social justice that contradict professors' abusive actions.

6. For further discussion in a Woolfian context see the linked essays by Rohman and Delsandro, 2022. These essays followed upon Rohman's keynote address about gendered abuse in academia, at the 2021 30th Annual International Conference on Virginia Woolf.

7. See Khoo 2010; and "Tall Poppy" and "Misogyny and Abuse in the Academic Library Workplace," in this volume.

8. For examples in this volume, see "Survival Analysis" and chapters by Cheshire and Carr.

9. For an important example of how moving into an administrative role heightened one academic woman's awareness of these issues, see Mayock, 2016. Most of the chapters in this volume contain examples of administrative abuse

and enabling of abuse, but see especially Carpan, Ferarri, Zekri Masson, Pathak, Vogelaar, Countryman-Roswurm, Carr, Gallup, et al., and Banner, et al.

10. See "Shocked" and "Tracking Sexual Predators across Academic Institutions" in this volume.

11. See essays in this volume by Carpan, Ferrari, Pathak, Vogelaar, Countryman-Roswurm, Carr, Gallup, et al., and "Tall Poppy." Sara Ahmed also writes about the complicity of women in gendered abuse, in this volume's Afterword.

12. See essays in this volume by Carpan, Demandante and Miranda, and Countryman-Roswurm.

13. The coinage of the term *mutual abuse* and the use of DARVO strategies by Johnny Depp's lawyers in the Depp/Heard defamation trial of 2022—which she lost, despite a UK court's previous ruling in her favor—attest to the practical efficacy of such rhetorical techniques. Jennifer Freyd calls the use of DARVO by institutions such as universities "institutional betrayal," which she explores on her website. A recent CFP for a special issue on "Institutional Betrayal and Academic Trauma" for *ADVANCE Journal* illustrates the growing momentum behind work revolving around this issue. The essays in this volume illustrate that DARVO is a near-ubiquitous element of the complaint process, but see especially "Shocked," "To Make a Fuss," and essays by Demandante and Miranda, Vogelaar, and Gallup et al.

14. We thank Ahmed for the powerfully suggestive image of the *broken record* (*Complaint!* 41).

15. See Holland and Hewett, 2021, 3–8.

16. For the history of the Me Too (now "me too.") Movement and #MeToo, see Burke, https://metoomvmt.org/get-to-know-us/history-inception/.

17. See Holland and Hewett, "Rethinking the Curriculum," 2023.

18. See Alcoff, 2018; Freitas, 2018; Kantor and Twohey, 2019; Kulbaga and Spencer, 2019; Towl and Walker, 2019; Warshaw, 2019; Gray-Rosendale, 2020.

19. On how #MeToo harnesses the work historically done by personal narrative in feminist activism, see Holland and Hewett, "Introduction" in *#MeToo and Literary Studies* (2021); on how #MeToo extends and reshapes the power of the personal narrative to do political work, see Leigh Gilmore, *The #MeToo Effect* (2023).

20. See Perkins, 2017; Bean, 2018; Gay, 2018; Moulton, 2018; Noomin, 2019; Oria, 2019.

21. See also Chapdelaine et al.'s *When Will the Joy Come? Black Women in the Ivory Tower* (2023). As editors, we have chosen to capitalize "Black" and not "white." Throughout this book, capitalization of these terms may reflect the decisions of each contributor or the stylistic and societal norms during the original publication date of quoted material.

22. For an account of a successful use of the collective to bring about change on these issues at an Irish university, see Rose Foley and Micheline Sheehy Skeffington's *Micheline's Three Conditions: How We Fought Gender Inequality at Galway's University and Won*, which was about to be published as our book went to press.

23. Fleisher's memoir demonstrates keen awareness of this point (264).

24. For more on how gender abuse manifests in STEM fields, see Paula A. Johnson, et al. *Sexual Harassment of Women: Climate, Culture, and Consequences in Academic Sciences, Engineering, and Medicine* (2018) and the documentary film *Picture a Scientist* (2020).

25. See, for starters, hooks, 2004; Manne, 2020; and Onion, 2023.

26. See especially chapters by Countryman-Roswurm and Gallup, et al.

27. See Ferrari, 2020 for an intimate account of how Black women feel pressed to contort themselves in predominately white, academic spaces.

28. For a discussion of how institutions can support Black women academics as leaders, see Evans, et al.'s *Dear Department Chair: Letters from Black Women Leaders to the Next Generation* (2023).

29. For an excellent discussion of the various causes and consequences of such silencing, see *Presumed Incompetent*, pp. 10–14.

30. See also Rohman, 2020 for a discussion of tongues, silencing, gender, and race.

Works Cited

Ahmed, Sara. *Living a Feminist Life*. Duke UP, 2017.

———. *Complaint!* Duke UP, 2021.

Alcoff, Linda Martin. *Rape and Resistance*. Polity Press, 2018.

Anderson, Nick. "Academia's #MeToo Moment: Women Accuse Professors of Sexual Misconduct." *Washington Post*, 10 May 2018. https://www.washingtonpost.com/local/education/academias-metoo-moment-women-accuse-professors-of-sexual-misconduct/2018/05/10/474102de-2631-11e8-874b-d517e912f125_story.html. Accessed 15 Sept. 2022.

Anitha, Sundari, et al. "Feminist Responses to Sexual Harassment in Academia: Voice, Solidarity and Resistance through Online Activism." *Journal of Gender-Based Violence* 4, no. 1, 2020, pp. 9–23.

Bean, Lexie, ed. *Written on the Body: Letters from Trans and Non-Binary Survivors of Sexual Assault and Domestic Violence*. Jessica Kingsley Publishers, 2018.

Chalmers, Carolyn. *They Don't Want Her There: Fighting Sexual and Racial Harassment in the American University*. U of Iowa P, 2022.

Chapdelaine, Robin Phylisia, Asare, Abena Ampofoa, Thompson, Michelle Dionne, eds. *When Will the Joy Come? Black Women in the Ivory Tower*. U of Massachusetts P, 2023.

Chemaly, Soraya. *Rage Becomes Her: The Power of Women's Anger*. Atria, 2018.

Cottom, Tressie McMillan. *Thick: And Other Essays*. The New Press, 2019.

Davis, Shardé M. *Black in the Ivory*. U of North Carolina P, forthcoming 2024.

Delsandro, Erica Gene. "Notes on Bristling." *Modernism/modernity*, 6, no. 3, 2022: Orientations Forum (27 Mar.). https://modernismmodernity.org/forums/posts/delsandro-notes-bristling. Accessed 29 Nov 2022.

Evans, Stephanie Y., et al., eds. *Dear Department Chair: Letters from Black Women Leaders to the Next Generation.* Wayne State UP, 2023.

Feder, Toni. "Culture Change Is Key to Reducing Sexual Harassment in Academia." *Physics Today*, 2018. https://physicstoday-scitation-org.libdatabase.newpaltz.edu/do/10.1063/PT.6.2.20180615a/full/. Accessed 15 Sep. 2022.

Ferrari, Carlyn. " 'You Need to Leave Now, Ma'am.' " *Chronicle of Higher Education*, September 8, 2020. https://www-chronicle-com.proxy.seattleu.edu/article/you-need-to-leave-now-maam. Accessed 1 Dec. 2023.

Fleisher, Kass. *Talking out of School: Memoir of an Educated Woman.* Dalkey Archive, 2008.

Foley, Rose, and Micheline Sheehy Skeffingon. *Micheline's Three Conditions: How We Fought Gender Inequality at Galway's University and Won.* M3C Press, 2023.

Freitas, Donna. *Consent on Campus: A Manifesto.* Oxford UP, 2018.

Freitas, Donna. *Consent: A Memoir of Unwanted Attention.* Little, Brown, 2019.

Freyd, Jennifer J. "Institutional Betrayal and Institutional Courage." https://dynamic.uoregon.edu/jjf/institutionalbetrayal/. Accessed 13 Oct. 2022.

Gardner, Susan K. "Women Faculty Departures from a Striving Institution: Between a Rock and a Hard Place." *Review of Higher Education* 36, no. 3, 2013, pp. 349–70.

Gay, Roxane, ed. *Not That Bad: Dispatches from Rape Culture.* Harper Perennial, 2018.

Gilmore, Leigh. *The #MeToo Effect.* Columbia UP, 2023.

Gray-Rosendale, Laura A., ed. *Me Too, Feminist Theory, and Surviving Sexual Violence in the Academy.* Lexington Books, 2020.

Gutiérrez y Muhs, Gabriella, Yolanda Flores Niemann, Carmen G. González, and Angela P. Harris, eds. *Presumed Incompetent: The Intersections of Race and Class for Women in Academia.* UP of Colorado, 2012.

Hansen, Julie and Ingela Nilsson, ed. *Critical Storytelling: Experiences of Power Abuse in Academia.* Brill, 2022.

Harris-Perry, Melissa V. *Sister Citizen: Shame, Stereotypes, and Black Women in America.* Yale Up. ProQuest Ebook Central, 2011. https://ebookcentral.proquest.com/lib/seattleu/detail.action?docID=3420728.

Holland, Mary K., and Heather Hewett, eds. *#MeToo and Literary Studies: Reading, Writing, and Teaching about Sexual Violence and Rape Culture.* Bloomsbury, 2021.

Holland, Mary K., and Heather Hewett. "Rethinking the Curriculum: #MeToo and Contemporary Literary Studies." *The Routledge Companion to Gender, Media and Violence*, edited by Karen Boyle and Susan Berridge, Routledge, 2023, pp. 601–10.

hooks, bell, *The Will to Change: Men, Masculinity, and Love.* Washington Square Press, 2004.

Johnson, Paula A., et al., eds. *Sexual Harassment of Women: Climate, Culture, and Consequences in Academic Sciences, Engineering, and Medicine.* National Academies Press, 2018.

Kantor, Jodi, and Megan Twohey. *She Said: Breaking the Sexual Harassment Story that Helped Ignite a Movement.* Penguin, 2019.

Kelskey, Karen. Sexual Harassment in the Academy. *The Professor Is In,* 2017–18. https://docs.google.com/spreadsheets/d/1S9KShDLvU7C-KkgEevYTHXr3F6In TenrBsS9yk-8C5M/edit#gid=1530077352. Accessed 15 Sep. 2022.

Kolodny, Annette. "I Dreamed Again That I Was Drowning." *Women's Writing in Exile,* ed. Mary Lynn Broe and Angela Ingram. U of North Carolina P, 1989.

Khoo, S. B. "Academic Mobbing: Hidden Health Hazard at Workplace." https://www.ncbi.nlm.nih.gov/pmc/articles/PMC4170397/. Accessed 22 Sep. 2022.

Kulbaga, Theresa A., and Leland G. Spencer. *Campuses of Consent: Sexual and Social Justice in Higher Education.* U of Massachusetts P, 2019.

Libarkin, J. Academic Sexual Misconduct Database. 2022. https://academic-sexual-misconduct-database.org. Accessed 14 Sep. 2022.

Lorde, Audre. *Sister Outsider: Essays & Speeches by Audre Lorde.* Crossing Press, 1984, p. 41.

Maldonado, Marta Maria, and Katja M. Guenther, eds. *Feminist Formations* 31, no. 1, 2019.

Manne, Kate. *Entitled: How Male Privilege Hurts Women.* Crown, 2020.

Marshall, Gillian. "Rejected." *Chronicle of Higher Education.* 25 Feb. 2022. https://www.chronicle.com/article/rejected. Accessed 26 Sep. 2022.

Mayock, Ellen. *Gender Shrapnel in the Academic Workplace.* Palgrave Macmillan, 2016.

Moulton, Erin, ed. *Things We Haven't Said: Sexual Assault Survivors Speak Out.* Zest Books, 2018.

Niemann, Yolanda Flores, et al., eds. *Presumed Incompetent II: Race, Class, Power, and Resistance of Women in Academia.* U of Utah P, 2020.

Noomin, Diane, ed. *Drawing Power: A Comics Anthology.* Forward by Roxane Gay. Harry N. Abrams, 2019.

O'Donnell, Peggy. "The Sexism that Permeates the Academy." *Chronicle of Higher Education.* 17 October 2017. https://www-chronicle-com.proxy.seattleu.edu/article/the-sexism-that-permeates-the-academy/. Accessed 10 Sep. 2022.

Onion, Rebecca. "The Controversial Parenting Theory That's Showing Up in Court Everywhere," *Slate.com,* 14 Sep. 2023. https://slate.com/human-interest/2023/09/parental-alienation-syndrome-prove-laws-hannah-dreyfus.html. Accessed 30 Sep. 2023.

Oria, Shelly, ed. *Indelible in the Hippocampus: Writings from the Me Too Movement.* McSweeny's Publishing, 2019.

Patel, Fay, ed. *Power Imbalance, Bullying and Harassment in Academia and the Glocal (Local and Global) Workplace*. Nova Science Press, 2021.

Perkins, Lori. *#MeToo: Essays about How and Why This Happened, What It Means, and How to Make Sure It Never Happens Again*. Riverdale Avenue Books, 2017.

Pittman, Chavella T. "Race and Gender Oppression in the Classroom: The Experiences of Women Faculty of Color with White Male Students." *Teaching Sociology* 38, no. 3, 2010, pp. 183–96.

"Race/ethnicity of college faculty." *National Center for Education Statistics*. 2022. https://nces.ed.gov/fastfacts/display.asp?id=61. Accessed 26 Sep. 2022.

"Resources." *Battered Mothers Custody Conference*. 2022. batteredmotherscustody conference.org/resources. Accessed 26 Sep 2022.

Reyes, Victoria. *Academic Outsider: Stories of Exclusion and Hope*. Stanford UP, 2022.

Robillard, Amy E. *Misogyny in English Departments: Obligation, Entitlement, Gaslighting*. Peter Lang, 2023.

Rohman, Carrie. "Severed Tongues: Silencing Intellectual Women." *Modernism/ modernity*. 5, no. 2, 2020: #MeToo and Modernism Cluster (28 Sep.). https:// modernismmodernity.org/forums/posts/rohman-severed-tongues. Accessed 20 Nov. 2022.

———. "Woolf, The University, and All Sorts of Brutality." *Modernism/modernity*, 6, no. 3, 2022: Orientations Forum (26 Mar.). https://modernismmodernity. org/forums/posts/rohman-woolf-university-all-sorts-brutality. Accessed 29 Nov. 2022.

Roos, Patricia A. "Together but Unequal: Combating Gender Inequity in the Academy." *Journal of Workplace Rights* 13, no. 2, 2008, pp. 185–99.

Ross, Abbi. "Rejected: These Five Scholars Were Denied Tenure. Could They Move On?" *Chronicle of Higher Education*. 25 Feb. 2022. https://www.chronicle. com/article/rejected. Accessed 6 Dec. 2022.

Settles, Isis H., et al. "The Climate for Women in Academic Science: The Good, the Bad, and the Changeable." *Psychology of Women Quarterly* 30, 2006, pp. 47–58.

Shattuck, Shannon, and Ian Cheney, dir. *Picture a Scientist*. Uprising Production, 2020.

Stengers, Isabelle, and Vinciane Despret and collective. *Women Who Make a Fuss: The Unfaithful Daughters of Virginia Woolf*. Trans. April Knutson. Univocal Publishing, 2014.

Towl, Graham J., and Tammi Walker. *Tackling Sexual Violence at Universities: An International Perspective*. Routledge, 2019.

Turner, Caroline Sotello Viernes. "Women of Color in Academe: Living with Multiple Marginality." *Journal of Higher Education* 73, no. 1, 2002, pp. 74–93.

Warshaw, Robyn. *I Never Called It Rape*. Foreword by Gloria Steinem. Harper Perennial, 2019.

Wilcox, Dawn. *Women Count USA*. 2018. https://docs.google.com/spread sheets/d/1WLiGtRnFUxz_E9YiJETqD_yErNRITeZMxnTcZZHuMu0/edit#gid =0. Accessed 15 Sep. 2022.

Woolf, Virginia. *Three Guineas*. Harcourt, Brace, Jovanovich, 1966.

Wu, Lilian. and Wei Jing. "Asian Women in STEM Careers: An Invisible Minority in a Double Bind." *Issues in Science and Technology*, Fall 2011, pp. 82–87.

Young, Sarah L., and Kimberly K. Wiley. "Erased: Why Faculty Sexual Misconduct Is Prevalent and How We Could Prevent It." *Journal of Public Affairs Education* 27, no. 3, 2021, pp. 276–300.

Part One

Contexts and Systems of Abuse

1

Survival Analysis

Why Do We Vanish, Where Do We Go?

ANONYMOUS

Look, you who think the gods have no care of human things, what do you say to so many persons preserved from death by their especial favour?

To which Diagoras of Melos replied: "Why, I say that their pictures are not here who were cast away, who are by much the greater number."

—Cicero, *De Natura Deorum 89*

We pull into the field site midafternoon, August, fifteen miles down a rutted road somewhere in the Uncompahgre National Forest. My subcompact had balked at a couple of the washouts along the way, but I'd managed to crawl around them without rupturing my oil pan, following his battered mint-green International Scout up the dirt track, and here we are at the end of the road. My car bumps through the campground past a handful of battered picnic tables, scattered fire rings, the one pit toilet, ending up at the farthest camping spot. I'm looking out over ten acres of willow wetland bordered on all sides by rising ground and then ranks of ponderosa pine lifting off toward the twelve-thousand-foot peaks to the west, where the abrupt rise of the Continental spine meets the severe and cerulean sky. It's still dusty summer, but we're high enough now that the aspen are thinking about turning. No other cars or campers are here. We are as isolated as drivable roads will take us, and I'm alone with him.

His research trailer has been parked up here all summer—a battered aluminum two-bunker with state plates. He's here to trap birds in the last capture session of the season and has invited/commanded me to come to his field site to get orientated to his work before I start taking classes, working as a teaching assistant, and writing my own research proposal. He'd been insistent that I ride with him, not bring my own car, and already there was a tension over my simple expression of preference, but I'd held my ground, saying I needed to get back early to register and find a place to live.

He noses the Scout into a spot next to the trailer. Behind him I do a three-point turn and park facing back the way we'd come. Through the dust on my windshield I see him standing next to the driver's door of the Scout. His Wranglers wrap tightly around his thighs and his snap shirt stretches across the watermelon of his gut. Tan Stetson pushed back revealing the first third of his balding conical head. In the moment before I reach for my door handle I still believe in myself. Just barely, but enough.

When I had been applying to grad programs my biology professor asked if this potential supervisor was wearing a cowboy hat in his university catalog photo. This was well before the internet. "Yes," I had said and she rolled her eyes and asked about my other options. The only other possibilities were to study fruit fly genetics or take a position with a social scientist who invited me to tea at his house then tried to press up against me when I was leaving, his smelly beard stuffed against my face, saying he wanted to kiss me goodbye. Fat nope on him, even though he was at an Ivy.

I'd spent the month before in the Absarokas and the Beartooth Mountains, some of the most remote roadless terrain in the lower forty-eight states. I was at home in wild places, at ease and sometimes ferociously happy there—hanging food in grizzly country, being treed by belligerent moose, hearing Yellowstone Lake ringing in the predawn mist. I'd earned close to perfect scores on my qualifying exams, had TA'd organic chemistry in college, done independent research, and I was in love with Knowledge and ready to take it all on. In that crystalline high-country moment, it could have gone in a different direction.

While we pull out the Havahart traps from the back of his Scout he doesn't say much, doesn't laugh or joke, address me directly, or explain what he's doing. He doesn't say anything like, *Here is the trap, here are the research goals, here's what I'm thinking. Here are the birds, here is the home range, here is the way I frame the questions.* Let alone ask me how I am or what I hope to do. What doesn't happen is always as important as what does, and sometimes much more important. Missing that sunny late-summer afternoon: collegiality, communication, direct gaze.

He takes orange cheese puffs from a big plastic jug and puts a couple in each wire-mesh trap. Their supernormal brightness, the fat and salt, will summon the jays. He brings the birds back to campus and puts them in a windowless white room. They have phenomenal spatial memories, recall thousands of cache sites, and he is intent on measuring that capability. As we are putting out the first trap, a jay plummets down through the branches, cheeky, skittering through the air, calling, raucous like something wonderful is about to happen. What is a trap but a connivance, a false premise, deceit? From a lifetime's distance I can see that the graduate degree was the Cheeto ball that lured me into the wire cage of collusion with the system, of shutting up, of putting up.

I had first met him the day before: me, twenty-four years old, a newly minted grad student; him, decked out in neckerchief and cowboy boots though he sat in an office. *All hat and no horse*, as they say in Wyoming.

Back at the campsite, he vanishes inside the trailer. The sky flares up as the sun slouches over the hill, an incandescent beast on its way to somewhere else. I walk to my car, which I've lived out of for the summer, and pull out my cook stove and root around in my food box for a can of beans and the loaf of bread I bought yesterday. I start the fire with a single paper match, as if my mad field skills could possibly protect me now. August-dry, the twigs snap into fiery life.

I don't remember him coming out of the camper, maybe I was tending the fire, but he sits down on the picnic-table bench hefting a handle of Wild Turkey. He untwists the cap, takes a long pull, his round expressionless eyes on me. He's not talking, just staring. I take another five minutes to mess with the fire, then stand up, dust off my jeans, sit down at the far end of the bench. The light from the campfire refracts off the hazed wall of the aluminum camper then vanishes into the blackness of the Colorado sky. Wind picks up.

He hands the bottle across to me and says, "Drink."

All right, I think, *I see.*

"Oh thanks," I say and take the bottle and hold it. Years of living with mean drunks taught me that refusal can bring on aggression; I know that even the most graceful *Thank you, no* can be taken as confrontation, judgment. Best to take the offered bottle and hold it for a while, friendly-like. I give him a bowl of beans and bread and after holding the bottle of Wild Turkey while he eats, pass it back to him. He starts drinking steadily, not bothering with a mug.

I'd worked with men in remote locations a fair amount because science and outdoor life are like that, and I was skilled at using humor, taking a light tone. I tell a few small stories then start to ask questions, the kind most academics like to go on about. I'm going to take my best shot at talking my way through till first light when I'll head down fifteen miles of dirt road to the sunshine of the populated world. After a while it starts to feel like a hostage negotiation where I am both the hostage and the negotiator on my own behalf. I'm the coyote in the leg-hold trap and he is walking up on the set with a noose pole. The middle of nowhere, long before cell phones, and even longer before #MeToo was a whisper in the wind.

Since childhood I had known that if you feel fear it will show, and if it shows, you'll lose the contest, and for this reason fear is a fucking useless emotion. He pushes the bottle to me again, then slides along the bench ending up with his thigh pressed firmly against mine. Reaches out and grasps my shoulder. As he leans in, his face unambiguously close, the odor of cheese and unwashed jacket. Welcome to grad school. The funny thing is it did not feel like he was driven by any sort of actual desire, but more like he was picking up a dollar bill from a sidewalk or filling his plate at an all-you-can-eat buffet. The flavor of his reaching was, "Might as well."

Driving out in the dark risks wrecking my car and stranding me, but worse, I know that if I burn this bridge graduate school will be over before it even starts. I'd trained myself to push relentlessly toward specific goals, to put on my game face. *He's a smallish guy, at least there's that*, I think, *and I am brave and strong and know how to fight.*

There's the idea that wearing a provocative outfit incites the male gaze and thereby invites the male violation. Translate this to remote settings and the theory of provocation goes like this: *You are out here alone in this wild place by your own choice, are beyond help, beyond witness. Why would you have allowed yourself to be in this vulnerable position if you didn't want something to happen? Simple presence in wild places constitutes the provocation. So this is what you get.* Being in the wilderness with a small subset of men *is* the inviting outfit, and they somehow forget that if you weren't there you would not be fit for the profession. This is the double-bind of situational predation: You have to show up to get your chance. And when you do, it's read as a signal of willingness. What prey is ever willing? We survive.

Allied bombers in World War II suffered staggeringly high loss rates, with 50 percent or more of some squadrons shot down in a single mission. In response, the military analyzed the damage patterns on returned planes (Mangel & Samaniego 259) and added shielding to areas where anti-aircraft shrapnel holes were densest. They studied the attributes of the pilots, their crews, the flight patterns. And still the devastating losses continued.

Then Abraham Wald, a mathematician working on wartime problems as part of the Statistical Research Group at Columbia University,[1] made the counterintuitive recommendation to add structural reinforcements to the *undamaged* areas on successfully returning planes. He reasoned that when a plane is hit in its most vulnerable sections, it goes down, so the damage pattern that caused the crash can never be directly observed. By this reasoning, Wald recommended reinforcement on engine housings, a location where the safely returned planes showed almost no direct strikes. When his recommendations were implemented, the survival rates of Allied bombers soared.

The military's earlier focus on successfully returned planes is an example of survivorship bias—the logical error of focusing on objects (or people) that "made it past some selection process, and overlooking those that did not, typically because of their lack of visibility" (Hemprich-Bennett et al. 373). Survival analysis, whether in theaters of war, demography, medicine, or academic attrition, begins with a consideration of the *entire set of entrants to a cohort* because attrition cannot be understood by assessing the attributes of the survivors alone. The explanatory factors of attrition are written on those who never made it home. In no way am I comparing academic research pipeline problems to the stark heartbreak of wartime pilots losing their lives. Wald's insight is an accessible example of a common logical error, one that underpins meritocratic myths.

I got up before first light the next morning, got in my little tin can of a car and maneuvered down the track back to the main road. I registered for classes, rented a room in a boardinghouse. The rest of my time at the university I scheduled monthly meetings with my cowboy supervisor and sat on the hard chair in the corner of his office and reported on my progress. I'd stay for ten minutes, ask carefully prepared questions. He would answer monosyllabically. I submitted a research plan, moved ahead, unguided.

Halfway through my program I met his other female grad student who worked in another state. She had long pink fingernails and she wasn't talking. Fair enough; by then I wasn't talking either. After she defended her dissertation, she got a job as an animal control officer. Basically a dogcatcher. Once I saw her driving around the sleepy western town in the dog-catcher van staring blankly ahead, her long rose-colored nails tapping the steering wheel. Did she fuck him or not? Can't tell. Either way, going through the work of a PhD so you can noose-pole racoons seemed unfortunate.

In my second year I went to a professor I trusted and asked him how to transfer. He said that graduate school is a closed and intimate system built on personal relationships. Researchers in a field all know each other, and leaving a particular supervisor requires letters of recommendation and a cogent professional reason. He finished by emphasizing that the graduate degree is the essential credential required to move ahead in a field. I should put my head down, stay, and finish however I could. So I did. I stayed not out of any particular fortitude but rather out of desperation because I needed the teaching assistantship stipend and had nowhere else to go. When I submitted my thesis my Wild Turkey supervisor gave it back to me two weeks later with his single summary comment on the title page: "Too many commas." Which is actually funny when you think about it, because I do use a lot of commas.

Present-day statistics on harassment of female graduate students, staff, and faculty in science and technology are consistent with rates first measured thirty years ago: around 50 percent of those surveyed report some form of harassment (Rosenthal et al. 364). Some fields are worse than others. I might have been better off with fruit flies.

Another factor was the lack of protection and support from a powerful figure. Ideally this advocate would be the supervisor, but it could also be any ally with standing: father, brother, husband, uncle, colleague. This aegis component is difficult to quantify because it's as much about the things that are prevented from happening to a vulnerable early career person as it is about direct benefits. It's about guidance, but also protection from hostility. Protégé means "protected one." A sponsoring powerful figure vested in a young person's success is the essential reinforcement of the weak points on the aircraft of an early career. Other essential protective factors are, of course, social class, caste, money, race, network, institutional culture.

Even now, a lifetime later, a part of me still believes that if I had done something differently there would have been a better outcome. I'm ashamed in a complicated way, mostly because the story I tried to fortify myself with—that I was good enough—was not borne out by fact. I was also felled by the capitalist myth of meritocracy in which the blame for failure is placed on those who don't make it. We idolize *The Queen's Gambit*-like few who endure and triumph. Their stories of heroic perseverance, of profound positive contribution based on heart, skill, intellect, decades of grinding hard work and sacrifice are confusing because they suggest that if the rest of us had been just that much more unstoppable and amazing, we would also have triumphed. But Abraham Wald showed that the pilots of the planes that never came home were by all measurable criteria as qualified and able. It wasn't the quality of the individuals that determined their survival; it was an encounter with a lethally timed piece of incendiary material when onboard an inadequately reinforced aircraft.

All of this is relevant not only because of our own aspirations alongside those of our daughters, sisters, friends, and colleagues—but more importantly because science and technology professionals determine public policies, climate science responses, and research trajectories in a self-reinforcing cascade. These decisions occur across multitudes of essential domains—ones we all have a stake in, no matter how much we do or don't care about how science and technology are conducted.

Change requires the ability to understand Abraham Wald's insight that the fates of the unseen will always be deeply informative, especially if we are clever enough to look beyond the overt survivors. If we pause to look to the lost, we can better figure out how to rescue the remaining peers. Our job is to understand likelihood, cause and effect, survivorship bias, and that human talent has upper bounds when trapped in a system failure.

Notes

1. Bomber Command Museum, Nanton, Alberta, Canada. Bomber command loss rates, https://www.bombercommandmuseum.ca/bomber-command/bomber-commands-losses/. International Bomber Command Centre Archive, https://internationalbcc.co.uk/history/losses-database/.

Works Cited

Mangel, M., and F. J. Samaniego. "Abraham Wald's Work on Aircraft Survivability." *Journal American Statistical Association*, vol. 79, no. 386, 1984, pp. 259-67.

Hemprich-Bennett, D., et al. 2021. "Beware Survivorship Bias in Advice on Science Careers: For Objective Career Advice, Talk to Those Who Left Science as Well as Those Who Stayed. *Nature*, vol. 598, no. 7880, 373-74, https://doi.org/10.1038/d41586-021-02634-z.

Rosenthal, M. N., et al. "Still Second Class: Sexual Harassment of Graduate Students." *Psychology of Women Quarterly*, vol. 40, no. 3, 2016. Original doi: 10.1177/0361684316644838.

2

This Chapter Not Intentionally Left Blank

ANONYMOUS

3

Unbecoming the Other Me

A Female Academic Trapped in the Male Student Gaze

AIMEE PARKISON

As a young professor of creative writing, I was excited to teach my first screenwriting course, an undergraduate workshop with over twenty students. One of those students was an older man, around my father's age. Early in the semester, this student visited my office to apologize for staring at me.

"I have something I have to tell you," he said with a smile. "This is going to sound really weird. I wasn't sure if I should tell you, but I can't not tell you. I have this ex-girlfriend who looks exactly like you. You could be her twin. I can't concentrate in class. Every time I see you, I see her. You could even be her. At first, I thought you were her, but you have a different voice. You don't believe me? I'll bring you a photograph of her to prove it."

"You don't have to do that," I said.

"It's making me feel so strange to be here with you because I don't know if she's alive or dead. She's on drugs. She's an addict. She's a whore."

"What?" I asked.

"She's a whore, and you look just like her."

I began to receive emails from him, requesting that I call him at night using his personal phone number. He explained he was "very eager to please" me but wanted to make sure he was "doing the assignment" to my "satisfaction," his words full of innuendo. He began visiting my office hours to bring me photographs of his ex—or the woman he claimed to be her—in various poses in motel rooms and on beds.

Low-quality photographs taken with disposable cameras in bad lighting of cheap motels showed an uncanny resemblance between me and the woman. We were not just the same age, the same height, the same body type; we also had similar coloring, facial features, hair color, and hair styles.

That this was happening with a student in my screenwriting class intensified the sense of threat. Visual images are particularly powerful in the context of screenwriting, where one must imagine the script as a blueprint for a motion picture. This student seemed to be showing me stills from scenes in a movie about a woman who looked just like me, or perhaps a movie about me played by an actress who resembled me displayed in positions he wanted to put me in, where the mise-en-scène was sleazy.

Here's a montage of actual photographs he showed me, where the woman's face resembled my face:

1. Dressed in blue jeans and a leather jacket, the woman is sitting on the edge of a bed near a pack of cigarettes and a stack of money. In this dim motel room scarred by cigarette burns, she stares at the camera, unsmiling.

2. Near the car window, silhouetted in streetlight, the woman gazes at the distance, marking time.

3. In close-up, why is she crying?

4. Covered in a towel and wet, her eyes are empty.

5. Her right hand handcuffed to the hand of a man, her face is out of the frame, unfocused in shadow.

She was my doppelganger, a sex worker my student claimed he had engaged for sex. She went missing, addicted to street drugs, presumed dead. Exhilarated, he claimed to have created a website devoted to her decline with photographs of her being degraded while looking "exactly" like me.

Here are questions I ponder:

Was this about gender or age?

Was it about sex or power?

Was it about teaching creative writing, or even teaching screenwriting?

Was the woman in the photos real?

What messages was my student sending me, and why?

Why did it feel threatening?

What should I have done differently, knowing what I know now?

At the time, it never occurred to me that a professor could be sexually harassed by a student. Any sexual harassment between a professor and a student is assumed to victimize the student, since the professor has all the power. When it started to happen, I didn't recognize that I was being harassed and didn't know what to do or how to seek help. I mistook the situation for a crossing of boundaries that often happens in the arts, where conversations can be intensely personal.

Since I didn't realize that traditional power structures in academia don't hold true for female instructors harassed by male students, I couldn't rescue the younger me anymore than I could help her doppelganger in the photographs.

Even now, the power of the images the student showed me remains mysterious. I've wanted to understand what he was attempting to do to me, how he did it, and why. At the time, seeing the images felt invasive. I was being shown things I didn't want to see and being invited to see myself in images of another woman, images that were sexualized as well as implicitly violent and harmful to my sense of self.

These images gave the man who created them and showed them to me power over the woman in the photographs and power over me when I was invited to view the images and to discuss them. Because of the narrative context my student created and conveyed, these images were pornographic, a sort of forced sexual experience that was as unexpected as it was unwanted. "Pornography, in the feminist view, is a form of forced sex, a practice of sexual politics, an institution of gender inequality," claims Catharine A. MacKinnon in *Feminism and Pornography* (2000). Pornography isn't just about sex. It is about linking sex to power. When it comes to gender and power, "pornography institutionalizes the sexuality of male supremacy, which fuses the erotization of dominance and submission with the social construction of male and female" (171).

Perhaps because people believe what they see more than what they are told or what they hear, photography can be the ultimate weapon to disarm a woman of her power, especially in academia, where we think we are protected by our status and titles. My student was using photography to disempower me because he saw me in a different way than I saw myself and in a different way than I was supposed to be seen in my role as his professor. "Men treat women as who they see women as being. Pornography constructs who that is. Men's power over women means that the way men see women defines who women can be" (MacKinnon 171).

My student was using photographs to disempower me and to train me to see the world as he saw it. Pornography is often used to teach women things men want them to know, unwelcomed lessons that threaten a woman's view of herself. Discussing the role of pornography in undermining a potential victim's ability to avoid or resist rape, Diana E. H. Russell states that whenever "women are shown such materials, they probably feel more obliged to engage in unwanted sex acts that they mistakenly believe are normative" (81).

Essentially, in showing me photographs of a woman who looked like me allegedly engaged in sex work while imprisoned by addiction, my student was reinforcing his idea of male supremacy by showing me that he was superior to me. In *Our Blood: Prophecies and Discourses on Sexual Politics* (1976), Andrea Dworkin reminds us that our culture "is *male supremacist*: that is, men are, by birthright, law, custom, and habit, systematically and consistently defined as superior to women . . . a gender class over and against women . . . in every organ and institution of this culture. There are no exceptions to this particular rule" (51).

In my student's mind, what was truly odd was not that I looked like his ex but that a woman who physically resembled his ex was in a position of respect and authority over him in the role of teacher. He immediately set out to disempower me by attempting to reverse our roles in order to become my teacher by using pornography. By showing me things that I didn't want to see, he forced me to learn the world as he saw it and to understand my place in the world.

If I could revisit the past to give the younger me advice, I would tell her that no matter how much professional power or authority a woman is supposed to have due to her position and title, a woman is still a woman. Certain men will assume she isn't really in charge, and they will find a way to illustrate this to any woman who doesn't want to be the object of the male's desire. One way of doing this is for a man to embarrass a woman by reminding her of his sexual mastery of women he likens to her. The older a man is compared to the woman, the more likely his feelings of patriarchal entitlement will be heightened by a misguided paternal authority.

The question of how I should have responded as opposed to how I did respond is clearer to me now. At the time, I attempted to teach class as if nothing was amiss. Thankfully, the student dropped the class midsemester after explaining that he couldn't concentrate, behave appropriately, or learn anything from me because I looked like *her*. After his departure, other students in the class confessed their relief at his going, telling me that he had been "doing a line" of cocaine on his desk before leaving. I knew then my embarrassment was a warning. I should have taken action.

Today, I realize that my lack of reaction does its own damage. If existing systems of combating gender oppression fail and even harm women in academia, one of the greatest harms is not knowing what constitutes sexual harassment and how it disempowers us. Another harm is pretending everything is okay, or thinking like men—that if we do our job well, we will be respected and everything will be alright. Sometimes doing the job well isn't enough to gain respect, authority, or peace of mind. I had to learn that no matter how effective I was as a teacher, gender was always a factor in how students would relate to me. I might experience a type of disempowerment, disrespect, or vulnerability that male colleagues would not and in ways so strange, insidious, and improbable that even the best faculty handbooks might not anticipate them.

When these harms first started, I should have documented each transgressive occurrence and reported the student's behavior to an administrator and/or to the Office of Student Conduct, which would have looked into the student's records for any possible related history, while also updating confidential records with my report to protect other women. The university could have assigned a counselor or adviser to contact the student to discuss appropriate behaviors and offered me support. Many people who work for universities, in such places as Student Support and Conduct, HR Title IX Specialists, and the Dean of Students Office, offer faculty support if a student happens to fixate on a faculty member for reasons that have nothing to do with the class. The best services help students while helping faculty. For instance, Student Support and Conduct provides support to students who are experiencing mental health issues, relational conflicts, or behavioral issues, and is intended to be a holistic approach administered by professionals trained in intervention to address and prevent sexual violences; but these people cannot help a faculty member if she doesn't ask for help, and a faculty member cannot know to ask for help until she realizes help is available—and that she needs it.

Works Cited

Dworkin, Andrea. *Our Blood: Prophecies and Discourses on Sexual Politics*. Harper & Row, 1976.

MacKinnon, Catharine A. "Not a Moral Issue." In *Feminism and Pornography*, edited by Drucilla Cornell, pp. 169-97. Oxford UP, 2000.

Russell, Diana E. H. "Pornography and Rape, A Casual Model." In *Feminism and Pornography*, edited by Drucilla Cornell, pp. 48-93. Oxford UP, 2000.

4

Keeping Women in Their Place

Sexism in Religious Universities

RACHEL NOORDA

The intersection of higher education and religion reveals an environment of heightened sexism. The religious context compounds existing sexism in higher education because religious universities can also be less egalitarian than secular ones, especially if their corresponding theologies are highly gendered. Silencing, othering, and undermining are a few of the ways in which gendered abuse is manifest in this context.

I experienced gendered abuse during a job interview and application process as one of the top two candidates for a tenure-track position at a higher-education institution operated by the Church of Jesus Christ of Latter-Day Saints (LDS church). The LDS church, like many religions, is focused on traditional and limiting family roles (such as mother at home full-time with children) for cis heterosexual couples. Women cannot hold positions of power in the organization because they cannot be ordained to the priesthood. Queer couples are not allowed to participate in essential temple ordinances. Even seemingly progressive ideologies are approached through a patriarchal lens; for example, Heavenly Mother (the spouse of God, or Heavenly Father) is an "essential" deity, but her qualities or characteristics are rarely discussed. Moreover, the LDS church has recently condemned praying to Heavenly Mother (Renlund 2022).

Research has illustrated how patriarchy is manifest at the intersection of higher education and Christianity in Christian universities and
colleges. Such scholarship asserts that the value Christian culture puts
on motherhood contributes to prejudice against single, childless women
working in higher education (Dahlvig). The Christian virtue of humility
makes it more difficult for women to reconcile with their career drives
and leadership ambitions than men, likely because femininity for Christian
women is equated with being quiet, supportive, and unassuming, exacerbating imposter syndrome through these internalized beliefs (Dahlvig).

Lack of female faculty representation and gender-wage gaps are
evidence of institutional sexism. At LDS higher-education institution
Brigham Young University (BYU), only 34.5 percent of faculty were
women in 2019, whereas the national percentage for women faculty in
higher education in the US is 47 percent (National Center for Education
Statistics). Women faculty at BYU also earn 20.8 percent less than male
colleagues (Gonzalez).

Why does representation of women in academia matter? Poet,
essayist, and feminist Adrienne Rich argues that the patriarchal family is
replicated in the university, where teacher "fathers" train and encourage
student "daughters," leaving out the creative mother (139). One of the
primary reasons I chose to apply to the tenure-track position at BYU was
to increase representation of women professors there, which I had craved
to see as an undergraduate student at that institution.

The following autoethnographic essay of my own job interview
experience at BYU clarifies three specific ways that sexism manifests at
the intersection of higher education and religion: (1) my self-efficacy
and competence were undermined, (2) I was silenced and othered, and
(3) I was asked to maintain traditional gender roles. Because the power
dynamics at play here are important contextually, I will note that not only
was I a female candidate for the position in a department that had only
three women full-time faculty (out of roughly twenty full-time faculty),
but I was also a job applicant in my twenties, and therefore in a position
of little power already. I was also an active member of the LDS church.
My hope is that my experience will validate other women's experiences of
sexism at the intersection of religion and higher ed, but also that voicing
this experience might lead to reflection and change in religious universities. I conclude with actionable steps that a religious university (such as
BYU) might take to address misogyny.

Undermining Self-efficacy and Underplaying Competence

During the course of the multiday interview process, I had two informal lunches with professors from the department. Over one of these lunches, I was asked about my PhD thesis, and I proudly and confidently proclaimed that I passed my defense with no corrections. But the response to my confident remark undercut my competence and undermined my self-efficacy. One of the male professors in the room reframed and devalued the accomplishment, by pointing out that I had completed my PhD in the UK. "You wouldn't have passed with no corrections if you did your PhD in the US; it's much more rigorous here."

Later, after lunch, a professor in the department belittled me by drawing attention to my age and former student status at the institution. Since this was the same department where I had received my under-graduate degree, I had taken classes from many of the faculty who were now part of the interview process—and were potential future colleagues, should I get the job. Many of the faculty took delight in the fact that I had my start in their department at BYU, and I enjoyed chatting with them. But others used this opportunity to imply that I was too young to be a competent, knowledgeable colleague. One professor went so far as to search through his old class lists, find my picture from when I was his student, and then show it to everyone while we were chatting. I tried to laugh it off by saying, "Oh wow! I can't believe you found that. That's a blast from the past." To which he replied, "It was only a few years ago." By emphasizing my age and the number of years between my undergrad-uate degree and PhD completion, he again sent the clear message that I was underqualified and incompetent. By presenting my student photo to the committee members, he planted in their minds an image of me as not only young but also lacking the knowledge, maturity, and authority required for the position.

Undermining self-efficacy and underplaying competence are accom-plished through patronization and condescension. Bourabain defines patronization as "the undervaluation of women's presence and work by key constituents in a variety of ways." Bourabain's in-depth interviews reveal how women are undervalued in their roles as academics: "Although they have the expertise, they are often 'forgotten' to be included or to be addressed in a proper manner. . . . This invisibility is reinforced by undervaluing and unacknowledging their work and abilities. Their work is the result of 'luck' or the 'help of others'" (258). In this particular interview experience, my excellence in PhD work was minimized and written off as luck. Rather than addressing me and my expertise in a professional manner, the committee members dismissed my experience because of my age. While young male scholars are often encouraged and esteemed as wunderkinds, being young and female remains a barrier in academia (Archer).

Silencing and Othering

At a religious university, patriarchal structures of academia and religion are intertwined with and substantiated by doctrine. One of the common ways to keep current power structures in place is through silencing, making it difficult for women's voices to be heard. Unsurprisingly, Biggs, Hawley, and Biernat found that women who "felt silenced also expressed increased intentions to exit from academic careers" (394). Self-silencing is a coping mechanism sometimes used by women when confronted with sexist behaviors, but silencing (whether self-imposed or not) maintains the status quo and upholds patriarchal power structures. "Silence may be reflective of experiencing detachment and a lack of belonging," Biggs, Hawley, and Biernat note (398). During this job interview, I struggled to make my voice heard while committee members othered me, emphasizing that I did not belong in that community.

On the evening of the second day, I went to dinner with members of the department: six male faculty and me. While much of the discussion was unrelated to work, the gender composition of our dinner party was palpable. At one point, a professor addressed it outright, saying that because the department had so few women, department meetings became like "priesthood meetings." (In the LDS church, this term describes meetings that only men are invited to attend.) The professor went on to argue that because department meetings functioned like priesthood meetings, "You're going to need to speak up so you can be heard." Despite his attempt to package the hostile comment as kindness, he further demonstrated how isolated I was as a woman in academia, and the words became a thinly veiled threat. In that moment, I was painfully aware of how my status as a respected colleague was already being diminished even at the interview stage. The professor had masked his ostracizing in the "fatherly advice" of benevolent sexism, a destructive and tenacious form of prejudice

(Hammond et al.) that upholds gender inequality (Glick & Fiske) and is more difficult to identify and address because its perceived warmth masks patronization and power dynamics.

Upholding Traditional Gender Roles

The final process of the tenure-track job application at BYU is a meeting between the candidate and a General Authority: a man in a senior leadership position in the LDS church, usually from the Quorum of the Seventy or twelve apostles. I was asked to bring my husband with me to the interview. Given that I was the one applying to this job, not my husband, it did not seem appropriate that we were asked to attend the interview as a unit. This "request" illustrated that my identity as a wife and potential mother was more important than my qualifications as an academic.

Toward the end of the interview, which was held in the General Authority's office in Salt Lake City, I was asked to respond to a particular scenario question: if a female student came to me asking questions about why women couldn't hold the priesthood, what would I tell her? There was only one "correct" answer to this question, which I knew well from my own long history with the church. To criticize the gendered nature of priesthood power would not be an option. This interview question informed me that one of my purposes as a minority woman professor would be to uphold traditional gender roles and power structures not only in my own life and department but also in my advice to students.

Conclusion and Recommendations

Application process: Research has shown that applications by women are better received in gender-blind reviews of their application materials (Goldin & Rouse, Moss-Racusin et al., Savigny). Implementing a blind CV review process would be a good starting point in an overhaul of hiring practices at a religious university.

Interview practices: If women are silenced and othered even in the interview process, they are much less likely to accept faculty positions. As religious universities strive to increase gender equity and representation, it will be important for them to reexamine interview practices, such as including religious leaders and female applicants' husbands. Institutions also need to provide gender-inclusive training for hiring committees, especially those dominated by men, to target the following behaviors. *Credibility acknowledgment:* Being othered, silenced, and questioned as a colleague or potential colleague is demoralizing for women applicants at religious universities. If Christian universities want not only to treat colleagues of all genders equitably but also embody the teachings of Christ (on which these religious institutions and doctrines are built), then they must validate and celebrate the accomplishments of women as they do for men.

Communication training: Good people can enact gender bias. Lack of intentionality does not make sexist behaviors acceptable in the academic workplace. I did not speak directly with all of the faculty involved in this particular job interview about the sexist comments and attitudes, but I believe many of them would be surprised to hear how their actions and words had been so harmful. Faculty need training so that they recognize these behaviors, especially covert and benevolent sexism, in themselves and colleagues, so institutions can develop mechanisms for preventing and calling out harmful behaviors.

My interview experience for a BYU tenure-track position is best summarized by Savigny: "There is a cumulative, drip drip of routinized practices and discourses where women are marginalized, their contributions ignored or devalued, their role assumed to be that of inexperience which can result in their loss of confidence" (2017, 649). These seemingly small drops add up over time, over a career, and make it much more difficult for women to be successful and happy in academic positions, especially at religious universities.

Works Cited

Archer, Louise. "Younger Academics' Constructions of 'Authenticity', 'Success' and Professional Identity." *Studies in Higher Education*, vol. 33, no. 4, 2008, 385–403.

Biggs, Jacklyn, Patricia H. Hawley, and Monica Biernat. "The Academic Conference as a Chilly Climate for Women: Effects of Gender Representation on Experiences of Sexism, Coping Responses, and Career Intentions." *Sex Roles*, vol. 78, 2018, 394–408.

Bourabain, Dounia. "Everyday Sexism and Racism in the Ivory Tower: The Experiences of Early Career Researchers on the Intersection of Gender and Ethnicity in the Academic Workplace." *Gender, Work & Organization*, vol. 28, no. 1, 2021, 248–67.

Dahlvig, Jolyn E. "A Narrative Study of Women Leading within the Council for Christian Colleges and Universities." *Christian Higher Education*, vol. 12, 1-2, 2013, 93-109.

"Data Snapshot: Full-Time Women Faculty and Faculty of Color." *AAUP*, 9 December 2020, https://www.aaup.org/news/data-snapshot-full-time-women-faculty-and-faculty-color.

Glick, Peter, and Susan T. Fiske. "An Ambivalent Alliance: Hostile and Benevolent Sexism as Complementary Justifications for Gender Inequality." *American Psychologist*, vol. 56, no. 2, 2001, 109.

Goldin, Claudia, and Cecilia Rouse. "Orchestrating Impartiality: The Impact of "Blind" Auditions on Female Musicians." *American Economic Review*, vol. 90, no. 4, 2000, 715-41.

Gonzalez, Sydnee. "Gender Inequality in BYU Faculty More than Just a Numbers Game." *Daily Universe*, 22 October 2019, https://universe.byu.edu/2019/10/22/gender-inequality-in-byu-faculty-more-than-just-a-numbers-game/.

Hammond, Matthew D., et al. "Benevolent Sexism and Hostile Sexism across the Ages." *Social Psychological and Personality Science*, vol. 9, no. 7, 2018, 863-74.

Moss-Racusin, Corinne A., et al. "Science Faculty's Subtle Gender Biases Favor Male Students." *Proceedings of the National Academy of Sciences*, vol. 109, no. 41, 2012, 16474-79.

"The NCES Fast Facts Tool Provides Quick Answers to Many Education Questions (National Center for Education Statistics)." National Center for Education Statistics, https://nces.ed.gov/fastfacts/display.asp?id=61. Accessed 2 Aug. 2023.

Renlund, Dale. "Your Define Nature and Eternal Destiny." LDS General Conference, April 2022.

Rich, Adrienne. *On Lies, Secrets and Silence*. London: Virago, (1979)1986.

Savigny, Heather. "Women, Know Your Limits: Cultural Sexism in Academia." *Gender and Education*, vol. 26, no. 7, 2014, 794-809.

———. "Cultural Sexism Is ordinary: Writing and Re-writing Women in Academia." *Gender, Work and Organization*, vol. 24, no. 6, 2017, 643-55.

5

The Snake

Surviving Misogyny in Tunisia

Souhir Zekri Masson

She shall crush thy head, and thou shalt lie in wait for her heel.

—Genesis 3:15

The epigraph of this chapter has many meanings in relation to my own story: "Snake" is the surname given to my harasser by his victims. Derived from the Bible, the quotation describes the curse of the serpent and the Virgin (the second Eve) who conquers it to save humanity from (another) fall. The third meaning, more optimistic, relates to the snake's rebirth by shedding its skin. My harasser represents the snake of sexual harassment, a ubiquitous threat that keeps reappearing everywhere, all the time. On the other hand, I also turned into a snake, for I succeeded in crushing sexual harassment, at least psychologically and physically, and being reborn as a new woman.

When I returned to Tunis from Glasgow after my defense to implement the final revisions of my PhD dissertation, I was very hopeful about my future career. Once the external reviewer approved the final version, I would finally become a doctor in English studies. Nine years earlier, my master's defense in Tunisia had not gone well due to a corrupt jury. This academic achievement had given me back my confidence in myself and my writing and research skills. I knew that, this time, I had been judged appropriately, following strict standards, by professional and well-meaning persons.

But in order to teach in my own country, I still had to sit for a national exam that would allow me to access a tenured position at university. The exam went smoothly, as it had taken place only four months after my defense, so my perspective on my research and four-year teaching career was solid and clear. I had failed to ask around for information before filling in the list of desired faculties and institutes, and only chose those located in the capital, confident that my exam score would allow me to rank among the best (and so access the universities closest to home). To my great dismay, this did not happen. When I received the official assignment, I read the words "Faculty of Letters of K.," and I thought I'd faint. I cried for days on end. It wasn't because I didn't want to teach in a distant city, as I had already worked in more remote places farther south, such as Gafsa or Sfax. Besides, I had very close relatives in K. As things turned out, being able to see my favorite cousin more often would prove to be a huge consolation.

K. has always been the historical capital of Islam, where religious conservatism rules and women's movements and behavior are very restricted, and at the same time, as I would find out later, it is very morally corrupt. I had had a strict education as a child, was even a practicing Muslim until I reached my early teen years, so I knew exactly what moral guilt and fear meant. But at the age of sixteen, I suddenly craved freedom, and an irrepressible revulsion for everything restrictive or religious took root within me, forever to stay. I knew all that was socially forbidden me, like smoking in public or joking with men, so at K. I had to adjust my behavior and hide my true liberated self, as I had been doing for the last thirty years. Nevertheless, I tried to recover some of my optimism: I loved academia and teaching, so I felt this assignment would be worth it.

I met my would-be harasser, whom I will call AB (after Agatha Christie's ABC murderer), on my first day of work in September 2012. I remember being surprised by his sinuous, snake-like gait, as if he had no skeleton, and his unprofessional familiarity. Since he didn't introduce himself as a teacher, I thought he worked in administration, which meant I wouldn't be seeing much of him. He insisted on giving me a tour of the premises, then he gave me his phone number "in case you need help." I wasn't suspicious of friendliness back then, so I wasn't on my guard with him. The first few months went rather well: the students were nice and

I was given freedom in devising my courses and choosing the literature subjects I preferred. In fact, I was happy for the first two years as I took part in conferences and was appreciated by most of my colleagues.

What would happen near the end of the second year sounds like the plot of a tragedy. The current head of department, who had been kind to me so far, resigned in protest of some administrative issue. One of our male colleagues, OA, volunteered during an urgent meeting to replace him temporarily. OA soon offered me the position of master's coordinator, allowing me to simultaneously become a member of the scientific committee. Considering K.'s social and misogynistic narrow-mindedness, all such changes were unacceptable to my patriarchal entourage as they afforded me "too much power" for a newbie academician, a woman in her thirties who had just obtained her PhD from Scotland, and who, on top of all that, came from Tunis, *the capital*, with all its fantasies of Westernized temptations and freed womanhood. Later I would find out that, as a divorced woman, I was also a social threat, as I was seen as no longer a virgin and therefore "easy." Unfortunately, my constant smile and happy disposition reflected the image of a naive, unsuspecting person and events started taking an evil turn.

Members of the scientific committee are elected or appointed and review academic matters. As a result, AB's attitude started metamorphosing. On some occasions, he would stop me in one of the corridors, yelling: "How come you get to be part of the scientific committee? You can't represent me!" On other occasions, he asked other colleagues "not to cooperate" with me, going as far as using verbal and physical intimidation to sabotage the meetings I organized. A few weeks after my appointment, an academic coup d'état took place. I was told that the dean was forced, also through intimidation and physical aggression, to appoint AB as head of department. Everyone was taken aback and the long dictatorial "rule" of AB, "the snake," began.

The administrative harassment escalated, insidiously. AB went back to his unctuous behavior and kept inviting me to "come to my office," saying "let's discuss issues in my office" and "I need to see you outside of the university because I have things to tell you." My polite refusals and offers to talk right there in the hall led to a first punitive measure, a form of administrative warning, ironically called in Arabic "drawing attention," in which he falsely accused me not only of refusing to "coordinate with the head of department" but also of repetitive unexcused absences. I was outraged to have my serious professional attitude so unjustly judged and tainted. I knew perfectly well I had done nothing wrong. It was a "discreet" form of sexual harassment at first, and I thought: "Well, this happens every day to every Tunisian woman; there's nothing I can do." But his position as head of department had increased his delusion of greatness and his actual power. He was apparently convinced that every woman in the department would fall into his arms.

After the exams, I received a strange phone call from the Board of Higher Education requesting my presence in their office the following morning. I was friends with N., the current vice dean at the time, so I called him to try to understand what it was all about. He told me "Something terrible is going to take place; I think you're going to be questioned about your exam marks." My heart pounded so hard that I could almost hear it inside my temples. I had no idea what was coming but a terrible anguish overwhelmed me.

My mother offered to drive me to K., as I was too nervous to deal with the two-hour trip on my own. We arrived to the Board's whitewashed building and I went in alone. Three men and a woman, including the president of the Board, were waiting for me. His first words chilled me to the bone: "You are accused of having forged another teacher's signature and of illegally modifying student exam marks on official scripts."

I couldn't understand what was happening. An administrative lawsuit had been filed against me and I didn't know who was at the origin of this blatantly false accusation. Like a suspect, like a thief, I was being grilled, intimidated by such threats as "I can have you erased from higher education" and "Why don't you admit it? You felt sorry for these poor students and were just trying to help them." Nothing could stop the flow of my tears—tears of surprise, shock, disbelief, and utter despair at such attacks on my professional and personal integrity. I had always done my best to follow regulations with utmost honesty. I couldn't stand to be subjected to such unfair treatment. So I kept crying and denying their "facts," until the president started talking about how the head of department "certainly couldn't let such an affront be tolerated in our faculty at K."

The picture was being made clearer and clearer. The president handed me a folder containing copies of exam scripts displaying my written marks, some of them scratched out and rewritten, together with the testimonies of two of my colleagues: the panel head and a woman colleague named A. I had made a mistake while changing my mind about some of the scores: teachers are supposed to add a signature and rewrite the final score in full letters. It is also the duty of the panel head (the teacher who collects marks for the administration) to point out such mistakes, but he didn't do so, to ensure the fault was mine only. A. was now accusing me of having kept the exam scripts out of her sight for "at least half an hour" to supposedly modify marks and forge her signature. I later heard that she herself had been threatened and blackmailed into writing her report. To make a long story short, I had to provide detailed answers on a questionnaire to defend myself and then undergo a second cross-examination involving a direct confrontation with A. But this time, I was ready. I had had access to the file thanks to a friendly intervention and was able to determine that no one, other than myself, had written anything on the scripts. My confidence in my ability to prove my innocence strengthened my resolve to have the signatures analyzed by a professional, as I was left-handed and A. wasn't. A. was nervous and kept saying that she had done her job and I had not. This whole masquerade ended with a double warning to A. and me.

At the beginning of this painful experience, I had doubted and blamed myself for my lack of meticulousness. But as I started experiencing sharp feelings of injustice, I began seeking definitions of what "harassment" really meant. I needed to do something about this constant undermining of my mental integrity, something radical that could lessen the burning pain and frustration about AB's impunity. Many other women colleagues had filed official complaints against him before, but none won their case. Besides, I needed to be completely sure that in filing a complaint I would not be risking further humiliation: it would be my word against his and I had no clear evidence to prove what he was doing to me. Ironically, I came across the right explanation while watching an American TV series, *Drop Dead Diva*, when the protagonist, a woman lawyer, said in court, "When a male supervisor turns a woman colleague's place of work into a hostile environment, it is considered sexual harassment." I was at once reassured and disheartened: accusing my boss of sexual harassment was morally valid in my mind, but only legally valid in the United States.

After the end of the exam mark investigation, I hardly spoke to anyone at work, and a long bout of sadness and depression overtook me. I had dreamy visions of sticking knives into AB's guts and flanks. I was scared of the person I was becoming through all this: my smile faded and my heart hardened as I dreaded the trip to K. a little more every week. Still, my teaching and student meetings were brief but uplifting respites from the stifling atmosphere in the department. I clung to those as for breath, and to the unfailing support of my family, friends, and husband.

One morning, my elder brother told me, "I feel like K. has changed you completely. You're not your own self anymore, you know?" I was shocked. I had not been aware of such a fundamental transformation. I thought to myself, "Do you really want to be that person? How long is this situation going to take?" I didn't want to be estranged from my happy, optimistic spirit. I wanted to be recognized by those closest to my heart, most particularly by myself.

My first decision was to speak again to all my colleagues, including those who had framed me. I thought that forgiving them would help my healing and lessen the mental isolation that had been stifling me for the past few weeks. I also resumed my academic writing—which had been at a standstill for the whole duration of this affair—and saw a pending article published. I applied for the associate professor position, and was first (obviously) rejected by the head of department, but ultimately his attempt to block me from promotion was to no avail, and I was promoted. These were both concrete and symbolic acts that revived my spirits, putting life back into my debilitated carcass, and I was slowly but surely finding my way back to the surface of life, both mentally and professionally.

Next I decided to move back to Tunis, where I had been born and raised. Of course, I had considered resigning altogether following the investigation, but I decided against it. After a few months of what felt like purgatory, I asked for an official transfer back to Tunis, knowing that, having only taught four years in K., my application could be rejected. The other problem was that AB was part of the official committee, meaning his agreement was compulsory. Fortunately, the vice dean, who had supported me throughout all this, was also part of that committee. I never knew the full details of what happened that day, but the vice dean told me after the meeting that he had pressured the committee to validate my transfer and "leave that poor woman alone." I accepted an offer to join what is now my current institution. There was light, at last, at the end of the tunnel.

I vividly remember the very last meeting I attended with the faculty of K. on 24 June 2016. I did not return to that city until my aunt's death in 2022. I am thankful every day for my new position, nearer home, and so promising with its new colleagues and fresh start. AB couldn't reach or hurt me anymore, I felt lighter, freer. I had filed three complaints in 2015 reporting what had happened to me in K.: at the Ministry of Higher Education and Scientific Research, at the Board (where part of the harassment took place), and at the teacher union, all of which fell on deaf ears. AB was apparently untouchable, corrupt since before the so-called revolution in 2011, adapting to each dictatorial regime's rules following Ben Ali's ousting. It did me good to put everything on paper, as I'm doing right at this moment, but ultimately I decided not to file a complaint with the more official administrative court, which would have meant more files and more confrontations. Sometimes I wish I had tried harder, but back then I was tired and needed to move on. I became pregnant one month after the final confirmation of my transfer reached me. I had been trying for a baby for more than a year and this second, brighter light finally ended my ordeal. I was born again with my son's birth.

Sexual harassment is dangerous, especially when it is not understood properly. I already knew street harassment, that uncomfortable pressure that makes you hate your own body and even desire its disappearance; it feels like a violent intrusion into a person's bubble of intimacy or safety. I felt that same discomfort and violation again every time AB looked at or talked to me, a sort of chill up and down my spine that made me want to vanish into thin air. I didn't know either form of harassment could be punished, so I ignored and trivialized it, like so many women who sadly internalize the fact that "they had asked for it," were "too beautiful" or "too alluring" or "too smiling." So often women choose to keep silent, allow their stories to be dismissed, or worse, hurt themselves. I don't blame those who keep silent because fear is the sad companion of harassment victims. I let go of the pain of this terrible experience, but I never surrendered. I have learned to resist, and defend myself and other women, by helping them understand that what is happening is not "trivial," and by verbally and administratively stopping any male colleague's attempts to intimidate me or turn my work environment into a hostile or uncomfortable one.

I hope that by reading my story, other women whose official complaints and unofficial sufferings have been blatantly ignored will find it in themselves to come forward and tell their stories as well. Although all the serpents out there may never be crushed, I hope that women in academia, especially those living in developing countries, can continue to dress as they like, speak their full minds, display a full smile, and, most importantly, be protected by clear and fair laws without risking the loss of physical and mental integrity.

6

Tall Poppy in the English Field

How Successful Women Are Mowed Down

Anonymous

Australians have a saying that the tall poppy gets mowed down. I was the tall poppy and the target of academic mobbing for twenty-four years. It wasn't only my height and self-respect that annoyed my English Department colleagues at the US university where I spent my professional career. My competence was also perceived as a threat: I was publishing more books and articles than my colleagues and was editor of a respected journal. Especially in teaching institutions with high course loads (four courses each semester, in my case), a woman's scholarly productivity may be penalized instead of rewarded when the majority of her colleagues are not producing scholarly work. Most academic-mobbing targets are high-achieving women with strong ethical standards and love for their work (Khoo).

Academic mobbing is "a non-violent, sophisticated, ganging up behavior adopted by academicians to 'wear and tear' a colleague down emotionally through unjustified accusation, humiliation, general harassment and emotional abuse . . . directed at the target under a veil of lies and justifications so that they are hidden to others and difficult to prove" (Khoo). Mobbing is far more common than typically understood, as it's tolerated and kept secret by its practitioners and victims, and sometimes whitewashed as "just the cost of working in academe."

Mobbing has a specific purpose, which is to ostracize the target until she leaves—whether by suicide or quitting (Leymann). The tall poppy cannot grow back after being hacked down; her only hope lies in transplant to greener pastures. Because of the fierce competition for an extreme scarcity of jobs in academia, however, targets of mobbing become stuck in their jobs. Most academics, especially in English literature and other humanities disciplines, cannot secure another position, yet they pay a high price for staying. While suffering the effects of ostracism and harassment, they're often unable to further their careers to make them more attractive on the job market. With lateral moves as a professor being sparse or nonexistent (and I did apply for all positions I might possibly qualify for), the main option for staying in academia is to develop leadership skills in hopes of being hired as a department or program chair at another university. But mobbing effectively blocks this professional development that might provide the only escape from abusive work conditions.

In addition to the professional costs of mobbing, the personal ones are significant. Long-term exposure not only robs the target of friends, a supportive workplace, and the joy and professional opportunities of their profession, but as a form of gaslighting, mobbing distorts the target's sense of reality. She may internalize the negative judgments of others and lose the social confidence that annoyed the bullies in the first place. After retiring early from my job to escape that trauma, I still suffer from PTSD. This manifests in an inability to trust individuals, institutions, and discussion forums that are intended to be free and nonjudgmental, but feel dangerous to me because I have experienced my speech being purposely misconstrued. I feel anxiety symptoms when I interact with a bully, especially when the power dynamic is tilted on their side, which means that giving feedback to them might worsen my situation. On such occasions, anxiety affects my sleep. I lack faith in organizations' complaint procedures because they have proven ineffective in the past and have even worsened my situation.

My intention in writing this article is to identify mobbing tactics so that readers may recognize them if they are present in their own work environments. These actions are unethical, unprofessional, and against written policy, but because of academic traditions, perpetrators get away with rationalizing or denying them. I will first describe four common tactics; then I will expand on three specific incidents that happened to me.

1. Slander. Three female colleagues were the instigators of the mobbing. The process began with sexually oriented slander that was passed among professors, and from professors to students. Some students who

had previously been friendly to me would suddenly begin ignoring me, particularly those working for my enemy-colleagues. Students would pass hours in their favorite professor's office, chatting, giggling, and whispering. The open-door policy didn't stop this pastime. This slander was one of the most egregious forms of mobbing since it interfered directly with my ability to do my job and the students' right to a fair education. By undermining a colleague's value as a teacher and human being, professors are able to decrease the enrollment of the target's courses and create an atmosphere of distrust toward her, which is personally and professionally damaging.

2. Ostracizing. My enemies prevented my friendships with other colleagues. Wanting to smooth their way, I would befriend new hires, being careful to avoid negative talk about the department or its established members. These new friendships would last only until they were noticed by my enemies, who would quickly warn new hires they must not be friendly with me if they wished to earn tenure. I learned that pretenure faculty were given an ultimatum by senior faculty: it was either me or them. This ultimatum extended even to part-time faculty members, one of whom applied for a full-time job and wasn't hired because she was friendly with me. This was unfair to her, and it was heartbreaking for me to lose friends because of slander and gossip. Ostracizing is extremely destructive to one's mental health. The practice effectively guaranteed that I would have no allies if I were to fight the injustices of this department, making collective complaint or action impossible for me.

3. Promotion blocked and sabotaged. After bringing two years toward tenure from my previous full-time teaching job, I was asked to give them back, ostensibly so my application for promotion and tenure would be successful in a later year. I didn't need any more publications to qualify for tenure. This request was effectively a demotion. It is a form of humiliation and harassment and a deprivation of the right to promotion's salary raise.

4. Work taken away. After tenure and promotion, I was denied leadership of committees and programs, though I volunteered for many such roles. I'm a scholarly person dedicated to research and teaching, so this might have been fine for me, except that it stymied my career. Only leadership experience would qualify me for other positions on the market, such as department chair or program director at other universities. Unless one is a superstar with a trendy monograph, one doesn't move laterally in the English field, except by taking on administrative roles. By denying me leadership experience, my colleagues kept me trapped in this difficult position and hindered my career.

Without diminishing the importance of scores of other instances of mobbing, I've chosen three incidents to highlight its insidious nature. When you are the target, it is difficult to understand such behavior and to believe that your colleagues are malicious. Once you realize this, it is hard to find allies and effective means to stop mobbing.

The Tenure Battle, Sexualized

In the years before my tenure application, the mobbing was apparent to me, but I did not realize the extent to which the enemy-colleagues would weaponize their gossip to deny me tenure. I was performing well in scholarship, service, and teaching, but the tenure committee described my student evaluation ratings in such a way as to make them look inferior. They didn't offer ways to help me raise those numbers, only using them against me.

I learned the true nature of the closed-committee discussion when a concerned colleague broke confidentiality and warned me of a scandal concerning my morality. Some female professors on the committee had accused me of sexual harassment of a particular male ("X") who taught in our department. X had completed coursework for the master's degree and was finishing his thesis. I liked X because he had a good sense of humor; I did not find him attractive or desire sex or romance with him. One of the enemy-colleagues had seen us playing racquetball at the gym and eating pizza in a downtown restaurant. I did not at that point understand that my friendliness with *any* person (colleague, student, townie, invited guest speaker) would be characterized as sexual and turned into scandal by colleagues looking for ammunition to get me fired.

The aforementioned concerned colleague asked X whether I had harassed him, and when X said no, my colleague asked him to explain this to the college dean. Without the concerned colleague's intervention, I would not have known that the denial of tenure was based on my colleagues' sexualization of me and my relationships. At each higher level of tenure review (dean, provost, president), the department committee's negative vote was affirmed, and tenure was denied. I appealed the decision. Thanks to a group of reasonable professors serving on the appeals committee, the vote was reversed, and I received tenure from a committee of ten professors who were not in my department.

Hospitality as Sexual Predation

After winning this battle, I thought my enemies would cease their warfare. Instead, they intensified their tactics as they looked for other ways to get me fired. (Meanwhile, I continued to apply diligently for other jobs each October, when the Modern Language Association Job List came out.)

One day, I was reprimanded by my female chair for an offense I still don't understand. After the evening talk of a guest speaker—who was a male professor from another university—another female colleague, who was in charge of transport, asked me to take over her duties so she could go home early. When I dropped off the guest speaker at his hotel, he asked whether we could continue our interesting collegial conversation. Going to a bar didn't appeal to either of us, so I invited him to my house for tea. When I informed my colleague, she immediately called the department chair (who was staunchly feminist) to complain. The next day the chair reprimanded me harshly for inviting the out-of-town guest speaker to my home, as it "looked bad." Was I framed for this offense? Could I have invited a female guest speaker to my home with impunity? If there are such rules in an academic department, they should be published so faculty know what is expected of them. Since the speaker and I were at equal "levels" of the profession, we should be "allowed" to enjoy social exchange without penalty. Is it impossible to understand that adult men and women can be friends, or did my colleagues just use the common assumption that they can't to impugn my character?

Weaponizing #MeToo

In midcareer, I began leading study-abroad trips—an opportunity allowed me only because the travel organization was external to our campus and therefore not subject to the mobbers' control. Our study-abroad trainer emphasized the need to make every student feel included. One way to keep folks engaged, he said, is to invite them to cultural events besides those on the syllabus. One afternoon, I took his advice and invited my class to see a film at the national film institute that evening. Of the three or four students who promised to attend, only one ("Y") showed up at our meeting place, the computer station in the hotel lobby. Coming from behind, she startled me at the desk where I was lost in email, so I said unguardedly, "Oh, you must be here for our date!" Of course, I meant the word as an "agreement to meet at a certain place and time to attend a cultural activity." Ours was an outing planned with several students and their instructor, clearly not a romantic date.

To reach the cinema, we walked through the rowdy crowds of the city's entertainment district, while I struggled to hear my student's words in the din. Arriving ten minutes early, we waited in the adjoining café. I offered Y a coffee and pastry, since she had no money—again, following instructions of the trainer, who warned us that students often run out of spending money, and we should pay for their snacks if we were so inclined.

Two or three years later, our Title IX investigator served me with a sexual harassment complaint filed by Y, then attending graduate school at another university. This occurred soon after the Brett Kavanaugh hearings, which had spawned an uptick in student sexual harassment complaints, according to our dean. Y claimed that the word *date*, plus the pastry and coffee I bought for her, the walking close and bending down to hear her on the way to the film, and then my "greeting her on campus" after our return, indicated that I had a sexual interest in her. The only example the Title IX investigator considered inappropriate was my use of the word *date*. I explained that I had meant "agreed-upon time to meet," and that I recognized it was an ill-chosen word. I had no sexual interest in the student. The investigator asked my sexual orientation, and I told him I am heterosexual.

The investigation dragged on past the six-month deadline, though the investigator contacted me only once or twice during that time. After her initial phone interview, Y refused to speak to the investigator. She would not provide any witnesses from her cohort of students on the trip. Instead, she provided the names of professors to whom she had confided her issues. The investigator's conversations with these three female professors, leaders of the mobbing campaign of the past two decades, caused him to conclude that they had coached Y to file the complaint.

Once she realized she had no evidence, Y withdrew her participation in the investigation. By law, a complainant can't stop an investigation once started, and the investigator had to proceed. Transcriptions of the professors' conversations with the investigator were in the report. They were unashamedly slanderous in sexualizing me and my intentions, not only during the trip, but throughout the entire period of my employment. The investigator made every effort to take this student's claim seriously but concluded that coaching by trusted mentors caused her to project a past trauma or harassment onto me. The investigator exonerated me of the charges.

When the case closed, I considered one avenue of redress: our school's new bullying policy. If I filed a complaint, it would pass through a long chain of reviewers, ending on the dean's desk for him to adjudicate. In the process, my complaint would be read by several faculty members, including the three bullies, who would retaliate against me. Thus, it was more efficient and safer simply to ask the dean to speak with the three female colleagues, telling them that their behavior would not be tolerated. He promised to do this, but never did. Instead, the colleagues' long-lived wish was fulfilled, and I left the university for good. I was three years away from my intended retirement age, but my mental health was more important than money at that point. After repeated unsuccessful attempts to rectify the situation, including complaints made to the department chair, discussions with the college dean, and consultation with the ombudsman, I understood that there was no avenue of redress in this university.

Although I mostly refrain from talking about this mobbing experience in order not to relive it, I do believe in the healing power of telling our stories. By writing this essay, I am letting readers know they are not alone. My advice to others is to fight academic mobbing as soon as it happens. Unfortunately, you must be willing to risk sacrificing tenure in your quest for justice. If enough individuals take action against this practice, we will eventually reach the critical mass needed for change. Public awareness, legal victories, and solidarity among victims will gradually change the environment.

An intelligent, optimistic English professor doesn't start her career believing that by rising to the profession's demands she will invite malicious attacks and long-term ostracism by her academic colleagues. Learning that such behaviors are not only possible but prevalent can infect a person with distrust, anxiety, and anger. Academia should not be such an unpleasant profession for tall poppies or any other blooms.

Works Cited

Khoo, Siew Beng. "Academic Mobbing: Hidden Health Hazard at Workplace." *Malaysian Family Physician*, vol. 5, no. 2, 2010, pp. 61–67.

Leymann, Heinz, and Annelle Gustafsson. "Mobbing at Work and the Development of Post-traumatic Stress Disorders." *European Journal of Work and Organizational Psychology*, vol. 5, 1996, pp. 251–75.

7

Misogyny and Abuse in the Academic Library Workplace

Reflections on Fifteen Years in American Academic Libraries

Carolyn Carpan

Little writing about women librarians exists, as Kathleen DeLong has noted, so that "the professional lives of women librarians are largely unknown, as is the importance of their contribution to the development of libraries and librarianship" (63). Also largely unknown are the many types of abuse that women librarians often suffer. In this autoethnographic article, I consider the relationship between misogyny and the abuse I experienced during my fifteen-year career working as a librarian in American academic libraries, how that abuse has affected me, and what we might do to stop it.

In recent years, academic librarians have publicly acknowledged that the kinds of bullying and mobbing I experienced happen frequently in library workplaces (Hecker et al.). Kaetrena Davis Kendrick found that bullying leads to low staff morale in academic libraries and is often long term (853). Bullies abuse by way of coercive control, "a repeated pattern of behaviour designed to undermine the autonomy of another individual" (Barlow & Walklate 2). Leaders use coercion to exert positional power, promote personal interests, squash dissension, and silence employees (Doe 106). In my experience, the power imbalance being preserved is specifically that of misogyny, which Kate Manne describes as "involv[ing] anxieties, fears, and desires to maintain a patriarchal order, and a commitment to restoring it when it is disrupted" (88). Both women and men are perpetrators of workplace misogyny and abuse, which is intended to silence, control, and disempower women. Just as women are coercively controlled at home by abusive men, they are also coercively controlled and abused at work by female and male leaders, supervisors, and colleagues.

Hannah Scott designed the Workplace Power-Control Wheel to illustrate the various forms of workplace abuse tactics, including intimidation, emotional abuse, isolation, minimizing, denying and blaming, using others, employer privilege, economic abuse, and coercion and threats. I have experienced versions of all of these kinds of abuse in academic libraries.

Figure 7.1. Workplace Power-Control Wheel. Source: https://socialscienceand humanities.ontariotechu.ca/workplacebullying/power-control-wheel.php. © Hannah Scott, 2022. Used with permission.

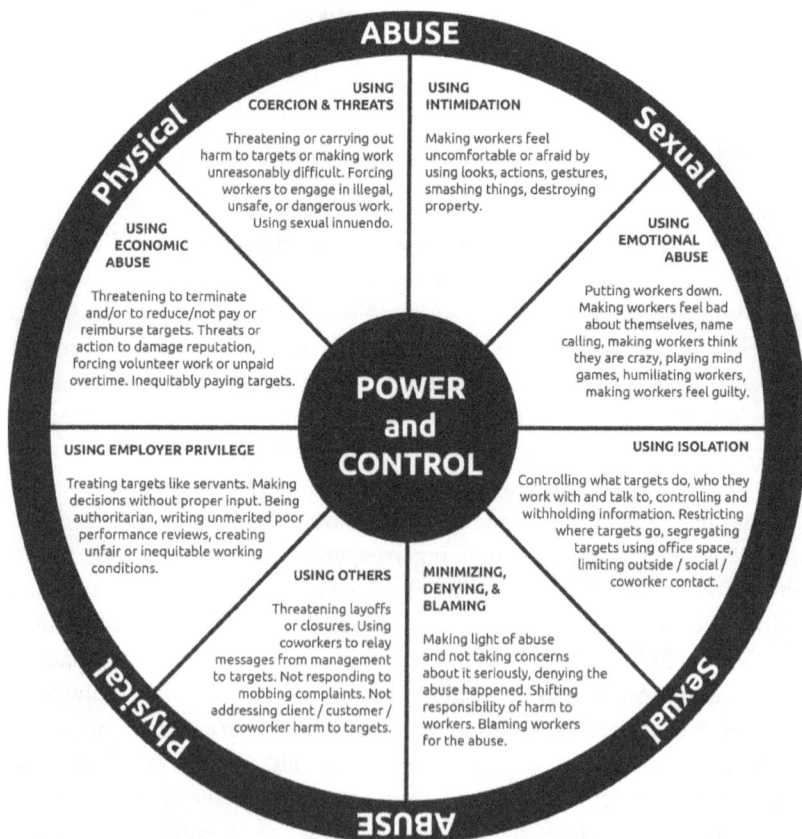

Intimidation

The occasional uncivil act—rolled eyes, pointed ignoring—can be excused by noting that colleagues are busy. But when such behavior is an everyday occurrence, it becomes intentional intimidation and a sign of disrespect. When it is clearly designed to comment on gendered power dynamics, it becomes misogynist.

Often, misogynist intimidation is dismissed as pranks. At one university, staff repeatedly canceled my hold on Sheryl Sandberg's *Lean In*, frustrating my attempt to read it. At another, someone exchanged my office name plate with that of a man's portrait, which was hanging near my office. These "pranks" told me that someone thought that as a middle manager, I was behaving like a man, which was not allowed, and that the library staff did not want me as a library leader. When I received a threatening phone call in my campus office, campus police found that it came from a colleague on a library phone. While this was explained as a prank aimed at another person, it came at a time when library staff were mobbing me, and I was truly frightened.

I also experienced intimidation as sabotaging of my work, when a colleague I had left in charge of a product demonstration at a conference damaged my relationship with the company representative. It was clear that the staff wasn't following my vision or leadership. But then, why would they when Library Administration also undermined my leadership?

Employer Privilege and Isolation

When the administration leaves you out of meetings, reassigns roles, and assigns work to staff that report to you, or doesn't give you information you need to do your job, these are intentional efforts to make you fail at your job. The library director at one university repeatedly left me out of meetings about staff members who reported to me, prompting colleagues to tell me they could see the director didn't respect me. Management also prevented me from doing my job, as when I was chastised for meeting with the Student Advisory Committee to discuss features they wanted in a building renovation.

Employers can bully by withholding needed resources, which happened to me when I requested a more ergonomic chair to deal with a diagnosis of repetitive strain injury. When a vendor brought me chairs to test, they left me their most expensive chair. The next thing I knew, I overheard gossip and rumors that I requested the most expensive chair on the market. I had never asked for the most expensive chair. I had asked for a chair that was better for me ergonomically than the one found in a storage closet. Their disrespect for my need for a chair was used as a way of letting me know they didn't want to provide me with the resources to do my job safely.

My colleagues also controlled and isolated me by withholding information and support. After dealing with a racist and misogynist attack on a student, I thought I had done everything to report the incident and support the student, but I later found out library staff knew the perpetrator was a student library employee. Instead of telling me so I could deal with the student worker, staff spent a semester managing the conflict between them and several Black students as a result of the incident.

When I took a temporary leadership role, I was isolated by my colleagues. One librarian told me I was being "thrown to the lions," meaning my colleagues had decided they were going to make work difficult for me. I ended up doing all the new work the dean assigned us because my colleagues refused to assist me.

Verbal Abuse

I regularly experienced verbal abuse, including yelling and snide comments. A library leader who often tried to bait me said to me, "I'm glad to see you're finally earning all that money I'm paying you!" Women are often paid less than men for the same work, and "men are significantly more likely to ask for a raise, a higher starting salary, and a bigger bonus, all of which contributes to gender differences in wages" (Gallop & Chamorro-Premuzic, para. 21). I was managing several departments at the time due to staff retention problems, while simultaneously leading searches to fill roles. I could never get ahead of the workload because I was leading job searches and managing problems other managers had abandoned. When my teams were able to successfully close a satellite library and move materials to another library ahead of deadline, library leadership was silent.

After a male colleague yelled at me, my manager called the attack an "interpersonal problem" instead of telling them to apologize and explain their concern. I was forced to meet with my manager and my colleague, and then alone with my male colleague, so we could "work it out." No one addressed the fact that I told Human Resources I was afraid of my male colleague. That job was over for me when the colleague closed a door and made a verbal threat against me. I did not report the verbal threat because of the lack of response I had previously gotten from Human Resources and my manager. What had been a great middle-management opportunity for me had turned toxic and I left the job.

Emotional Abuse

I experienced a full range of emotional abuses as a manager in academic libraries. For instance, I was told I took things "too personally." I was told during performance reviews that I was "too ambitious for both me and my staff" and I was "too Northeast." As Olin and Millett note, women library leaders are often told they are "too too" (para. 6). A colleague was allowed to submit their performance review focusing on how much they hated working with me.

Library administration and staff managed to bully me out of my chosen research field. Because I was a tenure-track academic librarian, conducting research and publishing were crucial for my career. Yet a library dean called my research and publication of books about young adult romance literature and girls' series an "obsession," library staff routinely belittled it with snide comments ("Carolyn is doing *research*" was said in a belittling tone), and a librarian who reported to me called me a pedophile because I read and wrote about young adult fiction. As a result of this vitriol, I turned down an offer to coauthor another book and ceased my research. Two decades later, my work is considered part of the canon of young adult romance literature (Allen 178-79). An article recently published in *Media International Australia* reported that a researcher replicated the content analysis methodology used in my master's thesis and an article I published twenty years ago (Bradshaw 2, 4). For becoming a significant scholar of the literature of girls and romance, I was ostracized in my job as a librarian.

Emotional abuse can cause moral injury, which Joseph McDonald defines as "suffering [resulting] from the violation of a human being's core moral principles" (7). I felt that moral injury over the course of several management positions in terms of the rejection of my concerted efforts to be an effective leader. Like many new managers, I made mistakes, including micromanaging and expecting people to do their jobs the way I would do them. As I moved from one management job to another, I tried not to repeat these mistakes. The management training I received at multiple institutions didn't help, as I had ten supervisors over ten years, and every organization wanted me to be a different kind of person and leader. One of the organizational management experts hired to work with me and my teams said to me, "You are not the problem. Library Administration is the problem"—and outlined the ways in which Administration was making it difficult for me to do my job, many of which I have recounted above. Over so many years, this repeated and pervasive mockery and undermining for doing my job, by those who were supposed to be supporting me in my work, became its own kind of gaslighting, in which I was systematically shown to be incapable of doing my job and undeserving of any authority.

But the most painful moral injury I felt was the rejection of my collaborative feminist leadership philosophy. Rather than leading by worshiping those above and abusing those below me in the power tree, I aimed to support colleagues in doing their jobs, find resources to help them do their jobs better, support them in tenure and promotion applications, and help staff get into library and information science programs. My colleagues seem to have found my approach threatening rather than supportive.

Economic Abuse

In several different organizations, when I took on leadership roles that required more responsibility, I had to persistently negotiate for increased compensation. A helpful session at the Association of College and Research Libraries Women's Leadership Institute in 2008 had warned me that I would be expected to do the work without more compensation, and I did find that it was given grudgingly. In one case, library leadership took advantage of the fact that I was on medical leave to ask if I would take on a leadership role. Compensation was never mentioned and I was too ill to think about it. Later I called human resources to let them know I had agreed to do the work and negotiated the compensation while I was on Family Medical Leave time. I was granted a reasonable stipend each month for taking on a leadership role. Another library leader grudgingly gave me a smaller stipend for the year I was formally head of two departments. When I was laid off from that organization, I lost pay, retirement, and health benefits, and I had to pay my share of the costs of moving for a new job. It was financially costly to me and the organization.

Coercion and Physical Violence

Threats of physical violence are a bully's most effective way of coercively controlling you. I never expected to experience physical threats against my life at work! A librarian told me to be afraid of a colleague who we knew owned guns, and that a former colleague had been scared of them. I had disciplined the librarian and they were unhappy with me. They thought I might leave if I thought I was at risk of violence from another colleague. I realized I had no choice but to leave because no one was protecting me from abusive and potentially violent colleagues in my workplace.

Misogynist body policing was also rampant. In every library where I worked, colleagues and leaders thought it was fine to comment on my body, weight, health, hair, clothing, and makeup. I was too fat, too skinny, dressed inappropriately, my hair was too curly, and so on. Once, such policing extended to sexual harassment, when one of my managers said, "You're looking good today" while eyeing my body up and down. A colleague who was nearby asked me later, "Did they really say what I think they said?"

Women in Library Leadership

Women aspiring to work in library leadership positions still face stereo-types, gendered expectations, and other obstacles to succeeding in lead-ership roles (Olin & Millett para. 1). DeLong has noted the slow pace of change in library management from male to female managers as a reason for barriers to women's library leadership (69). But no one ever told me I should expect to be abused by colleagues as my career advanced, solely because of my gender. As an advocate of user-centered libraries, I felt a sense of urgency for many years that libraries needed to change faster or be deemed irrelevant by faculty, students, and university administrators. Instead, administrators often led the bullying.

Navigating misogyny and abuse in multiple academic libraries left me feeling depressed, ashamed, exhausted, and burned out—with post-traumatic stress disorder, physical health problems, and a lack of confidence. Physical and mental health problems are frequently expe-rienced by bullying targets and they commonly lead to absence due to illness, poor work performance, low job satisfaction, and problems in personal and professional relationships (Marlowe et al. 42; Tsuno et al.

12). As I went from one toxic library to another, I disengaged from my work and considered leaving the profession. These are normal and rational ways to deal with toxic and abusive workplaces (Kendrick 874). This was the intent of misogynist and abusive leaders and colleagues, to wear me down so I would leave organizations, academic libraries, or the LIS profession altogether.

Conclusion

My experiences in three institutions over fifteen years illustrate how power, bullying, abuse, coercive control, and misogyny function together to maintain toxic organizational cultures in libraries. Abuse also keeps change leaders and feminists from succeeding in library leadership roles. It is important for me to tell my story so that current and future library leaders, managers, librarians, and staff know that abusing employees leads to problems beyond low morale.

Abusive and misogynist library leaders and colleagues tried to destroy my physical and mental health, my finances, my confidence, my spirit, my reputation, and my life. I dared to be my authentic self, a feminist, and a confident and strong leader. In so doing, I violated the patriarchal culture that is the foundation of libraries and universities.

We need a new kind of leadership in academic libraries, one that does not aim to control and destroy employees, but instead lifts them up and empowers them. We need library leaders and managers who understand power dynamics and who are willing and able to do the work of eliminating misogyny and abuse. Universities need to make it a priority to hire and support leaders in creating cultural change in library workplaces.

Works Cited

Allen, Amanda K. "Young Adult Romance." *The Routledge Research Companion to Popular Romance Fiction*, edited by Jayashree Kamble, Eric Murphy Selinger, and Hsu-Ming Teo, Routledge, 2021, pp. 168–90.

Barlow, Charlotte, and Sandra Walklate. *Coercive Control*. Routledge, 2022.

Bradshaw, Erin. "A Distressing and Peculiar Disease: Endometriosis in the Australian Press 1949–2011." *Media International Australia*, 2022, pp. 1–19. SAGE Journals, doi: https://doi-org.login.ezproxy.library.ualberta.ca/10.1177/1329878X221145974.

DeLong, Kathleen. "Career Advancement and Writing about Women Librarians: A Literature Review." *Evidence Based Library and Information Practice*, vol. 8, no. 1, 2013, pp. 59–75. Directory of Open Access Journals, doi: https:// journals-library-ualberta-ca.login.ezproxy.library.ualberta.ca/eblip/index.php/ EBLIP/article/view/17273.

Doe, Frederick. "Coercive Behaviour Management in Universities: A Comparative Analysis of Private and Public Universities in Ghana." *Journal of Business & Professional Studies,* vol. 13, no. 2, 2021, pp. 104–17.

Gallop, Cindy, and Tomas Charmorro-Premuzic. "Stop Criticizing Women and Start Questioning Men Instead." *Harvard Business Review,* April 18, 2022, doi: https:// hbr.org/2022/04/stop-criticizing-women-and-start-questioning-men-instead.

Gardner, Dianne, et al. "An Exploration of Gender and Workplace Bullying in New Zealand." *International Journal of Manpower,* vol. 41, no. 8, 2020, pp. 1385–95. Emerald eJournals Premier, doi: https://doi-org.login.ezproxy. library.ualberta.ca/10.1108/IJM-02-2019-0067.

Hecker, Thomas E. "Workplace Mobbing: A Discussion for Librarians." *Journal of Academic Librarianship*, vol. 33, no. 4, 2007, pp. 439–45. ScienceDirect, doi: https://doi-org.login.ezproxy.library.ualberta.ca/10.1016/j.acalib.2007.03.003.

Kendrick, Kaetrena D. "The Low Morale Experience of Academic Librarians: A Phenomenological Study. *Journal of Library Administration*, vol. 57, no. 8, 2017, pp. 846–78. Taylor & Francis Online, doi: https://doi-org.login.ezproxy. library.ualberta.ca/10.1080/01930826.2017.1368325.

Law, Margaret Z. *Cultivating engaged staff: Better management for better libraries.* Libraries Unlimited, 2017.

Leiding, Reba. "Mobbing in the Library Workplace: What It Is and How to Prevent It." *College & Research Libraries News*, vol. 71, no. 7, 2010, pp. 364–66, 384.

Manne, Kate. *Down Girl: The Logic of Misogyny.* Oxford University Press, 2017.

Marlowe, Carolyn, Huat Bin (Andy) Ang, and Muhammad Akhtaruzzaman. "The Long-Term Effects of Workplace Bullying on Health, Wellbeing, and on the Professional and Personal Lives of Bully-Victims." *New Zealand Journal of Employment Relations*, vol. 46, no. 2, 2021, pp. 31–51.

McDonald, Joseph. "What Is Moral Injury? Current Definitions, Perspectives, and Contexts." *Moral Injury: A Guidebook for Understanding and Engagement,* edited by Brad E. Kelle, Lexington Books, 2020, pp. 7–20.

Motin, Susan Hubbs. "Bullying or Mobbing: Is it Happening in Your Library?" *ACRL 14th National Conference Proceedings.* Association for College & Research Libraries, 2009, pp. 291–97. American Library Association Institutional Repository, doi: https://alair.ala.org/handle/11213/16925.

Olin, Jessica, and Michelle Millett. "Gendered Expectations for Leadership in Libraries." *In the Library with the Lead Pipe*, 2015. http://www.inthelibrary-withtheleadpipe.org/2015/libleadgender/.

Scott, Hannah S. "Workplace Bullying Power Control Wheel." *Workplace Bullying Project,* Ontario Tech University, 2022. https://socialscienceandhumanities. ontariotechu.ca/workplacebullying/power-control-wheel.php.

———. "Extending the Duluth Model to Workplace Bullying: A Modification and Adaptation of the Workplace Power-Control Wheel." *Workplace Health & Safety*, vol. 66, no. 9, 2018, pp. 444–45. SAGE Journals, doi: https://doi-org. login.ezproxy.library.ualberta.ca/10.1177/2165079917750934.

Tsuno, Kanami, et al. "Victimization and Witnessing of Workplace Bullying and Physician-Diagnosed Physical and Mental Health and Organizational Outcomes: A Cross-Sectional Study." *PLoS ONE,* vol. 17, no. 10, 2022, pp. 1–14. *Directory of Open Access Journals*, doi: https://doiorg.login.ezproxy. library.ualberta.ca/10.1371/journal.pone.0265863.

8

"Tell Me More"

When Bleeding on the Page Isn't Enough

CARLYN ENA FERRARI

Some problems we share as women, some we do not.

—Audre Lorde, *Sister Outsider*[1]

Little White Myths

"Watch out for the insecure white men." When I began my career in higher education, women of all races pulled me aside and gave me this advice in hushed tones. They still do. Sometimes they name a particular insecure white man. The Insecure White Man who voted against their tenure. The Insecure White Man who is the micromanaging department chair that purposely gave them terrible teaching schedules. The Insecure White Man who called them the "diversity hire." While the women I have encountered have been candid about the dangers of white men, I have yet to meet someone willing to be as candid—and cautionary—about *white women*. And if I'm being honest, I have had the most conflict with white women throughout my career, especially those operating under the feigned solidarity of "feminism" or "womanhood." Certainly, these Insecure White Men exist, and in no way do I intend to minimize white patriarchal supremacy. However, I do want to push back against the pervasive

79

misconception that in academia only white men are the problem and that white men are the sole perpetrators of gendered abuse.

In his 2020 *New York Times* op-ed titled "How White Women Use Themselves as Instruments of Terror," Charles Blow poignantly critiques this dominant narrative, writing, "We often like to make white supremacy a testosterone-fueled masculine expression, but it is just as likely to wear heels as a hood." Blow wrote his op-ed in response to the May 25, 2020 Central Park bird-watching incident in which Amy Cooper, a white dog walker, called the police and made false accusations against Christian Cooper, a Black birder, after he asked her to leash her dog.[2] Blow was not speaking about academia, but his critique rings true. In my first higher-education position, my harasser was a white woman. My colleagues and my institution did not view her actions as harassment and did not see her as an abuser. But I did. And I still do.

Documenting a Crooked Room

In 2010, I began working as an academic adviser for a small, private institution. My direct supervisor was a white woman who had been at the institution for nearly three decades and served in a variety of roles and now ran a center that housed academic advising and student support. During my interview, she seemed genuinely excited about my candidacy and all but confirmed that I had secured the position. As a first-generation college graduate myself, I was excited to be working with underrepresented and first-generation students, many of whom were on academic probation and (mis)labeled as "at-risk." It was an all-women office and though I was not the only woman of color, I was the sole Black woman. I was young, twenty-six. And this was my first "real" job. I was intimately familiar with racism, but I did not yet know how important—and isolating—being the only Black woman would be.

I transitioned into my position seamlessly. I learned institutional policies and procedures quickly, and I connected with students immediately. My academic probation caseload was shrinking, which I credited to my ability to connect students with necessary resources. Though my "official" caseload was smaller, my office was buzzing. Students regularly stopped by my office just to chat, and their infectious laughter could be heard throughout the building. What was once a place that only "certain types" of students had to visit turned into a social space. I was succeeding.

My students were thriving. I thought my supervisor would have been thrilled, but, instead, she seemed annoyed. My friend, Sachi, gave me the wisest advice that I still use today: *document everything*. And so, I did. I was documenting what I initially thought were "microaggressions": not greeting me in the morning, shutting her office door in my face, praising my colleagues' achievements while ignoring mine, and walking away while I was speaking to her. When students asked, "Why does your boss hate you so much?" I realized it was not all in my head, and what I was experiencing was anything but "micro." I was trying to stand up straight in a "crooked room" (Harris-Perry 29).[3]

To write this essay, I revisited the files that contain the documented incidents of harassment. Some I remember with detail and clarity. Others I recall vaguely and suspect my body is protecting itself from excess trauma. Three incidents still haunt me, and I wish back then I had been armed with the language—and healing meditations—of Black feminism and critical race theory to help me process and contextualize what was happening to me.

The first incident took place about a year into my position. My colleagues and I were meeting with a representative from the regional college accreditation commission. One of the questions posed was how our office supports students of color, namely, African American students. My supervisor answered, "Well, Carlyn is attractive and is . . . what do you call yourself? You're not African American. What do you call yourself?" The representative looked stunned. Angry and embarrassed, I fumbled through an answer about mentoring programs and various student support initiatives.

The next day, my supervisor came to my office. I foolishly thought she was going to apologize. She told me she had just met with the college president, who shared that she was happy to have a Black woman in our office representing higher education. Laughing, my supervisor said she told the president that I am "statuesque" and "attractive," and I especially attract African American young men into my office, which is an unintended consequence of my hire. "But, hey, whatever it takes, right?" She could barely contain her laughter. Some of my colleagues overheard. They came out of their offices and joined in the laughter. My office was directly across from the lobby, and I locked eyes with one of my student receptionists, who was also a Black woman. We were the only two not laughing.

I reported these incidents—and *dozens* of others—to the academic dean and human resources office. They made excuses for my supervisor's "odd sense of humor" or provided misogyny-tinged advice: *She's obviously just jealous of you because you're young. Just ignore her.* I was stuck in a cycle of what Sara Ahmed calls "*strategic inefficiency*" (91), in which my emails, formal complaints, and requests for follow-ups were either "lost" or met with radio silence. It became clear to me that the institution was willing to protect her even in the face of blatant racism and sexism.[4]

"Tell Me More": Explaining as the Other

The incident that made me contact an attorney took place during my third and final year working for the institution. We had concluded our weekly staff meeting, and my supervisor asked everyone to stay in the room. She stepped out of the room and returned with something that was wrapped in white tissue paper. She laid the folded tissue paper on the table and opened it, revealing lacey pink thong underwear. It was soiled. Looking at me and laughing she said, "Carlyn I found your underwear. You left your underwear out *again!*" She was laughing big belly laughs. So were my colleagues. While wiping away tears, she told us she had found the thong underwear while she was out walking earlier in the day. "Wanna tell us what you were up to this weekend?" The underwear was dangling from her index finger, and she reached her arm toward me expecting me to take it.

I went to my office to collect my thoughts. I had to confront her.

I knocked on her door, and she invited me to sit down. I remained standing. "I just want you to know that I know you meant it as a joke, but I did not find it funny at all. It offended me," I said.

She leaned back in her chair and crossed her arms. "Tell me more," she said.

She wanted me to convince her that she had done something wrong. I explained that being associated with underwear found in public and referencing my weekend implies sexual deviance and promiscuity. Had it been a pink clock or a pink water bottle, it would've been different. I felt myself growing hot as I said that I wasn't okay with being associated with lewd behavior, and that joke was inappropriate and unprofessional, especially in front of my colleagues.

"Well, I'm sorry you misinterpreted my joke," she said flatly. "I didn't mean for you to take it *that way.*"

That evening I contacted an attorney.

I realized then that, collectively, the incidents I had documented—in particular, the comments about my "tight pants," my "pretty little heels," and my "sexy blue shirt"—were her attempts to reduce me to a sexual object. My success angered her, so she decided to sexualize me. My supervisor thrust upon me what Patricia Hill Collins calls a "controlling image," which is "designed to make racism, sexism, poverty, and other forms of social injustice appear to be natural, normal, and inevitable parts of everyday life" (70). By summoning stereotypes of Black women's perceived hypersexuality, my supervisor suggested that her actions were not harassment. They were *warranted*. In other words, I was asking for it. What also became clear was that she was not aware of her positionality, not just as my supervisor but as a white woman. Kim McLarin explains the danger of this ignorance: "Put simply, white women have power they will not share and to which they mostly will not admit, even wielding it. . . . Moreover, white women simply don't see us. Not in the ways necessary for true sisterhood" (20).

Not Enough ~~Blood~~ Evidence

Several months after filing a legal claim, my lawyer called me with difficult news: "We're going to have a hard time proving that this is racial *and* sexual discrimination." I had submitted over one hundred single-spaced pages of documented incidents, emails, and notes that I had been compiling over three years.

Crying, I said, "I bled all over those pages. What more do I need to do?"

"I'm sorry," she replied. "There's just not enough evidence." She was right.

She had received a response from the college's attorney. I was also being accused of sexual impropriety, and the college's attorney cited an incident in which I allegedly brought condoms into the workplace. I chuckled in disbelief. I knew exactly what was being referenced. I had gone to brunch with a colleague, a white woman who I thought was a friend, and she mentioned that her boyfriend was coming into town. Our conversation turned to contraception, and she mentioned not having any condoms. "Oh, you can have mine!" I quipped. "They're just collecting dust!" I remember laughing with her when I stopped by her office after hours. I texted her, and she said she was working late and told me to stop by. It was just the two of us in the building. I handed her a gift bag with the condoms inside. We hugged and I told her to enjoy her time with her boyfriend. I will never know why she shared this moment. All I knew is that it was being weaponized as evidence of my sexual impropriety and deviance. We briefly stayed in touch after I parted ways with the institution, so I could have asked her why. Perhaps it is my naivete and hope that I did have a genuine friendship with this woman, but I do not think she was being malicious. Or, perhaps, as Kim McLarin bluntly suggests, the "why" boils down to race: "This is what Black women know: when push comes to shove, white women choose race over gender: Every. Single. Time" (22). That she felt it was appropriate to share this information with the college's attorney even after acknowledging—and witnessing—the racist, sexist treatment I received, let me know that she was comfortable being complicit. And that is just as dangerous and insidious as my supervisor's actions.

In hindsight, I realize that the documentation was about far more than recording incidents of harassment. I was also tasked with making myself *legible*. My institution could not see my supervisor as a harasser because she was a white woman, and they could not see me as a victim because I was a Black woman. They did not understand that though we were both women, our experiences and relationships to power were vastly different. As Audre Lorde explains, "Thus, in a patriarchal power system where whiteskin privilege is a major prop, the entrapments used to neutralize Black women and white women are not the same" (118). Furthermore, as Kimberlé Crenshaw argues, I was uniquely poised to bring such a case forward precisely because of my identity: "Black women—the class of employees which, because of its intersectionality, is best able to challenge all forms of discrimination—are essentially isolated and often required to fend for themselves" (145). I often wonder how things might have turned out if instead of sharing that anecdote my colleague had chosen to share the multiple incidents of harassment she witnessed. I don't blame her for not doing so, but maybe her voice would have been the additional evidence I needed.

Conclusion: Bleeding on the Page

In September 2020, I wrote an essay that appeared in the *Chronicle Review*, in which I shared how I was mistaken for a prostitute while on an interview for an academic job and thrown out of a hotel ("You Need to Leave"). I used this story to frame my experience as a Black woman in academia and talk about why I left my previous higher-education institution. It was a risky move for a junior scholar, and I braced myself for the backlash. A woman wrote to me expressing both gratitude and frustration. While she commended my bravery and storytelling, she expressed sadness about how often Black women have to offer up their hurt, trauma, and pain as testimony or evidence of systemic racism. She is right, of course. I wrote back saying that I wished we did not have to "bleed on the page" for people to take our experiences seriously. I told myself never to write another essay like that again.

While I genuinely appreciate the personal invitation to participate in this collection, there was—and still is—a part of me that knows that people understand that academia is a bastion of white supremacy. And they simply prefer it that way. I recognize that no matter how many examples I provide and how many theorists I cite, some will not believe me (and Black women, in general). As Tressie McMillan Cottom explains, the denial of public legibility and credibility for Black women is especially acute: "At every turn, black women have been categorically excluded from being expert performers of persuasive speech acts in the public that adjudicates our humanity. As women, black women face challenges of appealing to rationality in public discourse because our culture has decided that women are irrational and emotional. Logic and reason are beyond our biological and cultural programming" (20). Cottom further explains how through the act of writing, Black women can "fix their feet"—that is, "claim legitimacy in a public discourse that defines itself, in part, by how well it excludes black women" (19).

I didn't want to write this essay. I had to. I needed to "fix my feet." And, yes, I've bled again. Maybe one day it will be enough.

Notes

1. Epigraph from *Sister Outsider: Essays and Speeches by Audre Lorde*, "Age, Race, Class, and Sex: Women Redefining Difference," Crossing Press, 1984.

2. In choosing to capitalize "Black" but not "white," I draw on historian Martha Biondi's explanation, as she deftly and elegantly articulates the historical and political significance of this choice: "Black is capitalized because it is used much as 'Negro' or 'African American' is used. As a proper noun, it reflects the self-naming and self-identification of a people whose national or ethnic origins

have been obscured by a history of capture and enslavement. Similarly, 'white' is not capitalized because historically it has been deployed as a signifier of social domination and privilege, rather than as an indicator of ethnic or national origin." The direct quotes in which "Black" is not capitalized in this chapter may reflect the decisions of each author as well as the stylistic and societal norms during the original publication date.

3. See the Introduction of this collection, page 15, and Melissa Harris-Perry, *Sister Citizen: Shame, Stereotypes, and Black Women in America*, chapter 1.

4. Ahmed describes *strategic inefficiency* as the "unexplained and excruciating delays" (91) that are employed to exhaust a complainer so that they will withdraw their complaint (93). This tactic, Ahmed explains, is illustrative of how institutions work and how they are reproduced (100). See *Complaint!*, chapter 2, pages 91–100.

Works Cited

Ahmed, Sara. *Complaint!* Duke UP, 2021.

Biondi, Martha. *To Stand and Fight: The Struggle for Civil Rights in Postwar New York City*. Harvard UP, 2003.

Blow, Charles. "How White Women Use Themselves as Instruments of Terror." *New York Times*, May 27, 2020, https://www.nytimes.com/2020/05/27/opinion/racism-white-women.html?searchResultPosition=1. Accessed 20 July 2023.

Collins, Patricia Hill. *Black Feminist Thought: Knowledge, Consciousness, and the Politics of Empowerment*. 2nd ed., Routledge, 2000.

Cottom, Tressie McMillan. *Thick: And Other Essays*. The New Press, 2019.

Crenshaw, Kimberlé. "Demarginalizing the Intersection of Race and Sex: A Black Feminist Critique of Antidiscrimination Doctrine, Feminist Theory and Antiracist Politics." *University of Chicago Legal Forum*, vol. 1989, no. 1, 1989, pp. 139–67, http://chicagounbound.uchicago.edu/uclf/vol1989/iss1/8.

Ferrari, Carlyn. " 'You Need to Leave Now, Ma'am.' " *Chronicle of Higher Education*, September 8, 2020, https://www.chronicle.com/article/you-need-to-leave-now-maam. Accessed 29 July 2023.

Harris-Perry, Melissa V. *Sister Citizen: Shame, Stereotypes, and Black Women in America*. E-book, Yale UP, 2011.

Lorde, Audre. *Sister Outsider: Essays & Speeches by Audre Lorde*. Crossing Press, 1984.

McLarin, Kim. *Womanish: A Grown Black Woman Speaks on Love and Life*. Kindle ed., Ig Publishing, 2019.

Part Two

Resistance and Consequences

9

Mad Woman in the Ivory Tower

The Continuous Costs of Speaking Up
after Professor/Student Abuse

Sarah Cheshire

Throughout the process of writing this piece, I have found myself circling back to the same questions—questions that have plagued me since I first went public with my own story six years ago: *who, or what, are these narratives for? What are the potential costs of continuously asking survivors to put their most intimate traumas on public display if doing so does not result in material change? After a story enters the public domain, what happens to the person who tells?*

I will not go into detail here about what my undergraduate creative writing professor did to me. I will say that events followed a script that many young women artists and academics will find familiar: deep psychological grooming guised as "creative mentorship," the compulsory divulgence of secrets. A pen on a page became a hand on a thigh, a musty office became a musky moonlit living room. The boundary between personal and professional blurred each time he scoured one of my poems with his authoritative gaze, saying *I want to help you tell your story.*

I will not discuss in depth the fallout of what my undergraduate creative writing professor did to me, although it too followed a familiar pattern: the struggle to be believed after initial disclosure, the ensuing

subtle and not-so-subtle snubs for opportunities, promotions, and recommendation letters, the inevitable self-doubt intensifying into relentless
cycles of crippling depression and simmering rage. As harrowing as his
physical violations were, nothing prepared me for the cognitive dissonance
that emerged as I struggled to make sense of the betrayal: how had I let
the same man who taught me the power of language convince me of
the necessity of my silence? At what point did my stories—my fragile,
nascent process of coming into my voice as a young writer—become his
weapon of manipulation?

At some point after graduating from college, I convinced myself that
the only way to wrest back the power that my professor held over me was
to keep telling the story, over and over, regardless of who was listening,
regardless of the vastness of the void into which I was screaming. The more
respectable the company, the more graphic I got with details. Narrative
became a mechanism of distancing, disconnecting from the true impact
of what had happened to me. I told the story the way he taught me to
write—as if it were an animal to be tamed, an object to be conquered, a
grotesque force to be made aesthetic, marketed for consumption. Despite
my attempts to speak my truth on my own terms, his imprint seemed
indelibly stamped on my creative process.

Entering graduate school, I found myself creatively paralyzed. Every
time I sat down to craft a new poem or story, I felt his gaze leering over
my shoulder, and froze under its weight. The only way to shake the gaze,
I thought, was to write through it. So I wrote what he did to me. First, I
wrote fragments. The fragments became poems. I workshopped drafts for
peers and professors, who called the words *beautiful*. The poems became
a chapbook, then an award-winning essay. I wanted to be proud after I
released the story into the world, but instead I felt something like guilt:
what does it mean to make beauty out of brutality?

As the tides of #MeToo began to swell my second year of graduate
school, so too did the imperative to *tell*. This time, the story felt larger
than me; with the act of telling came a fleeting possibility of change. For
a moment, newspapers and magazines were deluged with stories like
mine: the charismatic older teacher/coach/boss/pastor/father figure. The
promising young female protégée. Private meetings gradually descending
into physical transgression. The specific trauma generated when institutions
collude with powerful, abusive men to enforce silence.

The programs of academic conferences suddenly boasted panels with
titles such as "Trauma as Metaphor" and "Telling the Truth Slant: #MeToo

Approaches to Understanding Memory and Rupture in the Poetry of Emily Dickinson." After leaving one such panel at a national literary conference, I stumbled across my former professor's book on sale at the bookfair. In a burst of audacity, I waved a copy at the sales representative: *Do you know that this man is a sexual predator? This is what he did to me.* She seemed concerned and took my email address. I never heard from her again.

Shortly thereafter, when more survivors came forward and the professor was finally dismissed from his position, I tweeted my story at a famous author who had recently edited a widely distributed anthology featuring one of the professor's essays. She messaged me directly in response, expressing profound empathy for what I had gone through and a desire to support young female writers and survivors: *I would love to read and help promote your work. Will you send me a sample?* I accepted the offer; then the thread fell silent.

Almost a year after the 2017 spread of #MeToo, when I was the creative nonfiction editor of a literary magazine, an assistant editor justified rejecting a submission with the assumption that readers had already had enough: *the writing is of good quality, but we've just had so many submissions lately in which sexual violence is the central theme.* A sardonic part of me wanted to request a rubric.

Tell me: what makes a "good" sexual abuse story? Shock value? Syntax? Proximity to a legal definition of "truth"? Linguistic eloquence? A linear plot? Should the prose be sexier? Should the narrative voice come across as more innocent? Is there a "correct" way to write, and speak, about sexual abuse? If so, who is the arbiter?

I kept writing my story and speaking my story, but the words felt increasingly hollow. When I found my former professor's book on sale again a year later, at the same conference bookfair, I did not vocalize my concerns to the sales representative. Instead, I tucked a copy of my own chapbook into the stack of his books, inserting my story into his, and walked away.

At graduate-student teacher training that same year, higher-ups in my department announced they were adding "personal memoir" as a recommended essay assignment category for freshman writing courses. When I heard this, I also heard my undergraduate creative writing professor's voice in the back of my head: *I want to help you tell your story.* I recalled the ways in which he used these words to extract my vulnerabilities, erode the boundary between personal and professional, and prime me for exploitation; I recalled the panic attacks I started having senior year, alone in my dorm room, after submitting assignments. I wanted to ask: what responsibility do we have to students after they share? How do we square a pedagogical desire for authenticity in the classroom with the reality that none of us is a trained mental health professional, the campus counseling center is currently operating on a monthslong waitlist, and the school has a total of two psychiatrists serving a student body of nearly forty thousand? Is it ethical to create learning environments that normalize personal disclosure if we aren't equipped to tend the wounds that might reopen through the narrative process?

On a Friday morning, my second semester teaching, one of my freshman students showed up to class with puffy eyes, matted hair, and visible bruises polka-dotting her neck. After class, she pulled me aside in a frenzy: *I don't know what happened last night.* She told me she remembered talking to a guy at a fraternity event, sometime after sunset. He handed her a drink. The world went blank. *Can you help me? Please?* I walked her, slowly, to a resource center across campus. As she disappeared through the revolving doors, I imagined her entering an endless tunnel where the waiting room should have been. I wondered: what will become of her story? Will her words get swallowed within cinderblock walls and echoing hallways, like those of so many before her? When she comes out the other side, will the story still belong to her?

Later that afternoon, the tenured professor who oversaw my graduate teaching assignments helped me fulfill my duties as a mandated reporter and called me *brave.* He also knew my story. Three months later, I approached this same professor with a critique of what I perceived to be heavily misogynistic undertones in a reading he had assigned for a graduate pedagogy seminar. The critique wasn't meant to be personal. I was merely hoping to engage in discourse—that's what academia's for, right? (Looking back, I wonder: how was I still so naive?) Suddenly, his demeanor went cold. *My buddy wrote that piece,* he said, taking his phone out of his pocket and placing it on the table between us. *Do you want me to call him right now and tell him he's a creep, too?*

I realized then that there was no transcending my story. I had become the girl who told: the story had become me.

Sometimes on bad days, I find myself playing out some version of the following scenario in my head:

> Tomorrow, or maybe twenty years from now, a young student enters my office. Maybe the student is my daughter. Maybe she is my past self. Tentatively, she tells me about

something a professor did to her. An older man, renowned in his field—perhaps a self-proclaimed feminist, a poet with a penchant for "elevating young new voices" and an uncanny ability to manipulate words. She trusted him to help her find her voice. She uses euphemisms to mask an internal paralysis she hasn't yet named as *fear*. She asks me: *what should I do?*
Speak! I tell her: *Your words are power. Your story matters.*
And then what? Does the scene end there?

In some versions of the scenario, I feel compelled to follow up with a warning.

> *You might be asked to tell again, and again, and one more time just to "clarify that one detail" (are you sure it happened like that?). Maybe you'll tell the story until it stops being yours, until the words become deadweight in the back of your throat. Maybe they'll swallow your story and spit it back in your face as a deformed version of itself, or force you to watch as they smile and run it through a paper shredder in the corner of an eerily sunny administrative office. You will walk through the world with the story mapped across your body, stamped in invisible ink on the front page of your résumé. You will wear it as a scarlet letter.*

I've spent many sleepless nights wondering if speaking my own truth was "worth it." If I'm being completely honest, I'm still not sure. On the one hand, I can't say with confidence that telling made my life better in the long term—in fact, I'm almost certain that I'd be further along in my career had I kept my mouth shut. On the other hand, I cannot imagine the insidious havoc the story would have wreaked on my mind, body, and psyche if I had left it to fester in prolonged silence.

I will not go into detail about what my undergraduate creative writing professor did to me. Quite frankly, I'm tired of telling my story. I'm tired of watching the stories of other survivors get voyeuristically consumed and exploited for outside gain, only for abusive men to retain their power at the end of the day. I'm tired of being called *brave* while fighting tooth and nail for the resources necessary to survive and heal.

I recently gave birth to my first child—a daughter. I would like to imagine a world in which I can encourage her to *speak* without caveats, disclaimers, or fears. Right now, however, I only feel one thing for certain: narrative in and of itself is not enough.

10

Muffled Voices

Creating Safe Space in a Toxic Department

RIFAT SIDDIQUI

Needing Safe Spaces

Scrolling through my phone, I came across an image that I took five years ago. It was a hand resting on an old wooden table, but there was something unusual about the image. It was a hand with a scratch, a scratch that exposed the layers beneath the skin revealing the flesh and blood within. It was my student's hand. I was a junior faculty member in Bangladesh, and it was my first time teaching this course with the first-semester graduate students. One of my students came to me crying one afternoon right after I finished teaching my class on media and cultural theory. I shared my office with four male colleagues, and I could not offer this student a chair to sit in because there was no place for her to sit. Her words were getting interrupted by her continuous hiccups, and she was trying hard to maintain her poise. I took her to the adjacent empty room so that she could feel more at ease. She took a seat and showed me her hand.

"After you finished your class . . ." she was still hiccupping. "We were all talking about the upcoming test, and I said we shouldn't request to change the dates. It's been four months already since we started this semester and I said if we don't sit for the exam, we will get stuck in a

95

session jam[1] again." At this point it was obvious that her classmates were trying to delay the exam, and they were planning to demand that I postpone the exam date. I gave her a glass of water and encouraged her to continue if she felt better. She took the glass, drank, wiped her face, and continued. I could see that she had been physically assaulted. She kept crying while telling me that one of her peers slapped her and called her names while others joined in. The back of her left hand was smeared with blood. I immediately took a photo of her hand to preserve the evidence and brought out my first aid kit, which I used to carry in my backpack because the department had none. After disinfecting her wound, I applied a Band-Aid. The classmates who assaulted her were political activists who supported the ruling party of the country, and I had no power to get involved in such a situation. I was a woman in a strict patriarchal society, and I was a newly appointed temporary lecturer, so my opinion didn't matter to my senior colleagues. Because I had zero political involvement, I knew no influential people. *I wish I could help her*, I thought. I told her, "You are safe here, don't worry."

She did not want to take this matter to the disciplinary committee of the university. She was scared because they had threatened to beat up her boyfriend. She was worried about her and her boyfriend's safety and asked me what to do. She had come to me because she had been attacked right after my class and wanted to inform me about it so that I could take necessary action against the culprits. I listened to her as she cried and shared the incident with me. I told her about the options she had. If she wanted, she could take this to the disciplinary committee and place a formal complaint against them. I assured her if she needed me to testify, I would be there, though the chances of her classmates getting punished was low because of who they were. The university administration rarely punishes student politicians who represent the ruling party. While I advised her that she could certainly submit a formal complaint, I stopped to look at her face.

In that split second, I was thinking about the severity of the repercussions she would face if she reported her attackers. I was thinking about those numerous violent incidents on university campuses that affected the physical and mental well-being of female students. I couldn't stop thinking of the myriad news reports on bullying, harassment, and sexual assault where the culprits were student politicians representing the ruling party. They received no punishment for their crimes. Media representations of those incidents almost always focused on the victim rather than the culprits, and the law enforcement agency often spared them due to their involvement with the ruling party.

Choosing Silence, Choosing Safety

As I comforted her, I told myself to calm down and not make a hasty decision. I walked her through the possible ways to contain the situation. I informed her about the procedure of filing a formal complaint to the university disciplinary committee, which was an overwhelmingly long process. The institution we were in lacked formal protocol for the prevention of gendered abuse or sexual assault on campus. We only had a "complaint committee" that students could turn to after they were sexually harassed. I was worried she might face severe consequences if she complained, so I advised her not to file a formal complaint. *I am doing this for her safety*, I said to myself. She was a hard-working student who never missed a class and frequently showed up for student hours. Her top priority was her education, and she certainly didn't want to endanger her future by giving up her studies.

I despised myself for advising her to stay silent. *I am a terrible teacher*, I thought. *What have I become?* Compromising my values is not what I learned as a student, and I am not the kind of professor who teaches students to swallow their pride and learn to adjust in a corrupted system that will ultimately corrupt them. And yet, here we were. So, I did what I had to in that situation. I told her to bite her tongue, control her emotions, and think about her future. If she could endure the present, she would be able to graduate successfully and achieve her goals.

I was troubled by my conviction that I did not have the power to tackle situations like this. I also thought of my dead classmate who was murdered on the last day of our senior-year final exam because of his political ideology. I could not shake the thought of how deadly a student's political affiliation could be.

Looking back at this photo now, I feel pathetic. As the youngest recruit and a temporary lecturer in the department of English, I had no one to put in a good word for me so that I could get a permanent position in the department. I am terrible at networking, and I never actively participated in the teacher's political association[2] where all the networking happens. Obviously, I had no chances of getting recommended by someone from the higher administration due to my lack of political involvement, and I never even tried to get a recommendation. Flattering was not my forte (and it's still not), so I had scarcely anybody who could support me in difficult situations. I had very little power to handle student misconduct on my own.

In Search of Justice

I could not help but think of the consequences this student would likely face if she made up her mind to report her assailants. So I decided to take matters into my own hands. As I sympathized with my student, I searched for ways to punish the assailants. With the help of their class representative, I informed them that they were not allowed to step into the same space where they assaulted one of their peers. As all this started because they wanted to postpone their exam, I notified them that their exams were postponed indefinitely, meaning I would no longer give them a chance to sit for an exam. Did they try to push back and make another demand? They did not, because they knew I wouldn't grade their papers even if they submitted them. I made sure none of the assailants could attend my class and if they did not attend classes, they had to retake the course again the next year. I also informed my colleagues of the assault, without revealing the name of the accosted student, to make them aware of this situation.

I kept treating the assailants like criminals, but in reality, they were also my students. I did not try to get an explanation from them, and my own infuriated response to violence blocked my ability to make unbiased decisions. Were these acts of revenge? I questioned the ethics of my own actions. I am certain that those culprits wouldn't have crossed paths with me after the incident, and I would never allow them to take my course. This was my way of avenging the victim. I often wonder if I made the right decision by doing this, by exploiting my own position.

The assault of "an anonymous" student by political activists didn't matter to my colleagues. I am certain of this because they followed the same political ideology, and the student leaders of political groups were their minions. Some of my colleagues enjoyed the attention they received from their minions. It made them feel special, like gods. Turning a blind eye to the political activists' frequent misconduct was very common for them. Such neglect of the students was typical of the department, which was lacking in many ways. Ours was a tiny department that did not even have a proper restroom for female students. We had only four classrooms full of wooden benches and tables, each room accommodating over a hundred students and offering few resources for them. The department was on the third floor of a shaky building that had wide cracks in the walls. There was no seminar room, no conference room, no library, not even a lounge where students could sit down and talk. Nobody ever thought it necessary to have a seminar room or a library for students of this department. I once asked my senior colleague what we were doing to support students' mental health issues. He hastily replied that he was serving as the counselor, but nobody ever came to those sessions. It was just a burden to him because he wasn't getting paid for this extra work. I realized mental health crises do not exist for these faculty members, and they lack compassion to assist students in crisis. This was one of the many ways the university was failing its students. The infrastructure of the university lacked resources to recognize the severity of gender discrimination and mental health issues and barely had any support for students. I was appalled but did not have the guts to say anything to them.

I did not know where students could turn to talk to someone. No one did. Meeting with a counselor was not something everyone could afford to do partly because no one has time to acknowledge the significance of mental health, and our society trained us to prioritize getting a good job and attaining so-called success in life. No one has ever thought of constituting a safe space. When I first thought about expressing the necessity to have a safe space, I knew it wouldn't be easy. *How do I make people understand a topic that they have never thought of? How do I inform them about a certain practice that they never considered essential?* I wrestled with these questions. This was something bigger than I expected when I began trying to help my student, and I did not have the resources or the support to do it alone.

There were times when I thought it was possible to have a safe space at the institution, if only I could endure all the retaliatory mistreatment from certain colleagues of mine and care enough for my students. The retaliation came in the form of verbal humiliation and the false accusation that I had deliberately missed lectures. Spreading malicious rumors, they tried to threaten my already vulnerable position of a temporary lecturer who could be dismissed without much explanation. Despite all that, I wanted to create a safe space for my students, where they could share their concerns. So I became their safe space. I was there, without any formal training, without any resources, just listening to my students and being there when they poured their hearts out. I listened and listened and listened. They shared their deepest concerns and stories, and I made sure the door was closed before they began. Together we formed our own kind of enclaved safe space. My senior colleagues did not approve of it, and I could not care less about their approval. The toxic environment of the department suffocated me, and I searched for ways to resist my irritating coworkers. I stopped entertaining their unfair demands. They ordered me to assist them with their official tasks. I agreed and sneakily walked away from arbitrary obligations. I did not want to participate in the toxic environment and become like them. I wanted to be better for my own sanity.

Still Searching for Safe Spaces

A few years later, when I was doing my second master's in women's and gender studies in Iowa, I conducted research on the concept of safe spaces among college students of Bangladesh. I asked several students from my former department in Bangladesh about their idea of a safe space. None of them was familiar with the concept of safe space. I wanted to make sure that they understood my question and could talk openly without hesitation. I was certain that these students would never associate sexuality or sexual identity with a safe space, as they are discouraged from thinking about their sexual orientation, not just because the topic of sexuality, including heterosexuality and homosexuality, was taboo in the conservative societies of Bangladesh, but because homosexuality was punishable by law.[3] I asked them once again, "What is your understanding of a safe space?" They didn't know, so I explained what a safe space was and what it could be. I could tell by the looks on their faces that they yearned for one.

Safe spaces allow people to express concerns and experiences that can be difficult to share. My former institution lacked proper resources and compassion to build a safe space for students, so I wanted to do something, particularly for the students in my department. Students and I were silently suffering in the department and shared a mutual feeling of distress, and this fellow feeling encouraged me to constitute an enclaved shelter. The young woman that came to share her experience with me also motivated me to create a safe space for students like her. Students who were vulnerable, who had no ties to the dominant political group and who were struggling to articulate their concerns came forward to participate in it. They reached out to me because of my public stance against bullying, harassment, and gender discrimination. It was important that the safe space we built was secret, to protect students from repercussions. Due to the extremely toxic environment of the department, where faculty members played favorites and political-activist students bullied other students, it was the best way to build a safe space. As a woman in academia, my experience taught me that it is incredibly difficult for women to work in a corrupted system where their agency is denied, and their voices are muffled. In a corruption-engulfed system like this, the only way out is resistance formed through enclaved safe spaces.

Notes

1. A session jam is a prolonged delay in academic activities, including class, exams, as well as closure of the university, which is a very common occurrence in the state-run universities of Bangladesh. Session-jam hampers scheduled academic activities, postponing the regular rhythm of academic life and, as a result, students fail to graduate on time.

2. Teachers' political associations are a very common practice in Bangladeshi state-run universities where teachers who share political ideology come together to form an association. This association helps them to express a collective opinion and express their demands, which often contributes to change in greater national issues beyond the university. Teachers' political associations can also influence the decisions made by the academic senate, as the members of such associations also serve as senate members.

3. According to Bangladesh penal code 377, which was replicated according to an 1860 British law, sodomy is punishable by law. The punishment for being homosexual in Bangladesh is life sentence or imprisonment for up to ten years. To learn more about this law from a government database, visit the following link: http://bdlaws.minlaw.gov.bd/act-11/section-3233.html.

11

Rocking the Boat

Experiences of "Silencing" from the Global South

Darlene Demandante and Raphaella Elaine Miranda

As of writing, there is no existing documentation in the Philippines about gender-based harassment in academia, even though multiple forms of gendered abuses persist within it. Moreover, discussing these issues proves challenging due to the lack of conceptual tools and a suitable vocabulary to articulate our experiences. Often, we find solace in sharing our stories within small circles of individuals who have faced similar adversities. Our contribution of this piece is our resistance against the culture of silence surrounding gendered abuse in academia, as we openly speak up about some of our experiences.

We also write this to celebrate the women philosophers who helped us make sense of these experiences and the communities that helped us challenge them. Through the art of critical storytelling, we aim to defy conventional expectations associated with "philosophical" works. This narrative serves as a powerful assertion, breaking the silence imposed on us by our philosophical upbringing. It comprises two personal accounts: one from a graduate student sharing her experiences of misogyny and misrecognition, and another from a teaching staff member facing micro-invalidation and silencing by her colleagues.

Misrecognitions: A Graduate Student's Experience

(Raphaella Elaine Miranda)

During my first year as an undergraduate philosophy student, I already observed that most of my philosophy professors were male. I belonged to a class where the gender profile of the students was generally equal, but most of the women in my class were interested in pursuing law after our bachelor's degrees. The equal gender profile also did little to affect our professors' syllabi and the discussion topics of the class. The philosophical canon taught to us was still predominantly male, save for discussions on Simone de Beauvoir's philosophy (but this was always in relation to Jean-Paul Sartre's). The women in my class were also extraordinary; their works had a deep resonance with their personal experiences, and they managed different organizations while being academically accomplished. Their brilliance was often overlooked because our professors focused on bright male students who confidently carried themselves. These male students were always the first to raise their hands to answer the professors' questions, and they would be the ones who followed them out of the classroom to ask more questions after class.

When I pursued an MA in philosophy, I felt the need to garner recognition as an academic. This desire for recognition was mostly animated by the need for validation and a need to belong to a community. In my formative years in graduate school, I volunteered for multiple projects in my department to prove my competence. I had a lot of experience organizing, and I thought this would be a meritocratic, fair way of gaining recognition. As a woman in academia, I knew there were many unspoken rules about how to act or not act around peers. Part of these unspoken rules was to avoid being the only woman in a room full of men, regardless of your relationship with them. In contrast to my thoughtfulness around these interactions, it was apparent that male colleagues my age carried themselves more candidly. They could not only sit with our professors and talk to them with friendly ease, but they could also easily schedule drinking sessions and get invited to coffee even if they didn't do any committee work.

I confided these fears to a former male colleague, and I was reassured that I was recognized as a "promising academic" regardless of my gender. At the time, I thought deeply about what it meant to be considered a promising academic. Years down the line, I arrived at a realization that this meant that I met the conditions of being a good philosopher as defined by the people I wanted recognition from. Part of these unspoken conditions was to separate me from my philosophical work. I should foremost be a disembodied philosopher, not a woman philosopher. The irony of this, however, was that the division of labor in philosophy departments was still gendered. When I asked older female colleagues about their experiences, their narratives verified that committee work was an expectation, a "rite of passage" that we all went through. For male scholars, doing well in committee work likely helps promote them to positions that support their academic formation, while for female scholars, this could mean that they will be taking notes in all the upcoming departmental meetings and doing more committee work.

The reality of being a woman in academia is one of precarity and carefulness. I don't only have to think about the quality of my philosophical work but also how I carry myself. I found myself worrying not just about the quality of my answers in class or my understanding of philosophical texts, but I also had to worry that my dress wasn't too short or that my shirt wasn't too tight. Despite my carefulness, I would still hear comments about how "inappropriate" I looked (and this justified certain people's disapproval of me). Even worse was that I would be the subject of misogynistic jokes from male classmates. One incident carved itself into my core memory: over drinks, some of my classmates at the graduate school made a joke alleging that the only reason why my graduate school professor called me to answer his questions was because I had an "improper relationship" with him. These were classmates I never said more than a few words to and whom I had never met outside of class. They made this "joke" when I wasn't there to call them out, and it was only relayed to me by one of my friends. I barely even knew their names. I doubt they knew more about me than I did them, but it was unbelievably easy for them to weaponize my womanhood against me.

I had to develop my philosophical prowess while simultaneously developing a thick skin to develop resilience against the pervasive misogyny in philosophy. An acceptance of my femininity seemed detrimental to my philosophical work, and it was a discomfort that sat with me for the first three years of my graduate studies. I found myself faced with a paradox of misrecognition: I am recognized as a promising graduate student without consideration of my gender, and yet I am policed because of my gender.

At the time, I had already identified myself as a feminist, but I did not have any philosophical concepts to help me recognize what I had experienced. It took years and multiple conversations with women colleagues to realize I was at the receiving end of repeated cases of misogyny and silencing. Kate Manne defines misogyny as functioning to "enforce and police women's subordination and to uphold male dominance" (Manne 19). The comments that targeted my appearance were well-crafted attacks meant to keep me "in my place" as a subordinate to my male colleagues in our classrooms. Being assigned to hospitality and registration committees was based on the misogynistic assumption that young female graduate students were best suited to entertaining guests and conference participants.

Microinvalidations Disguised as Objectivity: A Professor's Experience

(Darlene Demandante)

When asked to write about gendered abuses in academia, my initial inclination was to define what constitutes an abuse, how certain abuses are considered as gendered, and what makes the gendered abuse unique to my Southeast Asian context. Typically, this is considered a good method of philosophizing in as much as it attempts to come up with an objective, rational account of gendered abuses without resorting so much to the subjective narration of experiences that is often discouraged in philosophy. My inclination to pursue this approach reflects a broader issue in philosophy—the hesitancy to fully acknowledge and integrate embodied experiences. As philosophers, we have been conditioned to suppress our personal experiences to gain credibility as serious thinkers. The prevailing image of a philosopher as a male, able-bodied, contemplative figure with an air of calm reason further reinforces this bias.

Unfortunately, in the field of philosophy, women who express their emotions can sometimes face unfair labeling as mere "complainers" and be subjected to microinvalidations masked as demands for objectivity. Personally, I have experienced instances where I doubted my own encounters with misrecognition and found myself gaslighting myself about my own experiences, dismissing them as mere subjective impressions or work-related concerns.

In certain situations where I felt uncomfortable and had the urge to speak up, I found myself regulating my emotions and conforming to the expectations of how a "rational academic" should behave and what topics "rational academics" should discuss. The fear of being labeled as overly emotional and, consequently, irrational, compelled me to remain silent, seeking solace in the superficial comfort that pacifism brings about.

Labeling women's struggles as mere "complaints" serves as a tool to silence us, undermining our experiences while our male counterparts are not only permitted but also given serious attention when they express their "valid" concerns. This double standard perpetuates a cycle of inequality within academia. The common response of appealing to rationality is often an attempt to reshape the incident to align with the worldview of the majority, allowing the person making the appeal to remain oblivious to uncomfortable truths (Saba 149). In doing so, I often purposely blinded myself to my own experiences and those of others, all to maintain a facade of high functionality even when I was silently crumbling under the weight of my struggles.

This proves that objectivity comes with a price: the denial of one's own emotions, the invalidation of one's own doubts and sense of discomfort, and being forced to conform to standards set by patriarchy. My experience coauthoring a report with female colleagues about the status of women in our department brought these challenges to light as we sought to address issues of sexism and gender inequality. These issues included instances of sexual objectification, the use of sexist language, assumptions of inferiority, restrictive gender roles, denial of sexism's reality, and the invisibility of sexist humor, all of which we and some of our students faced.

For months, we painstakingly crafted the narratives, attempting to present them in an "objective" manner, believing that backing them up with theory would lead to better acceptance, as narrating experiences was often perceived as "drama." Additionally, despite all of us being women, the group encountered disagreements, with some prioritizing peacekeeping while attempting to maintain balance by also discussing stopgap measures. Part of the struggle in acknowledging our experiences stems from past mental conditioning, where we were repeatedly told that gender was not an issue in our department, as we were all judged based on our capabilities and merits, irrespective of gender. I now realize how untrue this statement was, given that male colleagues did not face the same hurdles in receiving promotions, and they enjoyed the benefits of working in academia without the added responsibility of family caregiving and other historically biased patterns that granted them more opportunities to assert themselves.

I vividly recall how presenting the report to the department became a retraumatizing experience. As a colleague read the report to the group (despite the fact that a copy of it was already circulated in advance), an uneasy silence filled the room, leaving us unsure of our male colleagues' thoughts and feelings. The silence felt like an empty, uncomfortable void, creating an atmosphere where we were compelled to continue speaking, yet sensing that our words were falling on deaf ears.

This challenge is particularly pronounced in our Filipino context, where the boundaries between professional work and personal life are often unclear. Within our department, colleagues embrace a familial approach, treating one another like family rather than coworkers. However, this familial dynamic can also give rise to certain individuals wielding disproportionate authority and commanding undue respect. Regrettably, this can result in personality politics permeating academic departments, wherein influential figures become resistant to constructive criticism, viewing such feedback as personal attacks rather than opportunities for growth and improvement.

I also clearly remember being warned about the consequences of the report. I was told by a senior faculty member to be more cautious when I call out male colleagues, as I might offend them. The warning is reminiscent of what Marilyn Frye (1983) writes in "A Note on Anger," that instead of focusing on the harm that has been committed, the perpetrator turns the complaint into an assessment of character and sanity of the wronged woman in question, part of which is perhaps about what the perpetrator thinks justifies the wrong. The senior faculty member was more concerned about offending those who would be called out than the actual harm that had been caused by the male colleagues who needed to be called out. It is also as if the male faculty members are so powerful they could reverse the narrative of harm.[1]

My experience confirmed my intuition that speaking up about abuses in the academic workplace is a complex gesture. Not only does the existing literature fail to adequately address this issue, but it also overlooks the fear of damaging personal relationships. Despite enduring experiences that caused me to doubt my worth as a scholar, I felt hesitant to speak out, as I found myself caught in a mentally taxing, draining, catch-22 situation.

Resistance and Communities of Care

The two of us have actively sought ways to address the identified problems by joining supportive communities where we can carry out our work without feeling unsafe. Through these communities, we have found strength in solidarity, fostering an environment that allows us to express ourselves freely and without fear. Some of our efforts were not initially planned but naturally fell into place and complemented each other. Despite lacking a formal strategy, these spontaneous actions seamlessly merged and propelled us forward.

In 2020, we coedited a special issue of *Kritike: An Online Journal of Philosophy* with the topic on "Women and Philosophy: An Initial Move Towards a More Inclusive Practice of Philosophy in the Philippine Context." This is the first collection of writings by Filipina philosophers compiled in a journal, pointing out the struggles and, simultaneously, offering a step in resisting a hostile environment in the Philippines that makes it challenging for women thinkers to thrive.

Over time, we established reading groups with women working in and interested in philosophy. Together, we engaged in thoughtful discussions and created a supportive intellectual environment. Our first reading group considered Kate Manne's *Down Girl: The Logic of Misogyny* during the pandemic lockdown in 2020. Women philosophers from different academic and nonacademic institutions also joined the group, and we shared our appreciation for the text as well as its resonances with our own experiences. This also led us to realize that the challenges we experienced as women philosophers in our institutions were not isolated cases but were part of a pervasive system of misogyny in the Philippines. Subsequently, we hosted a one-time reading group during Women's Month in 2022. The articles we read were Kristie Dotson's "Tracking Epistemic Violence, Tracking Practices of Silencing" and Josephine Acosta Pasricha's "Doing Philosophy in the Philippines: Rereading the Canon through Feminism."

A pivotal factor in our resistance was the establishment of Women Doing Philosophy (WDP)—through this group, we connected with brilliant Filipina philosophers who share similar research interests, leading to fruitful collaborations. Currently, we are working on several projects, including a journal special-issue proposal titled *The Philippine Condition: Threads of Critical, Decolonial, and Feminist Contentions*, and a forthcoming book, *Resilience: The Brown Babe's Burden*, under contract with Routledge. In addition, The Beyond the Ghetto! (BTG) subgroup was also founded as a platform to celebrate women philosophers and to encourage their active inclusion in philosophy classrooms.[2] A vital aspect of our practice in WDP is to engage in workshopping our ideas within a safe and supportive space.

Our efforts extend beyond academic work: a crucial element of our resistance involves engaging in care work and supporting one another. In WDP, we host spaces for writing sessions (Shut Up and Write!) and also for processing some of our traumatic experiences in the institutions where we work. These efforts serve as both productivity and solidarity spaces for us. Throughout the writing sessions, we check in on each other's progress, help each other work around the challenges that hindered our work, and celebrate our accomplishments. WDP is just one of the spaces we are familiar with, but it is essential to acknowledge that there could be other efforts and initiatives taking place elsewhere of which we may not yet be aware.

These shared spaces with women made us feel safe and *seen*. These women-only spaces revitalize our love for philosophy by reminding us that the hostilities we experience in philosophy are a by-product of the structural injustice in practices of philosophizing in the Philippines and not in philosophy itself. In contrast to the silencing, misogyny, and micro-aggressions we experienced in male-dominated philosophy spaces, the spaces we share with women respond to our plights with care, compassion, and empathy. These spaces also encourage us to work on philosophies that make sense of our unique, embodied experiences as brown women philosophers.

Notes

1. Another example of what Jennifer Freyd calls "DARVO"; see "Shocked" in this volume [editors' note].

2. Webinars and newsletters by Filipino women philosophers can be accessed through Beyond the Ghetto's website, https://beyondtheghetto.substack.com/.

Works Cited

Demandante, Darlene, and Marella Mancenido-Bolaños. "Women and Philosophy: An Initial Move Towards a More Inclusive Practice of Philosophy in the Philippine Context" *Kritike: An Online Journal of Philosophy*, vol. 14, no. 1, June 2020.

Dotson, Kristie. "Tracking Epistemic Violence, Tracking Practices of Silencing." *Hypatia*, vol. 26, no. 2, March 2011, pp. 236–57, https://doi.org/10.1111/j.1527-2001.2011.01177.x.

Frye, Marilyn. "A Note on Anger." *The Politics of Reality: Essays in Feminist Theory*. The Crossing Press, 1983, pp. 84–94.

Manne, Kate. *Down Girl: The Logic of Misogyny*. Oxford UP, 2017.

Pasricha, Josephine. "Doing Philosophy in the Philippines: Rereading the Canon through Feminism." *Karunungan*, vol. 21, 2004, pp. 71–82.

Saba, Fatima. "On the Edge of Knowing: Microaggressions and Epistemic Uncertainty as a Woman of Color." *Surviving Sexism in Academia: Strategies for Feminist Leadership*. Edited by Kirsti Cole and Holly Hassel. Routledge, 2017.

Women Doing Philosophy. *Beyond the Ghetto*. https://beyondtheghetto.substack.com/.

12

To Make a Fuss

The Chronic Predator in Higher Education

ANONYMOUS

In the early 1990s, a fellow sessional instructor and I made the decision to address unwelcome behaviors from a senior academic in a humanities department at a Canadian University. Our goal was simple: to be treated with respect and accorded the space and time to teach our classes, complete our dissertations, and pursue our academic careers. We also knew we were not his first targets and would not be his last, unless someone made a fuss. We thought we had procedures available to us to disrupt and reform his ongoing, invasive behavior. We had support from our department head and from a sexual harassment prevention office, and its policies and procedures. We had generous access to counseling services. However, efforts at informal resolution were met with hostile responses from him. When, as a result of this hostility, disciplinary measures were set and maintained by the dean for several months, conflict escalated to the level of crisis.

I still struggle to understand how a request to refrain from commenting on a female colleague's appearance, and to stop habitually engaging her in conversations about sexuality, could provoke retaliations for more than a year, while also drawing colleagues and administrators into the conflict. Despite the degree and duration of this escalation, I remain convinced that we were correct to make a fuss, to try to disrupt what was at least a decade's-long pattern of gender-based harassment.

In writing about these events now, I am irritated by inadequate labels. Specifically, to speak of a "harasser" implies harassment limited to one or a few workplace relationships over a short time frame. Yet frequently, as in this case, a harasser is a chronic predator, whose ongoing, habitual behavior is based on (1) careful identification and pursuit of numerous vulnerable individuals; (2) long-standing cultivation of an environment supportive of his behaviors; and (3) a sense of entitlement to impose harassment and resistance to corrective measures so vehement as to suggest obsession or some form of illness or chronic condition. My experiences with this case indicate that the chronic predator represents a particular challenge for universities.

In this essay, I refrain from naming the individuals, the department, and the institution. These specifics do not define the issues or remedies. I also largely avoid narrating my experiences from thirty years ago. Instead, I maintain a distanced and impersonal stance to describe chronic predators and universities as their ideal environment. I sometimes interrupt this generalized discussion with real detail. On the basis of this case, I point to preventative and potentially corrective measures available in academic environments, measures that stem from policies and processes for the prevention of harassment and discrimination. Expanding education about the mechanisms available to address harassment and discrimination continues to be a prominent recommendation for all workplaces including university campuses ("Bringing Harassment" 13–15; Rubin et al. 81). Furthermore, we still need to emphasize that universities must appropriately resource sexual-violence prevention initiatives, even as they have come to be viewed within the broader context of policies and processes addressing harassment and discrimination based on race, sexual orientation, gender identity, and dis/ability.

However, to disarm or even prevent the formation of the chronic predator, a pervasive cultural shift is needed so that the workplace becomes an environment toxic to the chronic predator. Bystander intervention, pervasive uptake of education on all forms of harassment and discrimination, leadership training (including mental health training), and the removal of blockages to institutional memory are essential. Exclusive reliance on reports filed by targets and victims cannot continue. I therefore agree with the recommendations by Rubin et al. (79–81) that universities cultivate a "culture of listening" through regular surveys that ask students and staff about their experiences, and that harassment prevention officers have the authority to file cases (89). To help complete the culture shift, all in positions of privilege and security must call out predatory behavior. Such measures could render universities inhospitable to chronic predators.

It is likely that, fundamentally, the chronic predator seeks power over others and the pleasure this produces. The university is an ideal location for a chronic predator because it presents large and continually refreshed numbers of targets. Every year there are new students, new staff, new academic colleagues. Vulnerable targets for the chronic predator are those who might be flattered by a senior scholar's attention and whose complaints of harassment are likely to be dismissed, ignored, or trivialized as misapprehensions, delusions, or lies designed to cause trouble or attract attention. Targets are therefore likely to be those perceived to have "lower rank" in the university hierarchy. Those students, colleagues, and staff whose intersecting identities are marginalized due to race, nonbinary gender identity, nonheteronormativity, or alternate ability will be more vulnerable wherever these identities affect perceived credibility.

The vulnerability of the target (or the predator's fixation on a particular target) likely increases to the degree that they engage with the chronic predator. If, for example, a target graciously accepts a comment on their appearance, the predator will intensify his comments or deliver them before a wider audience. After all, such a comment in private goes a certain distance toward reducing a target to their physical attributes, but one delivered to a junior instructor before an audience of students goes much further, undermining their academic achievement and their professional presence in the classroom. If a target engages with the predator in academic conversations about sexuality—a perfectly legitimate topic in many if not all humanities and social sciences settings—the chronic predator may seek to engage in more personal discussions and to do so in more private settings. To push much further is perhaps too risky, for the chronic predator must not be removed from his preferred environment. Therefore, while he will press for engagement that demonstrates his power to impose on others, these engagements cannot exceed deniability. If his behavior is called out for scrutiny or censure, he must be able to convince others that the complaint is a simple misunderstanding between friends and/or respected colleagues.

Even if flattery about physical attributes is no longer a preferred tool of the chronic predator as it was thirty years ago, intellectual flattery remains a serious threat, perhaps to students especially. The "compliment" of a request from a scholar for an academic opinion, or for an evaluation of a course in progress, will attract targets. A student, drawn aside into a private space like a professor's office, might find themselves exposed to more than a request to assess how a course is going.

The chronic predator expends considerable energy over the course of their career to secure peer allegiance and thereby ensure an atmosphere conducive to their predation. The loyalty of allies translates to sympathetic responses and a tendency to assume that accusers are misunderstanding or exaggerating, if not deliberately persecuting their alleged harasser, who is, his allies will readily insist, a highly respected scholar. The chronic predator might take pains to attend and speak up at events, lectures, seminars, or meetings where attendees are critiquing the very systems of oppression at work against the predator's target group. At such events, the chronic predator might confess their sins, which they have been compelled to recognize by the speaker's presentation, using body language to reinforce their shame—a hanging head, pinched shoulders—and express their humble but firm resolve to reform. A measure of the predator's successful environmental grooming could be how quickly their peers will defend him, assuring all present that he could not possibly have anything to confess or reform. The chronic predator's grooming will extend to sexual harassment prevention officers, who, upon witnessing the predator's display of contrition, might believe their work on a complaint file is done: "Oh, but he said he recognized his errors and promised to change."

That there have also always been colleagues who saw through the chronic predator's facade, but did not expose it, shows that a different culture is possible. Education and training for justice in the workplace must be extensive and pervasive enough that all who perceive predation know that, even as bystanders, we can respond in ways that will support, rather than merely pity or mock, the plight of targets. Bystander intervention requires that leadership have the training needed to respond appropriately: colleagues in leadership positions must know exactly the steps needed to support reports from bystanders *and* targets. In cases of chronic predation, policy must allow administrators to act without a formal complaint from a victim, as recommended by Cowan (36) and Rubin et al. (89). Administrators must have access to records that speak to the chronic predator's long history of harassment, and therefore letters of discipline can never be completely expunged from university records, and nondisclosure agreements must not be used to silence victims.

The chronic predator might believe he is entitled to his preferred modes of behavior, or perhaps he develops an addiction to the pleasure he gains from them. Self-deception, entitlement, addiction—something powerful drives the chronic predator's vehement opposition to any attempt to stop him. Therefore, faced with even the loss of one target, along with a challenge to his carefully cultivated veneer of respectability among his peers, the predator may seek out other allies. If his efforts are unsuccessful, he will likely escalate, especially if he has invested many years grooming targets and his environment.

Within days of my fellow sessional instructor's attempt to address and stop his harassment, I received an unprecedented phone call from him at my home. He requested I meet with him to counter recent attempts to create a toxic atmosphere in our department. Because these "attempts" were my fellow sessional's complaints against him, I refused to meet. The next day, I found a handwritten and signed note from him in my department mailbox, requesting a meeting and adding that I could have the department head present, as my fellow sessional had done, or the "entire [provincial] legislature," but he "strongly advised against it." After the dean and department head were informed of this, he was ordered to cease all communication with me and my fellow sessional instructor.

For the chronic predator, administrators must be remade as allies should his behavior weaken or break his relationships with them. So the predator might adhere to the disciplinary measures and after a suitable period, ask for reconciliation with his former targets. He may play the victim, claiming the "feminists" have made him a target of academic mobbing. In our case, though he complied with the dean's order to stop all communication with us, he announced to everyone his disdain for that order: when one of us passed by, he would dramatically step aside, flattening himself against the wall. He raised his arm in a Nazi salute behind my back. Persecuted, apparently, by the worst of fascists, he posed as the good guy. He found reason to defy the disciplinary order, claiming he "just had to" tell me how impressed he was after observing my daughter at a department social event.

The chronic predator's escalation might encompass colleagues' family members. As early as possible in such an escalation, mental health professionals must be authorized to intervene. University leadership must be trained and empowered to reject procedures that place the whole community at risk while protecting the rights of a predator. Failure here has consequences, as it did in my experience.

It is the last day of classes, April 1995. I arrive in the department and am immediately directed into the office of the department head. I and my fellow sessional instructor have been ordered by a senior university administrator to leave campus and not return until it would be safe. Handwritten letters had been delivered to the dean and the department head that morning, detailing how the chronic predator had been unjustly subjected to improper and unwarranted discipline and stating his hope that the spouses and families of the dean and department head "would be OK." The two letters were signed using the name Valery Fabrikant.

Less than two years before the events I describe here, in August 1993, Fabrikant had been sentenced to life in prison for murdering four of his academic colleagues and assaulting one staff member at Concordia University, in 1992.

The senior administrator who had determined the immediate institutional response to those letters later told me they recognized that their response was wrong: we were sent home; the predator was allowed to teach his classes. Wrong indeed. If there was not then and there, there should be now and everywhere, a university code of professional ethics that specifies that even veiled threats of violence are cause for immediate dismissal. It must simply be intolerable that any member of a university community should remain part of it after identifying themselves using the name of a convicted murderer. That someone who makes such threats would be allowed into classrooms full of students must be inconceivable. However, the matter should never have escalated to such a crisis.

I doubt that a cure for the chronic predator is possible. My experience suggests that prevention is essential, not only for the well-being of targets, but for the long-term mental, emotional, and professional well-being of one who might become a chronic predator. The university must become a place where a predator cannot find targets and allies and therefore is unable to invest years of effort to groom targets, to generate an enabling environment. To effect such a culture shift, our rights to a healthy and just academic work environment must be pervasively understood so that we can all respond effectively to every instance of harassment. To be effective bystanders, we need trained leaders who are willing and able to provide support, including from agencies and professionals outside the university, as well as properly resourced and trained campus teams for prevention of harassment and discrimination ("Bringing Harassment" 14; Cowan 32–36). Finally, the culture shift required to prevent the formation of chronic predators cannot rely on those who are vulnerable as targets of harassment to speak out. Instead, we must cultivate a pervasive culture of listening: those of us in academia who enjoy the safety of privilege in whatever form must be the ones who ask, listen, remember, and, when necessary, make a fuss.

Works Cited

"Bringing Harassment on Campus out of the Shadows." ["Lever le voile sur le harcèlement sexuel et la discrimination sur les campus."] *Bulletin: Canadian Association of University Teachers/Association canadienne des professeures et professeurs d'univérsité*, vol. 68, no. 8 Nov. 2021, 10–15. https://www.caut.ca/sites/default/files/november-2021-bulletin-final-online.pdf. Accessed 9 Sep. 2023.

Cowan, John Scott. 1994. "Lessons from the Fabrikant File: A Report to the Board of Governors of Concordia University." Retrieved from https://www.concordia.ca/offices/archives/stories/fabrikant.html. Accessed 9 Sep. 2023.

Rubin, Janice, et al. 2023. *University of Prince Edward Island Review*. Retrieved from https://www.upei.ca/about-upei/independent-third-party-review. Accessed 9 Sep. 2023.

13

Too Woke, Too Radical, Too Unforgiving

Queer Resistance to the Patriarchal Panopticon

NANCY PATHAK

Education and work should provide the individual with dignity and security, not enable some to overpower others. I entered academia with this hope. My dissertation was on the democratization of human spaces. My PhD supervisor taught me that the greatest learnings of a social scientist come not from books but from experiences, often evoking the same sentiments as bell hooks in *Teaching to Transcend*. I expected my new workplace, the political science department in a top college of Delhi University, to be a liberal space. Instead, I found an unfathomable gap between theory and praxis in academia. To my surprise, this elite institution was interested only in ivory-tower discussions by academics who used their privileges to appropriate stories from the margins rather than lifting others up.

The Prelude and Buildup

I was appointed as assistant professor (guest) at a leading college of South Campus, Delhi University, where I was immediately shown my place in the hierarchy of a system that exploits non-tenure-track faculty members much as the US adjunct system does. As a contractual worker with no security or welfare provisions, as dictated by government of India policy, my

121

safeguards were nil, though the qualification and selection criteria for guest faculty were the same as those for permanent faculty. Guest appointments have to be renewed by the head of department (HOD) every semester, leaving young academics dependent on the whims of their HODs. Tenured faculty members treated guest faculty as the untouchables of academia.

I was the only guest faculty in the political science department, so I was ranked below all the others. The rules of my position were made immediately clear. My HOD told me not to speak to anyone from the department. He barred me from sitting in the staff room, restricting my interaction with other department members. I found refuge in the college library, but when the HOD noticed several faculty members interacted with me there, he drove me out of the library, humiliating me in front of everyone. The college canteen became the only place where I could sit, alone, before and after my classes. My HOD started coming there to speak to me about random things. Of course, I could not refuse to speak with him, since my future work in the department depended on his good favor. Through this routine isolation, he came to make me believe that he was my only supporter and everyone else in the department could be harmful to me. He portrayed us as "a team," provided I followed his instructions.

The Gaslighting

Reading about domestic violence enabled me to look back at the HOD's behavior and understand why he isolated me from my colleagues. In *Politics of Surviving: How Women Navigate Domestic Violence and Its Aftermath* (2021), Paige Sweet describes how abusers use gaslighting tactics to make their targets question their sanity, perception of reality, and ability to interpret events. In almost all cases, the perpetrator first cuts victims off from all supporters (270, para. 1). When I tried to share this understanding with another senior department member, she brushed it off, saying that "he is just like that," normalizing the harassment. I spiraled into further self-doubt and started believing my HOD. I understood that nobody cared about the rights or well-being of a contractual faculty member.

My HOD started calling me late at night, inquiring about my personal life. I tried to avoid answering those questions. Sometimes he insisted that I tell him everything, so that he could "help me." When I would not pick up the call, he would scold me at the workplace. He used the pretext of urgent work to make these late-night calls seem routine, but his reasons for calling were almost never urgent. On the following mornings he would try to pacify me, saying that scolding was only for my own good and he was just trying to protect me from others in the college, whom he described as "vultures." He projected himself as a supporter, asking all sorts of questions, and I soon told him about my poverty, my dire need for the job, and my research on gender rights and performativity. He then had all the information he needed to exploit my vulnerabilities. Women working on gender rights have often been rebuked as "feminazis" and "radicals," and soon I would be, too.

In *The Dignity of Women at the Workplace*, Michael Rubenstein determines that the likelihood of being sexually harassed is associated with the perceived vulnerability and financial dependency of targets. The most probable victims of harassment are women who are single, divorced, minorities, lesbians, or women with irregular employment contracts (117). Most of those aspects of marginalization described me, making me highly susceptible to abuse.

The Incident

The calls from my HOD became more frantic, and his questions became more personal, when an article was published in a daily newspaper celebrating my participation in a fashion show that was also a platform for body-positive activism ("A Walk to Set Fashion Free," Aggarwal 28 Feb. 2020). I had been writing a research paper on queer representation in fashion and performativity and had participated in several queer movements in India. Walking in this show as a body-positive model for the Fashion Development Council of India was part of my performance of queer gendered identity, as theorized by Judith Butler ("Performative Acts and Gender Constitution," 1988).

A week later, on March 5, 2020, even before I could finish teaching my classes, the HOD started calling me relentlessly. He asked me to meet him off campus, not disclosing the exact location. I was suspicious but too afraid to refuse his request. I started communicating only in text, so that there was a record. When I reached the metro station where he had asked me to meet him, he drove me to a suburb. At that point, I was very far away from my home and workplace, more isolated and vulnerable than ever. He asked me about the news article, inquiring whether I was a fashion model. I clarified that I was an activist who frequented fashion events to promote body positivity. He started threatening me, saying that the "vultures" in the department would not tolerate this kind of activism. Though I resisted the onslaught, he questioned me invasively about my queerness, for example, asking what clothes I wore for my performances. He convinced me that the "secret" of my queerness and my performance of it was safe with him, suggesting it was something to hide, though I performed openly and proudly.

By then it was late, but he kept taking me from one eatery or café to another, driving me farther from the main city and not allowing me to leave, even as midnight approached. Finally I declared that I would leave, but he insisted that he take me home rather than allowing me to get myself there. Instead, he drove me even farther away, to the border of another state, without asking or informing me of where he was going. We were on a completely dark road, with no one in sight. Later I used Google maps to find that the road was taking us to a retreat resort. When I protested, he said, "I have not had a fun night out in a long while." I expressed disgust and clear my desire to go home; he responded by commandeering me to participate in his "fun night." After many more protests, he finally turned the car back toward the city. I rushed into my home. Looking from our balcony, my flat mate and I were horrified to see him downstairs, walking back and forth from our house to the street again and again. Meanwhile he was calling and texting me, despite my message asking him to leave me alone.

I spent that entire night sleepless, fearful, and avoiding his frantic calls, while he continued circling my house. In this situation, my education could not protect me. I was just another terrified woman being stalked by an entitled man. Worse, he had made it clear that I was being targeted for my identity, activism, and my work in queer politics.

The Complaint

Early the next morning, I called a senior professor in the department. She heard me patiently this time. Something so appalling had to happen before my complaint registered for her. She told me that my HOD had also been making advances on students. When I approached the college principal regarding the issue, she said that her hands were tied. I had to make a formal complaint with the Internal Complaints Committee (ICC), which was required by the government regulation of 2013 Prevention of

Sexual Harassment (POSH) act (*Handbook of Sexual Harassment* 2015). When news of the incident spread, another senior female professor asked me to "forgive him." I learned another lesson: academic hierarchies matter more than gender solidarities.

The Roleplay of Binaries

Catherine MacKinnon points out the "dominance perspective" in which sexual harrassment is commonly understood as manifesting sex differences defined by the power differential of dominance and submission (162). Margaret A. Crouch further notes that MacKinnon categorizes the causalities of sexual harassment into the quid pro quo and hostile environments created by gendered hierarchies (16). With this same binary logic, the Prevention of Sexual Harassment Act of 2013 was also created. It reifies workplace gender roles into binary power play.

The POSH Act does not provide for queer representation in these ICC proceedings. It only allows the nomination of at least one woman from the marginalized castes and tribes designated by the government as "schedule" categories (as per chapter 3, section 7, subclause (c) of the POSH Act, 2013). Queers do not qualify as marginalized categories for them. In fact, not just the ICC constitution but the entire legal concept of gender and identity in India omitted constructs of queerness. And my queerness was the primary point of blackmail used by the perpetrator. My queerness was discussed repeatedly during the legal proceedings of the ICC case, without any queer representation in the committee to understand it. Further, I was facing a legal committee that was handling the proceedings as dictated by the moral standards of the POSH Act of 2013—though homosexuality was not decriminalized in India until 2018 (*Navtej Singh Johar v. Union of India*). I was technically a criminal in my own harassment hearing.

The Burden of Truth: Proving One's Victimization

Another regulation that governs these proceedings, DU Ordinance XV(D), allows the victim to be punished if she fails to prove her accusations. The proceedings for my complaint pitted the victim against the institution, rather than providing a legal avenue for the victim to attain justice. With one exception, no witnesses spoke the truth, fearing institutional action against them. Instead, I had to depend on technology to establish my innocence, using our Google locations from the terrifying night to prove that I was not lying; the perpetrator was. Soon the committee realized that the punishment under the POSH act was extremely grave for the crimes that had been proven. The Indian Penal code section 354A allowed imprisonment for up to three years, a fine, or both for the crimes proven. So the committee refused to execute the ICC proceedings according to that act and instead followed DU's Ordinance XV(D), dated September 30, 2003. That ordinance allowed the perpetrator to walk away with a slap on the wrist: he was suspended for two months without detention and told to write an apology letter, which I never received.

Other pressure tactics were also employed throughout the proceeding. Various people on the committee and providing evidence questioned my merit, belittled my work on queerness, and assassinated my character. I was frequently asked why I met my HOD off campus, though he was not censured for asking me to do so. They kept asking me why I sat in his car and stayed so late, without acknowledging how my HOD misused his authority to force me to do so. When I warned them that he also sexually harassed students, I got no response. No one cared about the safety of the young people who interacted with this person within the framework of teacher-student power relations. The POSH Act defined sexual harassment as an act of power, yet the committee never acknowledged the perpetrator's domination and humiliation as harassment.

Case Won, Justice Denied

I emerged from the proceedings victorious, having proven the crime committed by my HOD on March 5, 2020. Then my job contract was terminated immediately, without any explanation. My pay was withheld. My academic career seemed to be over. People who once declared themselves my friends started communicating with me only away from public sight. Feeling defeated, I went into therapy, which I could not afford. I was diagnosed with clinical depression. My own parents shamed me for deciding to file the complaint and defending myself in the hearing. They believed I did not come from a social background that allowed me to choose justice over my livelihood. An entire family had been pushed to choose between dignity and survival.

The Homecoming

Picking myself up, I decided to apply for other jobs. The news of a small fish who dared to fight a shark had spread throughout Delhi University like wildfire. After completing more than sixty unfair interviews, I interviewed for a position at a college known for its feminist politics and academic excellence. It was a big brand for someone so small, so I had little hope of getting the job. As the interview ended and I dragged myself out of the room, the college principal stopped me and said, "Wait! You can't just leave." I hesitated, then apologized for something I seemed to have done wrong but failed to understand. Everyone in the room smiled and the HOD said, "We need you! You've come to the right place." I knew then that they knew what I had been through at my former institution. It was as if each one of them had experienced something similar. The principal patted my back and said, "Welcome to your new academic abode." It felt like an overdue homecoming for a broken traveler.

This experience taught me that when the system fails a victim, only the gender solidarities and sisterhoods outside systemic hierarchies come to protect them. People have been struggling for better accountability and safeguards against sexual harassment at Delhi University since the 1990s. But patriarchal forces in the institution keep pushing them back by abusing the absence of inclusive law or by exclusionary interpretation of the law. These forces prevail because of the lack of systemic support for harassment victims, especially those who identify as members of marginalized groups. Many capable women and queer folks have lost their careers because of this lack of protective policies and support, having been labeled as "radical feminists" and a danger to the dominant culture. I survived this trauma carrying a heavy responsibility to fight for those who were not as fortunate as I was in finally finding an inclusive space.

Works Cited

Aggarwal, Asmita. "A Walk to Set Fashion Free." *New Delhi: The Asian Age*, 2020. https://www.asianage.com/life/more-features/280220/a-walk-to-set-fashion-free.html. Accessed 28 Feb. 2020.

Butler, Judith. "Performative Acts and Gender Constitution: An Essay in Phenomenology and Feminist theory." *Theatre Journal*, vol. 40, no. 4, 1988, 519–31.

Crouch, Margaret A. *Thinking about Sexual Harassment*. New York: Oxford UP, 2001.

Government of India, Ministry of Women and Child Development. *Handbook on Sexual Harassment of Women at the Workplace*. Delhi, November 2015. https://wcd.nic.in/sites/default/files/Handbook%20on%20Sexual%20Harassment%20of%20Women%20at%20Workplace.pdf. Accessed 7 Aug. 2020.

MacKinnon, Catharine. *Sexual Harassment of Working Women: A Case of Sex Discrimination*. Yale UP, 1979.

Navtej Singh Johar v. Union of India. No. AIR 2018 SC 4321. Supreme court of India. 6 September 2018.

Rubenstein, Michael. *The Dignity of Women at Work: A Report on the Problem of Sexual Harassment in the Member States of European Community*. Office for Official Publications of the European Communities, 1988. https://op.europa.eu/en/publication-detail/-/publication/db562ac1-7ad0-4b57-92e1-6b48f5982cfc. Accessed 3 May 2023.

Sweet, Paige L. *Politics of Surviving: How Women Navigate Domestic Violence*. U of California P, 2021.

14

Shocked

Resisting and Rising above Abuse in Academe

(Karen) Irene Countryman-Roswurm

In the midsize city I call home, the local state-funded university acts as more than an educational institution. Rather, it serves as a powerful force in our business economy, professional development opportunities, and communal belonging.[1] All over town, college colors replace the waving of red, white, and blue; people proudly wear university attire, and vehicle plates and buses pronounce allegiance to the school mascot. The university sells a powerful dream, a pathway out of desperation and into a life of social connection and career success—particularly to those of us raised in the impoverished surrounding neighborhoods.

My childhood home and public school were just blocks from the university, which lured us poor kids into academe with free tickets to sporting and firework events. Born into generational trauma, I came home from school at thirteen to find my mother deceased by suicide. As an orphan, I spent three years displaced between foster homes, shelters, and the streets. At sixteen, I won legal emancipation from the state and began taking college classes to realize the promise of the recruiter's repeated claim: "Attending university will make you less likely to live in poverty, struggle with addiction, or experience violence; and more likely to have good pay and a healthy life."

After more than a decade of pursuing education while working full-time in child welfare with unaccompanied and trafficked minors, I earned a doctorate and was offered a tenure-track professorship in a social services department at my university. Having just given birth, and after fifteen years serving youth with childhoods similar to my own, I welcomed earning a living wage, a slower-paced lifestyle, and entrance into a revered community. But administrators, anxious to leverage my lived experiences, expertise in antitrafficking, national partnerships, and relationships with local donors, asked me to "start a center." Consequently, as an assistant professor learning to navigate academe, I also became the founder and executive director of the Center for Combating Human Trafficking (CCHT).

Never could I have imagined that answering the request to serve our university as a degreed professional would lead me to abuses more traumatizing than my experiences on the streets as an orphaned runaway. While juggling the demands of spouse and mother, I strived to exceed the teaching, research, and service demands of a tenure-track professor as well as establish a not-for-profit-like organization within the university—a world full of unfamiliar policies, politics, and practices. Worse, my sex, gender identity, age, race, faith, and (presumed) political affiliations became the target of hostility. With discrimination, harassment, and retaliation (DHR) straining my mental and physical health, I found myself confused, lost, and alone in figuring out how to obtain safe access to a career in academia.

Discrimination and Harassment

The abuse I experienced was so persistent and pervasive that it seemed the perpetrators had studied a rules-of-engagement handbook: deplete energy, degrade character, disconnect community, diminish identity, discredit pedagogy, devalue passionate pursuits.

It began as verbal attacks on my professional expertise and personal character. Dr. Fib, a department authority, led these attacks, beginning with a faculty meeting he organized to protest my new contract as director of CCHT. He implied not only that my credentialing was insignificant, but that I had prostituted myself to obtain my academic appointment by asking college directors, "What did she *do* to *get* a Center?" "Whose cock did she suck?" "Did she fuck you?" Fib also aimed his hostility directly at me, often calling me a "one-trick pony," which, as a Native woman, I found particularly offensive and dehumanizing since Native Americans have been treated as horses through the practice of blood quantum testing (HTLA 2020). Once, as I entered a meeting, he said to my colleagues, "She's got some ho boots on! I wonder if she used those ho boots on [my supervisors]!" One exceptionally traumatizing day, Fib disparaged me in similar ways—loudly throwing insults and accusations—in the commons full of lounging students and passersby. On another occasion, when I argued for the importance of collaborating with students on publications, he responded that "Native women are known for trading sex to get what they want!"

Faculty and students reported such discrimination and slander to me for years, recounting his assertions that I was exchanging sex for my career. One faculty member repeated his claim that, "You know she fucked them . . . she worked an 'Indian deal.'" Fib also made presumptions about my faith and political affiliation while insulting my work, saying, "Only crazy Christians and radical Republicans believe in this human trafficking crap." Numerous students reported that Fib referred to me as a "crazy prostitute," discouraged them from pursuing a practicum with CCHT and/or a thesis on human trafficking (HT), stated that individuals in our CCHT program were "not victims" but rather "promiscuous criminals," and shared his belief that "femicides are a lie because women are more violent than men." Students repeatedly reported their experiences to administrators in written form, along with peer signatures.

In addition to verbal harassment, I was discriminated against through annual performance reviews (APRs) and the tenure/promotion (TP) process. Year after year, Fib, and later his associate Lemming, discredited my pedagogy, downplayed my outstanding teaching evaluations, refused to consider my research and service related to HT, and insulted my professional identity through lengthy commentary. Dr. Rodent, a more senior administrator, attempted to reason with them through written rebuttals, but Fib and Lemming voted "no" for my reappointment and "no" against TP.

Reporting and Retaliation

The more I reported discrimination and harassment, the more authorities purposefully retaliated: relocate, reduce pay, remove connection; threaten, incite fear; delay responding, defend behaviors, deflect blame, demand self-sufficiency, destroy passions, deny abuses.

I consistently reported DHR to supervisors who made light of the abuses, suggested I "laugh it off," and joked that the sexual accusations were a "compliment." They told me to "Keep your head down and try to avoid harassment. When you aren't teaching, stay out of the department and don't attend faculty meetings. And on your record, tone down accomplishments so you don't further anger the guys." Describing their own problems in the university and with the Offices Intended to Address Equity and Abuse (OIAEA), Dr. Rodent and his associate Dr. Blub repeatedly instructed me: "Don't formally report. It will derail your tenure and ruin your career." Because "Nobody likes a whistleblower."

While following Rodent's instruction to be "discreet," I gradually became more vocal about the discrimination through annual APR reports and, ultimately, my TP evaluation. For five exhausting years I described my experiences of discrimination and requested assistance in letters to administrators in the college and Headmaster's Office and to faculty who served on the TP college and University Committee. I never received outreach from any administrator or OIAEA, and the DHR escalated.

While my department committee voted against TP, the college and university committees recognized the value of my work and recommended me for TP. As the first woman to earn TP in my department in several years, and the only tenured female department member at the time, this should have been celebrated. Instead, I received more hostility. In a rapidly worsening turn of events, Rodent retired and a new administrator, Dr. Ambush, was hired.

In our first meeting, Ambush declared, "The men in the department have concerns about you and your Center." Dismissing the DHR, he exclaimed, "You made tenure! You should just be happy! You are lucky to have your job and pay as a woman!" Shocked, I protested his statements. Within months, Ambush promoted Blub and Fib and announced a restructuring of CCHT. Ambush increased CCHT workloads by demanding changes to our website and reporting mechanisms. Causing confidentiality and safety challenges for survivors in our Pathway to Prosperity™ Program, CCHT offices were abruptly moved from our downtown location to mere doors away from perpetrators on campus. When concerned board members reached out, Ambush rejected their requests to meet. Furthermore, he denied my request to use vacation hours for professional development, refused or returned CCHT donor dollars, and breached the terms of my contract regarding access to a graduate assistant and receipt of compensation for grant-funded services rendered. When I sought resolution to these issues, Ambush yelled, "You are just a Russian doll in *my* college! You will just have to work until the work is done!"

In desperation, I filed my first of several complaints with OIAEA in December 2018. This too only inflamed matters. OIAEA was not transparent about my rights (including my ability to speak off-record, get access to files, request supportive or safety measures, and bring an adviser to interviews), responsibilities (to know how to define terms of discrimination and document abuses), or processes (including methods of reporting, timelines, and thresholds of harm). OIAEA itself was accusatory, hostile, and presumptive. One OIAEA agent excused the harassment as "simple locker room talk," asked whether Fib's racist and sexist statements were "because Native women are known to trade beads and things?" and repeated Ambush's justification: "You're tenured, so what harm did it do?" When I finally learned of, and advocated for, my right to obtain recordings of meetings with OIAEA, my initial interview was provided in three parts, clearly altered to omit critical evidence. OIAEA explained that "the batteries might have died . . . maybe once . . . or twice." There was no clear distinction of privacy or autonomy between OIAEA and administrators. Worse, OIAEA empowered abusers further by informing them that "her reports aren't rising to our level to investigate" while refusing to transfer me away from their supervision, thus enabling perpetrators to further gaslight and silence me.

Within a couple of months of my reporting to OIAEA and requesting new supervision, Ambush and Fib were informed that OIAEA had decided not to investigate my complaint and they would remain my sole evaluators. Soon after, Fib entered my office without permission, posted signs proclaiming ownership of my workspace, and broke several meaningful glass items displaying my name and credentials. OIAEA called Fib's behavior a "personnel issue" and directed me to resolve the matter with Ambush who, citing OIAEA's judgment that my reports did not deserve investigation, forbade me from bringing him such complaints.

I worked my way through the chain of command until I had exhausted all internal resources. The responses I received from top administrators, including women I had once respected, deepened my sense of unsafety, fear, and helplessness. Many women guessed Fib and Ambush were the key perpetrators due to their own experiences and a known history of unaddressed discrimination across campus. While I appreciated validation of my experiences, I was shocked when women in positions of authority shared threats of violent retaliation, sometimes in racist and heterosexist terms. Ultimately, every administrator I sought help from communicated their unwillingness or inability to assist me, was deceitful about their statements when later interviewed by OIAEA, and joined in the retaliation against me.

Finally, during a meeting with an even higher administrator, Dr. Rort, I begged for help. In response, he expressed the university's appreciation for me and my work and committed to abide by the terms of my contract. Then, in typical DARVO fashion ("Deny, Attack, Reverse Victim and Offender," Freyd 1997), Rort referred to OIAEA's judgment and warned, "We will abide by the terms in your contract . . . but those concerns of yours . . . you're gonna have to set it aside to move forward—it's gonna be *better* for you if you do." Rort followed up in email, "You should refrain from stating you have been harassed or discriminated against . . ."

I did not heed Rort's threat. Consequently, he retracted his commitment. Within months, those with the authority to put an end to DHR—those I had once trusted, worked tirelessly for, and depended on—breached my employment contract, attempted to silence me with a nondisclosure agreement, fired CCHT staff, closed the CCHT at the university, provided deceitful information about the closure to our donors, and withheld CCHT funds. Despite their repeated commitment to maintain my salary as they transferred me back into a sole professorship role, administrators also reduced my pay.

Exasperated and depressed, I sought assistance outside the university. I spoke with CCHT donors and board members, media covered rising concerns, and I formally sought assistance from the Board of Regents (BOR), who denied my request. Without options, I filed a complaint with the Equal Employment Opportunity Commission (EEOC) and Human Rights Commission (HRC). After rounds of investigations and failed mediations, EEOC issued a Right to Sue Letter, and I filed a lawsuit in October 2021, which brought additional layers of trauma: sleepless nights preparing materials, defendant deceit, legal manipulation, scare tactics, my resignation from a hard-earned tenured position, and forced silencing.

A Culture of Fear and Silence

At all levels, my experiences of DHR illuminate systemic oppression fueled by a culture of fear and silence: regulated power imbalances, protection of the status quo, restricted access to information and resources, valuing money over education.

Within the university, demographics—sex, gender, race, heritage, ancestry, culture, faith, political affiliations—greatly influenced the occurrences of and responses to DHR. While data demonstrates that 80 to 90 percent of all social workers are women (McPhail 2004; NASW 2020; Salsberg et al. 2020), my experience reflects McPhail's statement: "In fact, social work is more correctly described as a female majority, male dominated profession" (325). When I experienced the most severe DHR, only men were tenured in my department. The weight of work was carried out by several adjunct and non-tenure-track women, along with two other tenure-track women who were denied TP in the two years prior to my review. Thus, three men—Fib, Lemming, and Blub—held the power to weaponize their authority with what OIAEA referred to as "academic freedom" and "pedagogy" in the classroom, annual evaluations, and the TP process. Similarly, while I was being harassed, the two college administrators were men, four successive higher administrators were men, and a male OIAEA agent "reviewed" my complaint.

Even when non-white-male individuals were involved in my complaint, systemic oppression prevailed. Academics who profess to believe in social justice sat silently, laughed, or joined Fib in his abuses. When invited to speak truth to power in their OIAEA interview regarding my case, one female higher administrator obstructed the possibility of an investigation through lies that blatantly contradicted evidence. More painful than the deceit is the unchecked racism on record: "I'm not going to help her. I know she's Native, but she looks white, and I'm not going to waste my social capital."

After a year of requesting that OIAEA interview witnesses, the agent gathered statements from other faculty who confirmed the harassment and the value of my work. Still, OIAEA refused to facilitate a full investigation. Near the end of Fall 2019, master's students wrote a letter to university administrators and the BOR in which they documented Fib's "shockingly offensive behavior," including calling victims in the CCHT program "criminal whores," silencing objecting students, and triggering abuse survivors. Students wrote that Fib expressed "an undeniable hostility targeted against Dr. Roswurm and other females he would like to suppress." In response, the administrators scolded the students for sharing their concerns "across campus and outside the university," and the students, fearing their degrees would be refused, submitted to the reprimands. I then received a memo instructing me, against campus policy, to share concerns only directly with the department manager and never inform students how to seek OIAEA assistance. OIAEA claimed that Fib was "exercising his right to pedagogical freedoms."

In 2020, inspired in part by my reports of gender-related abuses, the student-led university paper wrote an article about Title IX. Authors reported that fewer than 7 percent of cases from the last two academic years resulted in formal investigation and report, an amount the OIAEA called "not unusually low." In 2021, the BOR and university ordered an audit of the Title IX program, which revealed that the university OIAEA was created in response to a previous 2017 private audit; there was only a 5.9 percent response rate to the survey in the current audit; and the percentage of cases that move forward was, contrary to OIAEA's claim, "surprisingly low." The survey also found that employees did not report abuses because they did not think reporting would solve anything, feared retaliation, and worried about being blamed, not believed, or treated differently.

This culture of silence was never more evident than in fall 2020, when I made my final plea for on-campus help in an email to four top administrators. I succinctly provided a timeline of the DHR and evidence, which they were already aware of and/or implicated in, and posed questions regarding their awareness of the abuses and the function of the academy in responding. My final question: "Are you ready, willing, and able to exercise leadership to not only help me but improve our campus community?" No one replied.

Stay Alive, Survive, Thrive

My experience of discrimination in academe has altered my worldview and modified who I am. At times, it has squashed my spirit and even clipped my wings. Yet, because I remember my ancestral and personal journey of breaking and putting back together, I have hope to heal. The following practices continue to support my transformational journey:

1. Pump the Brakes: Stop to breathe, experience your feelings, and purposefully act. Particularly when navigating the demands of reporting and litigation, ensure that you create space for intentionality. Your abusers, and even attorneys, may demand that you participate in twelve-hour depositions, aggressive mediations for weeks, and review and sign documents at 1:00 a.m. under duress. Remember: you are not the criminal.

2. Care for Yourself: Don't wait until abuses have ended or been resolved to prioritize healing and transformation. Implement self-care that increases your ability to self-regulate and self-soothe such as meditation, prayer, mantra

memorization; therapy, support groups; walking, gardening, cooking. Although I had never previously owned a dog, I adopted one and threw myself into training, cuddling, and loving the only *Justice* I will ever receive.

3. Educate: Seek, explore, and share information that (1) helps you put words to your experiences of DHR and institutional betrayal, (2) clarifies relevant policies and/or laws, (3) proposes response standards, (4) provides protective mechanisms and/or resources, and (5) illuminates methods of increasing institutional courage. One painful evening, I mustered the energy to rely on the academia I once believed in and found sheroes in Benya, Frey, Freyd (1997), and Pyke.

4. Expand: Develop and strengthen your identity outside your work institution. Read for fun, explore abandoned interests, learn a new hobby. Apply your gifts, talents, and resources in fresh ways. Remembering and discovering your whole soul self is critical to surviving, and even thriving amid abuses.

5. Lean into Relationships: The formal help-seeking process to address DHR has consumed approximately six years of my life. Leaning into relationships with my life partner, children, closest sister-girlfriends, and weekly yoga circle continues to help me rise above the pain. Few friends and family had any idea how to journey alongside me. But creating space in which to share a hug, laugh, or a simple "you are loved" gave me life.

Hope to Heal

When I consider what may have altered my experiences of DHR, Freyd and Smidt's (2019) description of "institutional courage" comes to mind: an active commitment to protect individuals who depend on the institution (for salary, housing, education, etc.), to intentionally seek truth and address abuses regardless of risks, and to transform the institution into a more accessible, equitable, accountable, and effective place for all individuals. Like Freyd (2018), I believe institutional courage is the antidote to institutional betrayal. Several practices can help us work toward transformation, healing, and courage in academia.

1. Build a Collegial Culture: When institutions do not address adaptive cultural challenges, those representing minority populations are often put in positions that make them vulnerable to abuses or force them to protect perpetrators. Combat the perpetuation of individualism and competition for limited resources by building a culture of support, encouragement, productivity, and safety. Leverage individual traits, skills, and lived experiences to foster relationships, trust, collaboration, and innovation.

2. Cultivate Courageous Conversations: Create space for uncomfortable conversations about concerns and creative ideas that may threaten the institution. Invite employees to facilitate discussions. Communicate a clear, accessible, and safe process to engage in brave spaces.

3. Speak Up: If you witness discrimination, intervene by asking the perpetrator(s) to stop and remind them of their professional purpose. Considering the level of safety, you might ask to speak elsewhere with the target of the abuse.

4. Document DHR: Include date, time, location, witnesses, quotes, or a description of the abuse. Keep copies of evidence on a device and in a location that is personal and does not belong to the institution.

5. Report: Merely informing someone about discriminatory comments or behavior against them, or repeating the abuse in casual conversation, causes further harm. Report DHR you experience or witness to all possible internal administrators, and do so until someone listens and acts. In the absence of institutional response, report DHR to external sources such as the Board of Regents, Equal Employment Opportunity Commission, and Human Rights Commission. Harness the power of (social) media while carefully choosing which identifying information to use or omit.

6. Take Collective Action: Building on a collegial culture, develop a network of trusted friends and allies committed to accessibility, human rights, and social justice. If you experience or witness abuses, use this network to engage in collective action and hold institutions accountable.

7. Administer with Knowledge and Care: Educate those who handle abuse claims about civil rights codes and Title VII and IX law. Train them about best practices for responding to DHR, including trauma-informed responses, psychological and physical protections, swift interventions, discrete and full investigations, autonomy between administration offices intended to serve victims of abuse, and prioritizing the victim. Provide in-house legal counsel to victims, and advocate for victim-service resources, as well as caps on perpetrator protection (which is often funded through Attorney General offices). Tax dollars should not, as they did in my case, fund multi-million-dollar defenses for state institutions and their employee-perpetrators, while victims/survivors are unable to fund strong legal teams and so sacrifice their careers for safety.

8. Support Survivors: Check on survivors of DHR and ask how you might help, demonstrating empathy and respecting their confidentiality. Offer to accompany them to report DHR. As we say in my culture, be a good relative.

9. Celebrate Whistleblowers: To dismantle codes of loyalty and mechanisms of fear and silence, develop a culture that encourages and cherishes whistleblowers. This not only helps heal the survivor, but strengthens the entire institution.

10. Evaluate: Facilitate, and share the results of, annual evaluations regarding DHR, assault, and perceived institutional courage.

As this manuscript ends, so does my pursuit of freedom from gender abuse in academe. I am walking away shocked, but I am not shattered. I can and will heal. Through courage in action, I have hope that academe can too.

Note

1. Legal terms, reached just before submission of this chapter, prohibit me from naming the institution or involved individuals, for whom I use pseudonyms.

Works Cited

Benya, F. "Treating Sexual Harassment as a Violation of Research Integrity." *Higher Education, Issues in Science and Technology*, vol. 35, no. 2, Winter 2019, pp. 56–59.

Frey, L. "When It Hurts to Work: Organizational Violations and Betrayals." *New Directions for Teaching and Learning*, vol. 153, Spring 2018, pp. 87–98.

Freyd, J., Smidt, A. "So You Want to Address Sexual Harassment and Assault in Your Organization? Training Is Not Enough; Education is Necessary." *Journal of Trauma and Dissociation*, vol. 20, no. 5, Sep. 2019, pp. 489–94.

Freyd, J. (11 January, 2018). "When Sexual Assault Victims Speak Out, Their Institutions Often Betray Them." *The Conversation*. Retrieved from https://theconversation.com/when-sexual-assault-victims-speak-out-their-institutions-often-betray-them-87050. Accessed 11 Nov. 2021.

Freyd, J. "Violations of Power, Adaptive Blindness, and Betrayal Trauma Theory." *Feminism and Psychology*, vol. 7, no. 1, 1997, pp. 22–32.

Human Trafficking Leadership Academy/HTLA (10 September, 2020). Class 5 Recommendations: How Can Culture Be a Protective Factor in Preventing Trafficking Among All Indigenous Youth? Retrieved from https://nhttac.acf.hhs.gov/sites/default/files/2020-11/HTLA%20Class%205%20Recommendations%20Report_508c.pdf. Accessed 11 Nov. 2021.

McPhail, B. "Setting the Record Straight: Social Work Is Not a Female-Dominated Profession." *Social Work*, vol. 49, no. 2, 2004, pp. 323–26.

National Association of Social Workers/NASW. "New Report Provides Insights into New Social Workers' Demographics, Income, and Job Satisfaction." Retrieved from https://www.socialworkers.org/News/News-Releases/ID/2262/New-Report-Provides-Insights-into-New-Social-Workers-Demographics-Income-and-Job-Satisfaction. 11 Dec. 2020. Accessed 12 Nov. 2021.

Pyke, K. "Institutional Betrayal: Inequity, Discrimination, Bullying, and Retaliation in Academia." *Sociological Perspectives*, vol. 61, no. 1, 2018, pp. 5–13.

Salsberg, E., et al. "The Social Work Profession: Findings from Three Years of Surveys of New Social Workers. A Report to the Council on Social Work Education and the National Association of Social Workers from Fitzhugh Mullan Institute for Health Workforce Equity, George Washington University, Dec. 2020. https://www.cswe.org/CSWE/media/Workforce-Study/The-Social-Work-Profession-Findings-from-Three-Years-of-Surveys-of-New-Social-Workers-Dec-2020.pdf. Accessed 10 Nov. 2021.

Smidt, A., and Freyd, J. (2019). The Institutional Courage Questionnaire (ICQ).

15

The Specter of Anonymity and the Shadow Labor of Complaint

ALISON E. VOGELAAR

"We are moving on," the university president proclaims in the first (virtual) meeting of the faculty assembly in 2021. "The poison pen has been taken care of." *The poison pen.* (I wince as the words slice through the screen, nicking my thin skin.) His announcement is followed by silence. They (the president, the faculty, the meeting) do move on, to the next agenda item.

Poison pen: a derogatory term that first surfaced in early-twentieth-century parochial journalism, and subsequently crime fiction, to refer to the anonymous author of critical, malicious, and/or accusatory letters.

Taken care of: a phrase that describes having dealt with a task or problem; a euphemism for murder.

As the only member of the twenty-five-person faculty whose employment has just been terminated, I am, of course, the poison pen: the "malicious" letter writer who was *taken care of*; the she-who-shall-not-be-named whose abrupt dismissal and excommunication after thirteen years as a full-time faculty member serves as a lesson to those who might also consider using their pens; the shadow muse inspiring a fervent commitment to "civil discourse" and "values" and a series of virtue-signaling task forces and social media campaigns; the ghost of ▮▮▮▮ University past.

I remain awestruck by the casual violence of the president's announcement and his spectators' (my colleagues') silence. Did it not strike them as

141

a bizarre way for the president of an academic institution to announce the dismissal of an employee? It's hard to read silence. Though much power is conferred on ghosts for their ability to silently haunt and terrorize, I haven't enjoyed being one: being looked through by former colleagues on the street (do they see me?); being wiped from the institution's documents and collective memory (was I ever there?); being left with a ghostly "gap" on my CV (what's my story?). I cannot help but entertain the thought that I "had it coming." It is, after all, a well-worn truism that filing a complaint or speaking up about abuses of power is "career suicide" (that is, *self-inflicted* harm). I knew this. Does this mean I was "asking for it"? Troubling thoughts.

As Sara Ahmed notes in *Complaint!*, my experience isn't uncommon. Those who are "willing to become complainers, to locate a problem" often become the "location of a problem," the thing to be *taken care of* (3). Even as I learn how common the contours of my story are, I have had difficulty trying to make sense of it, trying, as the president exhorted, to *move on*. Thanks in large part to the novel contributions of Sara Ahmed and Jennifer Doyle on the genre of "complaint" and "anti-harassment writing" in the context of higher education, I have come to see that "working-through" complaint, giving it "a hearing" is a far more intuitive (and ethically nuanced) project. In this vein, my contribution to this collection is the outcome of such a process of working-through.

I have drafted and deleted my story several times for this essay. (Am I being too dramatic? Am I telling the right parts? Am I being fair? Who cares? What is my point? What good will it do?) Telling my story feels narcissistic (I didn't have it *that* bad. Other people have more deserving stories). And yet there is something about "the poison pen" that keeps me committed to telling this story. Something about the ways that my story maps onto a "witch tale" that seems noteworthy in this fraught moment in women's history. Something about the association of a woman's work with witchcraft that feels poignant. I offer my story here in the hope that it helps shed light on the various forms of shadow abuse and shadow labor that have become mainstream in academia.

I was initially inspired to pen an essay about the perils and possibilities of anonymity because the use of anonymity was, in Ahmed's lexis, a "shattering experience" in my "complaint biography" (14). I wanted to give anonymity, a form of communication that is shrouded in silence, "a hearing." I sought to work through my experience of it because, as Ahmed so aptly puts it, "what is hard is close to what's important" (14).

As a scholar of rhetoric and resistance, I also wanted to take a theoretical lens to anonymity, to work through its rhetorical contours and consequences. Perhaps by doing so, I could work out why, instead of drawing attention to institutional abuses of power, the use of anonymity became the supposed abuse of power at which the institution threw its resources. Why, aside from a series of short-lived moral-panicky social media campaigns (#civildiscourse!) and a defanged and dysfunctional "task force" for diversity, equity and inclusion,[1] the only consequences seemed to be unemployment, humiliation, and a bit of excitement/distraction for the faculty and administration (who doesn't love a good witch hunt?). Why the principal harassers remain employed.

In the process of telling my story for this volume, my initial preoccupation with the singular act of "anonymity" has faded. In part, because it isn't that interesting, surprising, or consequential. (Of course, a person who works in a toxic environment and fears retaliation would choose anonymity when all other options had been exhausted. Of course, the misogynist leaders of a struggling institution who have repeatedly chosen not to "hear" complaints would jump at the opportunity for a witch hunt). Also, and with a bit of distance, I have come to see the ways in which I unwittingly played my designated part in a scripted story (did I choose anonymity or was it chosen for me?). In this vein, my story is less about the power or perils of anonymity and more about the gendered uses and abuse of shadow labor. A witch's tale if you will.

Becoming "The Poison Pen," or
Playing My Part in a Scripted Story

Since becoming "the poison pen," I have thought a lot about witches and the association of feminine labor with witchcraft. About the complex symbolic work witches do as sources of female power and persecution. About the fact that *tens of thousands of (mostly) women were tortured and murdered* by mere association with the word (most without a "hearing") and the fact that no one seems all that fussed by it. It's as if we think we've *moved on* . . .

Except, what if we haven't?

We are surrounded by accounts of gendered abuse in the news and in our communities. Contemporary struggles to expose and eradicate gendered forms of violence are consistently met with violent attempts to silence them and push them into the shadows. Women's legal right to our bodies is increasingly threatened. Feminized labor continues to be marginalized and un(der)paid. At a tiny liberal arts institution, in a wealthy, secular, developed nation, the president announced the abrupt termination of a long-serving female member of the faculty by declaring "the poison pen has been taken care of."

This is my abridged story.

In the beginning—or once upon a time—there was a young "lady professor" (that was how the most senior member of the faculty liked to refer to female faculty). In her first year at her first academic post, a student came to a meeting with a black eye and casually informed her that he had been beaten up by a fellow student because he was gay. Her shock was met with his confusion. "This is normal here," he said, *moving on.* She didn't. And so began the college's first Safe Allies program.[2] It didn't take long for her to learn that indeed harassment—including harassment by faculty—was "normal there" ("baked in," as one faculty member put it). Her early interventions were cautious and proactive (that is, lady-like, civil). Caution and proactivity are laborious. Her "complaint biography" was filled with more decisions *not* to complain than to complain. These decisions weighed on her. Over the years, the stories of sexual harassment "piled up" (Doyle). That's the thing with being a "feminist ear"—once the word is out that you will "hear," people sing to you (Ahmed 3). They became a sad chorus, on a broken record. Part of the difficulty of combatting institutional harassment is that most people don't hear the sad singing. Being a feminist ear is like hearing a looping chorus of frustration and rage over the PA system while most of the community walks around with earplugs. Jennifer Doyle calls this phenomenon "collective disavowal," about which she states, "It is not a question of knowing and pretending one doesn't know. It is more nearly not having the capacity to be present to what one knows." Harassment dynamics flourish in this context.

In 2018, the young lady was no longer young and a new chorus—righteous, indignant—had erupted onto the global stage: #MeToo. This time, when yet another student came forward with a story she'd heard many times before about being harassed by a particular professor, she and a fellow "lady professor" joined arms and made clear demands to the administration: update the mechanisms for reporting misconduct, provide resources for targets, educate the community, change the culture and leadership. As Ahmed notes, making a complaint is never one action; it often requires "more and more work," it requires "tenacity" (5). So these women were tenacious: climbing the "curious walls of indifference and resistance," winding through the dizzying "circularity of complaint" (35). Tenacity is laborious. Over the next two years there were provisional (cosmetic?) concessions: a Title IX officer (located in a different time zone on a different continent), a new (and equally problematic) reporting system, an online tutorial about sexual harassment, an ombudsperson, a search for a new dean. This last one gave them the most hope, for they had come to realize, slowly and painfully, that the dean was central in perpetuating the harassment. A self-described feminist and former faculty member who had also experienced gendered abuse, she was nevertheless enabling others' abuse because her own position of power in the system depended on her ability to *move on*, to never let any stories stick.

Then, in early 2020, the plague came and with it a series of radical changes: the administration canceled the search for a new dean, electing instead to retain the current dean and add five new faculty administrative positions conveniently held by the dean's closest allies. Shortly thereafter, my antiharassment collaborator was informed that her position had been terminated for "financial reasons." Following her dismissal, I filed formal complaints to the accreditation agency and the board. These complaints ended up being, as Ahmed puts it, "complaints about how complaints [were] handled" (23). Though the accreditation agency's complaints procedure required complainants to consent to nonconfidentiality, complainants could request confidentiality, which I did, but my request was denied without explanation. The complaint was instead handed directly to the dean, who shared the complaint with the named people (writing "FYI" in a group email). I learned later that the president instructed the dean to share both of my complaints with those named (citing "total transparency"). I was not granted such transparency and I was neither consulted about my complaints nor informed that the people I named as bullies and harassers were given my complaints. A colleague informally informed me of the dean's "FYI" email, but asked me not to expose him. I understood in that moment that my time was limited.

Thus was born the poison pen.

She pens several letters. Each details concrete abuses of power and reads like a desperate plea for help. Unlike the others, she does not sign these. Partly because she is afraid of retaliation, partly because they are the complaints of a collective, a chorus. She is struck both by how difficult it is to send an anonymous letter in the digital age and how inherently criminal it feels. She later files a "formal comment" to the US Department of Education and to the accreditation agency about these issues. Though it is too late to help the poison pen, the accreditation agency has formally changed its complaints policy to accommodate anonymous complainants and threats of retaliation. If she had to do it over, she would have consulted accreditors much earlier.

Whereas the young "lady professor's" complaints went more-or-less unheard, the poison pen's words registered loud and clear. But not as intended. Instead of combatting the abuses of power referenced in the messages, the administration decided to combat the messenger. "The poison pen" became a cause célèbre, a shadow being that had hexed the institution. She was railed about in meetings ("We will find you!") and whispered about in offices ("Did you hear . . . ?"). She became the imagined source of all external persecution and internal conflict.

Following weeks of silence from the administration, and after the campus was emptied for the summer holiday, a certified letter arrived in the mail: "Your contract will not be renewed" (financial reasons, it cited).[3] Aside from an email from a kindly office assistant about clearing out the office and returning keys, there was no further communication. No explanation. No condemnation. No responses to emails. No hearing. In order to get one, I promptly filed a wrongful termination lawsuit.

The Shadow Labor of Complaint

Filing a civil lawsuit is a tool of last resort. It is more labor, more terror, more expense. The process of monetizing injustice is demoralizing if not absurd ("$5,000 for harms to character . . .") The experience of reading the cruel and dismissive responses to my claims is humiliating. Other than walking away, however, this is my only recourse. I have been informed that very few wrongful termination cases are successful in my legal jurisdiction. Even so, I have decided to labor through this one final complaint in my complaint biography. One last chance at a hearing. One final act of tenacity.

As I was beginning my legal proceedings in 2021, I was also finishing an article about "care labor" in the context of higher education with two colleagues, both of whom were similarly disappeared during this time period. Inspired by the incredible demands for care brought on by the COVID crisis, our research explored the increasing demands for care in academia from the perspective of labor. Guided by feminist theory on care and reproductive labor, our survey research (collected in 2020) set out to "account for care" in the context of academic labor in the neoliberal university—that is, who performs it, for whom, why, and in what conditions? Unsurprisingly, our provisional findings revealed that care is unevenly performed by women and other members of marginalized groups and is, by and large, unaccounted for, invisible, and unpaid (see Dasgupta et al.).

During the same period, a package arrived on my front porch. Inside: Sara Ahmed's *Complaint!* It was a game changer as it elucidated the connection between themes in my work and worklife: complaint is (care) labor. And care labor, by design or by necessity, occurs in the shadows. As I was thinking about shadows and labor for this essay, I came across Ivan Illich's book *Shadow Labor* (1981), which uses the term to describe the unpaid activities (for example, housekeeping, caregiving, homework, and consumption) "required" by advanced industrial economies. Describing the inherently discriminatory nature of shadow work, he writes: "While for wage labor you apply and qualify, to shadow work you are born or are diagnosed for. For wage labor you are selected; into shadow work you are put. The time, toil and loss of dignity entailed are exacted without pay" (n.p.).

Over the past three years, I have often reflected on the countless hours I have spent laboring in the shadows, on "the time, toil and loss of dignity exacted" performing labor—hearing complaints, filing complaints, offering advice, writing letters of recommendation so that a student can transfer and avoid harassment, helping a colleague respond to her bully's emails—that cannot be listed on my CV, will never be paid, and are difficult to articulate, even to sympathetic friends and family. As Doyle observes, antiharassment writing requires a form of labor "for which the university cannot account. It is work that doesn't count. You do not get promoted as a scholar for doing this kind of work. In fact this kind of diversity work [. . .] can feel like a disruption of work. It is. Imagine putting 'filed sexual harassment complaint X, saw complaints process to its completion with ambiguous results' down on your CV!" (n.p.). Like other gendered absences on our CVs (often care or abuse-related), complaint and antiharassment labor haunt our careers and perpetuate the misogyny and inequity of academia. Only a "mad woman" would admit to shadow labor on her CV. Imagine it: "Awarded the title of 'the poison pen' after filing anonymous complaints about chronic harassment; was fired shortly thereafter." My best bet for future employment is to pretend, alongside my former employer, that none of the abuse *or* labor ever happened. In the choice between employment (livelihood) and truth, the truth rarely wins. As communities and institutions, we must find new ways to perform and account for complaint labor that neither cast complainants into the shadows nor force them into the dangerous spotlight. As individuals, we must stop playing our designated part in their witch's tale.

Even so, I've embraced my assigned pen name. Because they got one thing right: my pen is powerful.

Notes

1. The single POC faculty member on the task force was bullied into silence for flagging a tokenizing social media campaign. She eventually stepped down and was reprimanded by her white department chair for being difficult. She was terminated shortly thereafter for "restructuring" purposes.

2. She was joined by two colleagues in proposing and running the program, which was supported by a sympathetic new provost (who was let go the following year).

3. While we were informally recruited with the assurance that our contracts were "like tenure" in the foreign country in which the university operated, they were in fact short-term contracts.

Works Cited

Ahmed, Sara. *Complaint!* Duke UP, 2021.

Dasgupta, Poulomi, Alexandra Peat, and Alison Vogelaar. "Care in the Time of Covid-19: Accounting for Academic Care Labor." *Journal of Economic Issues*, vol. 58, no. 1, 2024.

Doyle, Jennifer. "Notes on Anti-Harassment Writing." *Trouble Thinking*, 12 July 2017, troublethinking.com/2017/07/01/notes-on-anti-harassment-writing/comment-page-1/.

Illich, Ivan. *Shadow Work*. Marion Boyars, 1981. Retrieved from https://theanarchist library.org/library/ivan-illich-shadow-work#toc7.

Part Three

Theorizing and Enacting Change as Individuals and Collectives

16

All My Skinfolk Ain't Kinfolk

The Politics of Solidarity in Black Academia

NICOLE CARR

We register academia's exclusionary and elitist structure with pithy one-liners. Plantation politics (Williams & Tuitt). Piled higher and deeper (Cham). Trauma track. The ivory tower. Publish or perish. And, the equally accurate: Publish *and* perish. As a Black woman professor, I have been searching for a lexicon to chronicle the internecine violence that Black women and men commit against each other in academe. When a senior Black woman professor disparaged my name at a national conference during a workshop, I needed this language. Because I had not been present at the workshop, the news traveled to me by way of a work colleague. Her visible shock at the comments spoken by the senior scholar confirmed their vitriolic intent. Initially, I greeted this information with sardonic laughter. Having fled my assistant professorship position in New York due to sustained career sabotage from a Black male professor and department chair of the Black Studies Department, I did not feign surprise. Even after reluctantly leaving my witty students from Harlem, Brooklyn, and Poughkeepsie to settle in Texas, I had not found the language for this abuse. In Texas, I simply vowed to keep my head down and mind my business. I did the same at the conference, leaving my hotel room only to eat, visit a few panels, and present my paper. It felt safer to retreat into myself as I had done when I was a girl, painfully shy and self-conscious of my deep voice. Still, the disparagement found me there.

I was seated at the bar, head buried in a book, when a Black woman professor greeted me, her innocuous "Is it any good?" spurring a nearly two-hour conversation ranging from death to poetry, mentoring, and teaching. Years later, I remembered the question she posed to me before we parted: "What do I do when the people who look like me have hurt me the most?" Since our paths crossed, I have purposely avoided answering this question. It is easier, acceptable even, to declare all the ways that white people in academia have hurt us. When we publicly name their toxic abuses we can be sure that the amen corner will commiserate, console, and protect us. But the rules within my beloved community urge against airing our dirty laundry, especially in front of mixed company. It is a traitorous thing. This is why, when the book editors approached me about writing an article for this collection, I hesitated. After all, only one of the editors is a Black woman. What would my people think of me?

My literary foremothers answered. Not only did Zora Neale Hurston's oft-cited "All my skinfolk ain't my kinfolk" emerge as a warning against assuming familiarity with other Black folks, but the biographical details of her life also illuminated the persistent intraracial tensions stoked by class, color, and educational status. Despite her literary talents, she remained especially aware of her humble country upbringing among northern, more well-to-do Black folk. In fact, Hurston was reluctant to enroll at Howard University, believing that the school represented "Negro money, beauty, and prestige" (qtd. in Boyd 104). Hurston, hailing from rural Eatonville, Florida, found these ideals worrisome. Ironically, one of the most creatively gifted minds had to be urged on by friends to realize that she was indeed "good enough" to attend Howard. Even as Hurston became involved in social organizations on campus, the clear rigid hierarchies manifested in various ways, as Ophelia Settle Egypt, an acquaintance of Hurston's, describes: "There were these three sororities. The AKAs (who really could dress beautifully), the Deltas (light skinned), and the Zetas (it didn't matter how you looked as long as you had brains). I had enough brains to get into Zeta. Zora Neale Hurston was there and she was a Zeta" (Boyd 106). Nearly one hundred years later, Toni Morrison described her experience at Howard as "welcoming," but the strict colorism enforced there shocked her: "On the campus, where I felt safe and welcome, I began to realize that this idea of the lighter, the better, and the darker, the worse . . . really had an impact on sororities, on friendships, on all sorts of things, and it was stunning to me" (Gross). I came to see Morrison's and Hurston's experiences not as criticizing Howard or Black-curated spaces as hostile, but as an opportunity to meditate on the nature of power among Black academics. What I have been struggling to name is how power moves through Black academics.

Having grown up in South Florida, I was prepared for the chilly breeze of white racism souring the hallways and classrooms as I pursued my master's and doctoral degrees. In the hallways, I was largely ignored by the white faculty there. Or, worse: misrecognized. One white male professor, certain that I must be the Black woman candidate interviewing for the open position on campus, warmly greeted me by the other woman's name. When my friend corrected him because I was too stunned to speak, he offered no apology. In the classroom, my attempts to make the courses on Samuel Beckett, Michel Foucault, and John Milton relevant to my own research interests were met with nervous smiles. One white male professor asked, after reading my paper on the Haitian Revolution, Fanon, and Foucault, "You aren't really advocating for violence are you?" His cold hostility necessitated that I seek out a Black mentor. As Black women professors Catherine Packer-Williams and Wendi Williams explain, "Black/ African women academicians often work in isolated career spaces in which the power of relationships and support can mean the difference between thriving, mere survival, or their collective demise" (Packer-Williams).

Initially, my gratitude for Dr. Abrams,[1] the sole Black woman professor in the department, soared. I took courses with her, met during her office hours, and offered my labor on the graduate journal she spearheaded. But when I inquired about working on the journal, she brushed me off. Instead, during our meetings in her office, she discussed her own graduate school experiences. Each time I tried broaching the topic of my involvement in the journal she directed the conversation elsewhere. Like Hurston, I began wondering if my Southern-inflected accent and first-generation status made her wary of working with me. Perhaps I was not smart enough after all. Southern Black people, as I know as well as Hurston did, often wear the legacies of Jim Crow segregation in the way that they speak. My maternal grandparents met in the Georgia cotton fields as children. As sharecroppers. Not only did I begin questioning whether I truly belonged in academia, but I also began considering whether Dr. Abrams, a Caribbean Black woman, registered my Black American identity in much the same ways that my Black Caribbean friends did when they were shocked by my intention to become a professor. They believed most

Black Americans to be lazy and "ghetto." Too uninspired to pursue higher education. My exclusion from the journal—despite my Cuban American colleague's inclusion in it—felt all too familiar. Frustrated, isolated, and alienated, I began doubting my career path.

It was not until Dr. Marshall, a Black male professor from Georgia, joined the faculty a few years later that I understood mentoring as key for Black doctoral students navigating anti-Blackness within academe while securing professional jobs within the academy. In addition to educating me on the inner workings of academia, Dr. Marshall utilized his power to advocate for me. When Dr. Abrams attempted to block my graduation, insisting that I had not made the proper adjustments to my dissertation despite her signing off on the final paperwork, Dr. Marshall assured the dean that my dissertation was stellar, as evidenced by my ability to secure a tenure-track appointment in the Black Studies Department in New York. This was the kind of radical mentoring championed by Toni Morrison: "When you get these jobs that you have been so brilliantly trained for, just remember that your real job is that if you are free, you need to free somebody else. If you have some power, then your job is to empower somebody else. This is not just a grab-bag candy game" (Houston). Often, we tend to confine mentoring to a set of tasks, but we must also consider it as the praxis of tapping into one's power base along racial, gender, and educational lines to "free somebody else."

In academia, there are plenty of opportunities to do so precisely because Black academics do not stand outside the bounds of wanting, desiring, and executing power. For years, as I would later learn, Dr. Abrams had been using her status to exploit, bully, and abuse graduate students. One student dropped out of the program altogether, never completing their degree. Another was forced to switch her major. So notorious was Dr. Abrams's abusive behavior that while attending a conference, I swapped stories about her with a Black PhD student enrolled in the current program. We were like two Army veterans baring war wounds. Dr. Marshall, however, disrupted Dr. Abrams's path toward power while he was there. As a Black male full Professor, Dr. Marshall outranked Dr. Abrams, an associate professor with fewer publications and less national standing in the field, and used the weight of his credentials to ensure that I could move on to the next steps in my career. Equally important, Dr. Marshall taught me a valuable lesson about advocating not only for myself, but also for others in less tenable positions.

This lesson proved useful in my first tenure appointment. When Dr. Dudley, a Black male professor and Chair of the Black Studies Department, attempted to ruin my career due to a minor disagreement, I understood his aggression as a manifestation of unchecked power. So, I recorded every interaction with him, even if the terse words were spoken in the hallway, sending emails to both my dean and Human Resources. To be clear, I did not actually believe that Human Resources would swoop in to save the day. In fact, Human Resources is often quite useless in these situations. So too was my dean, insisting that everything would simply resolve itself. However, my reasoning for cataloging every conversation was threefold. First, I put my Chair on notice—he would have to watch what he said around me or say nothing at all. Anyone who has been consistently harassed at work knows that the abuse often surfaces in seemingly mild conversation.

Second, I was building a legal trail of paperwork against my Chair in the event that I chose to sue him or the university. In this way, I made the workplace more bearable until I could secure employment elsewhere. Third, as Hurston warned, "If you are silent about your pain, they'll kill you and say you enjoyed it." By refusing to be silent, we can also disrupt the abuser's path toward power. In simply documenting the inappropriate comments he made about a fellow colleague's accent and religious beliefs, I argued that he was fostering a hostile work environment for not only me, but also Dr. Mahama, the Black Ghanaian professor in the department. Following a meeting with Dr. Mahama, I learned that Dr. Dudley had also threatened to not renew Dr. Mahama's contract. As I learned while pursuing my doctorate, power often leaves behind a trail of victims. Thus, we must not silo ourselves away from potential allies. Eventually, due to my email records corroborating Dr. Mahama's experience of discrimination, HR launched an investigation resulting in Dr. Dudley's removal from his position as Chair. At the close of the investigation, Dr. Mahama's contract was also extended for another two years.

Despite these wins, I am an incongruous figure in academia—ill at ease with the rankings, titles, hierarchies, and most bothered by the cowardly refusals to tell the truth. Fortunately, I study at the feet of my ancestors. bell hooks's insistence that "to be open and honest in a culture of domination, a culture that relies on lying, is a courageous act" has become a mantra for my wellness in academia (29). Still, I am self-conscious of my propensity for telling it like it is; academics dislike it. They prefer to overlook uncomfortable or painful things. As hooks writes, "Black folks find it easier to 'tell it like it is' when we are angry, pissed, and desire to tell the truth" (31). When the Black woman professor disparaged my name at the conference, I called her out in the all-Black women's forum where our earlier disagreement stemmed. I minced no words. The administrators of the group quickly closed the comment thread due to my use of the word *ass*, as in, "Your soft ass would say something like this."

In my family, fighting was a last resort, but a valid one if someone physically hurt me or my sisters. My mother did not tolerate anyone speaking ill of our family and we lived by the "Don't start nothing, won't be nothing" credo. However, as hooks notes, this style of truth telling can often lead to humiliating and shaming other Black people. Perhaps that is why, instead of owning her behavior, the senior professor denied any wrongdoing and refused to apologize, continuing to treat me dismissively at the conference, even though senior Black academics told her she should apologize to me. In receiving bell hooks's wisdom, I have since recognized in that situation my failure to extend grace to another Black woman and in letting my anger, though righteous, take precedence. "To heal our wounds," hooks writes, "we must be able to critically examine our behavior and change" (39). In examining my behavior, I have also embraced my fierce desire to tell the truth, even if I am gaslighted and tone-policed by other Black women, excluded in certain elite Black circles, or branded a traitor. As hooks warned, "There is no healing in silence" (25).

Often, power is a full room, a packed audience hanging on to the vaunted speaker's every word while other conference presentations go unattended. I witnessed this at a recent conference in which organizers scheduled a Pulitzer Prize–winning novelist's workshop at the same time as conference attendees' presentations. To be honest, I had planned on attending the novelist's workshop; however, after Dr. Walker, a fellow Black woman professor, attended my panel and we chatted afterward, I decided to express my support by appearing at her panel the next day. Predictably, the novelist's workshop was jam-packed, standing room only. The four-person panel I attended was far less popular. None of this would have mattered if the workshop had not been right next door to this presentation, the choir of laughter and clapping nearly drowning out the conference presenters despite their using a microphone. When I headed next door to request that the audience quiet down a bit so that we could hear the presenters, I had not known that it was *that* Pulitzer Prize–winning novelist's workshop. Or that the conference president would then visit the less-attended panel not because he was interested in the speakers, but to see who had the audacity to interrupt the Pulitzer Prize–winning novelist's workshop. Later, after realizing that I had committed a faux pas, an attendee at Dr. Walker's panel assuaged my embarrassment, insisting that I had done the right thing, "And it's pretty bad-ass to say that you told [insert famous author here] to be quiet."

Now, in writing this, I realize that I have been searching for the language to say that I do not belong in academia. I never want to feel at home in this space, inhaling this rarefied air. My grandfather's eyes would always water with pride whenever I told him everything was fine down at the school. But I was most proud of him. For working the land with his hands. For working construction on the university buildings that he would never be invited to attend class in. For telling me that one day water would flow under my hands without even pressing a button because he helped build the automatic bathroom sinks. Until I can free myself from academia, I will build monuments to my people by telling the truth. Don't care who it shames.

Note

1. All names have been changed.

Works Cited

Boyd, Valerie. "Zora Neale Hurston: The Howard University Years." *Journal of Blacks in Higher Education*, vol. 39, 2003, pp. 104–108.

Cham, Jorge. "Piled Higher and Deeper." PhD Comics. Piled Higher and Deeper Publishing, 1997. https://phdcomics.com/comics/archive.php?comicid=1.

Gross, Terry. "'I Regret Everything': Toni Morrison Looks Back on Her Personal Life." *Fresh Air*, April 2015. https://www.npr.org/2015/04/20/400394947/i-regret-everything-toni-morrison-looks-back-on-her-personal-life. Accessed 15 May 2023.

hooks, bell. *Sisters of the Yam: Black Women and Self-recovery*. London: Routledge, 1993.

Houston, Pam. "The Truest Eye." Oprah.com, Nov. 2003. https://www.oprah.com/omagazine/toni-morrison-talks-love/4. Accessed 15 May 2023.

Packer-Williams, Catherine, and Wendi Williams. "The Frenemy Project." *Feminist Wire*, 7 November 2012. https://thefeministwire.com/2012/11/the-frenemy-project/. Accessed 15 May 2023.

Williams, Bianca, and Frank Tuitt, ed. *Plantation Politics and Campus Rebellions: Power, Diversity, and the Emancipatory Struggle in Higher Education*. SUNY P, 2021.

17

In Defense of Remembering

SHANNON WALSH

I don't know if you remember me, but you should, he said. It was nearly twenty years after he had assaulted me and we were at my book launch. I had not spoken to him, or even looked in his direction in a crowded room, since what happened between us all those years ago. . . . *but you should.* It left me speechless. Did he mean I should remember him because of what happened between us, or because he was a prominent figure in the field discussed in my book? I could not tell by the look on his face or his tone of voice. It was jarring that he would appear at my book launch, at a small bookstore with only a few dozen people in attendance. Why here, why now? What was I being asked to remember, precisely?

In my essay, "In Defence of Forgetting," I write about the pressures of survivors to remember trauma, to expose themselves to retraumatizing, often for little gain. As I wrote then, "in a world of violence and trauma, forgetting is as elemental to human action and human life as is remembering. What if it is survivors who best know the benefits of forgetting and the dangers of collective remembering? . . . Who does remembering serve, in this moment?" (173). Can we still claim the space Audra Simpson calls "refusal": the ethical and political rejection of any form of reconciliation? As Simpson writes, "refusal comes with the requirement of having one's *political* sovereignty acknowledged and upheld, and raises the question of legitimacy for those who are usually in the position of recognizing" (11, original emphasis). At times I've wondered how aboveground reckonings have also allowed for a smoothing over, a liberal form of erasure that assuages guilt but often does little to repair or reconcile. Yet, if I'm honest, my own untold story has felt like an itch I have longed to scratch, but could not find its surface. Perhaps my time for remembering has arrived.

Twenty years earlier, during grad school, it didn't even cross my mind that I could tell anyone or say anything about what had happened. On that day, I showed up early to meet him in the lobby of his hotel, as he had asked me to. I was in my early twenties, and a scholar I really admired at that time had agreed to meet me for coffee and discuss my work. It was an absolute thrill to be able to talk personally with someone whose work I esteemed. I was shocked to discover later that this professor, more than twenty-five years my senior and married, would approach this meeting as a date. I was working on issues of gender-based violence in my research, and yet I tucked away the memory of what happened, telling only a few people, and avoiding him ever afterward.

Of all my feelings around my various experiences as a woman scholar, the feeling that stands out the most may be *disappointment*. The dream I had of being taken seriously as a scholar was so disrupted in my early career, it had lasting impacts on my sense of self-worth and legitimacy. I fought on, hardened, shifted course, and became wary of my male collaborators and interlocutors. I never trusted that intellectual interest in my work was not always also sexual inuendo. The experience of disappointment and diminishment by men I had admired in the academy became so incredibly frequent as to become unremarkable. When I first began my academic journey, I did not see that my gender came before my intellectual contribution. It was a disappointing lesson, but also one that perhaps opened up ways of seeing that had been less clear before. Sometimes, in the heat of an intellectual discussion with a female peer, the feeling washes over me that here, in this discussion, I am *human*. Not gendered. Not sexualized. *A human with ideas*. It has felt rare and precious. A gift.

When, a couple years ago, letters emerged that were signed by prominent faculty members defending an anthropology professor accused of groping, kissing, and harassing a graduate student, *his* name was among them. Something in me burst. It finally felt time I told a bit of my story, which does not begin or end with my experience of being forcibly confined for hours and then sexually assaulted by a man I regarded as a leader in my field. Gender discrimination and aggression have followed every twist and turn in my career, and in the careers of women around me. The sense that in these privileged spaces we must bear it, that complaint has no recourse, and that the academy would forever harbor perpetrators, is only now feeling like something we may truly start to see change. The personal is indeed political, as is the act of memory, storytelling, and, at times, forgetting. In what follows, I speak to both my own experience and the complicated dynamics of storytelling that accompany it, centered on memory, disappointment, grief, and ambivalence.

The Encounter

In those days, the early 2000s, *he* was the writer of an important text in my field. I first met him at a conference where I was presenting and he was giving the keynote lecture. After his talk, I approached him with excitement, as I often did to speakers after events like this. I asked him a few questions and told him how much I appreciated his book. He took my contact information and mentioned that he would be in Cape Town over the coming weeks, and that we could talk more when he was there. His work directly related to the topic of my master's thesis, and it felt like I was entering the terrain of academia for the first time and being taken seriously for my ideas. The first encounter had been encouraging and exciting.

A few weeks later, he sent me an email saying he would be in town. Would I like to meet up? He asked to meet in his hotel lobby. I didn't love this idea, but there was a café there, so I parked outside and waited, drinking coffee. When he came down, he immediately said that he wanted us to go elsewhere, and that I should leave my car and we would take his. I agreed. It was my first mistake in what felt like a series of mistakes to follow.

Once I got into his car, he proceeded to drive up the coast to Cape Point, a tourist destination and the farthermost point along the highway outside of Cape Town, driving along a winding road with the sea to one side off a long cliff drop. I tried to keep the conversation as professional as I possibly could, talking about the work: international regulations, Trade-Related Aspects of Intellectual Property Rights policy, the global pandemic, you name it. It was clear early on that an in-depth conversation was not what he had in mind. He stopped to look at the penguins. And then again, he stopped for a walk down the beach. It was cold and

I didn't really want to go, but he was persistent and insisted I take his jacket—another thing I really did not want to do. He was in his late fifties and I was twenty-five years old. It didn't even occur to me that morning that this man might have thought that he could take me on a date.

The day wore on and I realized there was nothing I could do to get out of the situation. I was far away from my car or any public transportation that I knew of. I felt trapped. There was nowhere I could get out, no way I could get back. So, I tried to make light of it and stay pleasant. I pretended as best I could that this awkward situation wasn't happening and tried to keep it as professional as possible. All I wanted was to get back to my car, but this was one of the most powerful men in my research area. He was a full professor; he had written a book that I was quoting at length in my own writing. I really did not know what to do.

As the afternoon faded into night, he pulled into a winery. The innuendo deepened. He told me he could give me a job working as a research assistant in his center. His wife was in England, he said, and they had an open relationship. I was appalled and increasingly sad, disappointed, insecure about why I was there, and unsure about everything that I was saying.

Finally, in the dark dead of night, he dropped me back at my car. It was now on a deserted street, dangerous at night. He walked me to my car, pushed me against it, and forcibly kissed me. I pushed him off me, and drove away quickly, trying to get hold of myself.

Afterward I just shook it off. I told a few people over the subsequent weeks and years but mainly I brushed it aside and buried it. I never spoke to him again, or looked at him if I saw him in a public or academic space. He did not acknowledge me either.

The Value of Memory?

Can storytelling lead to social change? This is one of the urgent questions I ask of my work as a filmmaker and writer all the time. Invariably, the answer I come to is "yes," even if the means to get there is often unclear. When #MeToo came around, I remembered the experience I have recounted above, and began to feel pangs of guilt for not coming forward with my story. Must I remember, and, in remembering, bear public witness? Was testimony an obligation for all of us who had experienced such things, and worse? I tried to justify my silence by observing that I hadn't heard any other women experience similar things so maybe not telling my story was fine and wouldn't put any other women at risk. The question remained: *Are my memories in fact owed to the public, an obligation of care?* Listening to other women's stories brought fresh perspective to my own. The stories were powerful, but did they create change? Would mine? We are told our stories matter. But to whom, and at what cost to the teller?

When does remembering make sense? We are in a moment when trauma and confessional modes of trauma retelling have become cultural currency. Remembering can be important, but should not be an obligation or a burden. Everyone has their own journey.

In her book *Run Towards the Danger*, Sarah Polley writes an eloquent account of her evolving thinking about not coming forward to tell her experience of sexual assault by Jian Ghomeshi and her fractured memories of the events themselves, writing, "So many of us who have been sexually assaulted know that remembering the truth, knowing the truth, and telling the truth about it is anything but simple" (101). Polley relates a moment when she encounters Lucy DeCoutere, who had gone to trial against Ghomeshi, and communicates to DeCourtere her intense feelings of shame for not having come forward. DeCoutere responds with the admission that she'd wished she'd better understood the toll herself. "No one prepared me for that," she said (97).

For my part, the experience of that long drive up the coast was a real disillusionment. A moment of revelation. It felt like a confirmation that I would not be judged by my work alone, if at all. I felt belittled and like I had been reduced to my body. I had experienced aggressive male behavior in other contexts, but I had held a romantic idea that it would be different in the academic world. I really felt that I was able to contend in the realm of ideas, but this belittlement and sexualization at that time in my life left an indelible mark on me.

He must have noticed at some level that I never spoke to him again, though we later overlapped at the same institution. He never attempted to approach me either. Only much later did I hear the rumors about his behavior that floated around the university. My experience felt minor, insignificant, unworthy. It all seemed par for the course, what must be endured, perhaps even forgotten. In a sense, I had internalized the academy's implicit demand that I forget, bury, minimize. By offering no space in which I could find respite or recourse, it provided no space for me to remember. To be institutionally at ease in the discomfort of a female body, I would have to forget the encounter. As Lauren Berlant writes of the citizen/nation relation, "Citizen adults have learned to 'forget' or to render as impractical, naive, or childish their utopian political identifications in order to be politically happy and economically functional" (29). At times, it is also in forgetting that we forge other worlds, reframe our experience, live on in the crisis of the ordinary.

It was only years later, post-COVID, when I was launching a book in South Africa that he appeared at my book launch. Before the launch started, he strode over and grabbed my hand, shaking it. *I don't know if you remember me, but you should.*

I don't know if you *remember* me, *but you should*, I could hear myself saying to him inside my head. You should remember the ways you have behaved. The things you've yet to be held accountable for. Ironically, it was this man, long lost in the rearview mirror of my life, who asked me to remember. In writing this account, I take his obtuse words and clarify them in my own voice.

I don't know if you remember me, but you should.

Works Cited

Berlant, Lauren. *The Queen of America Goes to Washington City*. Duke UP, 1997.

Polley, Sarah. *Run Towards the Danger*. Penguin Random House, 2022.

Simpson, Audra. *Mohawk Interruptus: Political Life across the Borders of Settler States*. Duke UP, 2014.

Walsh, Shannon. "In Defence of Forgetting." In *Memory*, edited by P. Tortell, M. Turin, and M. Young, U of British Columbia P, 2018.

18

How Black Men Can Help Eradicate Gendered Abuse on University Campuses

Kudzaiishe Peter Vanyoro

I write as someone who was a student in two Southern African universities between 2012 and 2022. In 2022, I attained my doctorate in critical diversity studies and I currently teach postgraduate and undergraduate male and female students. I currently occupy a position of power in the university. In this article I reflect on the misogyny I witnessed as a student and hope that bringing attention to it can help reduce rape culture in the university. In relaying the experiences in this chapter, I rely on my personal diaries between 2012 and 2014, and autoethnographic reflections on learning at a Zimbabwean university. I am a straight, cisgender, masculine-presenting man whose account should be considered one of past complicity with misogynistic structures. This method, dubbed "performing autoethnography," draws from Tami Spry's recommended "process of integrating the 'doing' of autoethnography with critical reflection upon autoethnography as a methodological praxis" (709). This approach understands that the body is a politically inscribed site of meaning-making (Alexander 90; Spry 710). In autoethnographic methods, the researcher is the epistemological and ontological nexus on which the research process turns (Spry 711). Having been institutionally immersed, my body is the medium for the autoethnographic research data used in the chapter to unmask misogyny.

Scholar Roxanne Bainbridge argues that indigenous researchers can employ an "epistemology of insiderness" to construct and theorize knowledge where one assimilates their life and understanding into the research (9). The "inward gaze" adopted in autoethnography allows researchers to create the self who has crossed and lived between borders (Bainbridge 9; Neumann 11). I am seeking to use my experiences to help readers understand personal and collective complicity in the university's power relations. Bainbridge also notes how, as a "complete insider," she could perform autoethnography by interrogating her connection to the research phenomenon by writing memories of her life story, which allowed engagement with the research phenomenon on both an experiential and an intellectual level (9). The contact between the experiential and intellectual produces a critical understanding of a social phenomenon such as gendered verbal abuse.

Dehumanization through Gendered Abuse in a Zimbabwean University Lecture Room

In a 2001 study of masculinity at a university in Zimbabwe, Tapiwa Chagonda found that "traditionally, the University male students (UBAs[1]) have tended to affirm their masculinities through activities such as heavy drinking sprees and sexual exploits, which involve going out and having sex with female university students (USAs[2]) or nonuniversity females (NASAs)" (48). Male students' methods of exhibiting their masculinities have sometimes tended to intrude on and subvert the human rights of other students, especially female students (Chagonda 48). Rudo Gaidzanwa cited a 1990 Senior Proctor's report at the University of Zimbabwe, "which chronicled incidents of knifing, sexual harassment ranging from rape to groping and whistling at women, alcohol abuse and public violence by students during demonstrations" (Chagonda 48). This is evidence of the deep-seated culture of sexual harassment at universities in Zimbabwe that creates a dehumanizing university culture.

Before being accepted as a student at the university under discussion, I heard multiple stories describing the high levels of unprotected sex and sexually transmitted infections at the institution. The university was dubbed "More Sex University" to revere these high unprotected-sex levels, which most media outlets always framed as irresponsible. The university earned itself this name because of the multiple sexually explicit videos circulated on social media almost yearly (Vries). Some of these sex videos have been criticized for being recorded without the consent of the women, yet the male students rarely get charged. When I arrived on campus, I learned immediately that the environment was sexist; therefore, men took up defensive, violent, and aggressive masculinity to be recognized. I was still in my early twenties and possessed no concrete vocabulary to name this experience.

During one of my undergraduate core courses, I attended a class taught by a young Black man, Mr. Matambo,[3] who had recently completed his master's degree at the same university. Matambo made a lot of sexual innuendos while teaching. He would also make inappropriate comments to some women in the class. While his toxic masculinity was stylized as "humor," it was also a method of reinforcing his masculinity (Chagonda 60). I captured one of Matambo's statements in class in my diary.

> Matambo is referring to how the underperforming students are not naturally gifted with the intelligence to pursue an honors degree. He always makes sure to make you all laugh before saying something wild. The classroom laughs. Then he proceeds to say the underperforming students had to force their way into the university even though their mental capacities were opposed to this. He likens the manner they forced their way into the university to the manner broke UBAs force themselves into the pants of USAs who turn them down. He concludes his speech with the words: *dzimwe nguva semu UBA ka unotomanikidzira kuti zviite, ndizvo here girls.* (Sometimes as a UBA you must force your way for it to happen, is that so girls?) A majority burst into laughter. (Personal diary, Mar. 2014)

While I was part of those who laughed, I look back at this incident today and cringe. I cringe because Matambo's words endorse sexual violence. While he set off with an academic reference, which undermined the mental abilities of low-performing students, he also sexualized his lecture. Through false solidarity with the "girls" in the end, he sought to validate the need for force by creating an illusion that the women in the classroom either (1) agreed with his suggestion on the necessity of sexual force or (2) have experienced male students who have used force and are okay with it. Matambo employed misogynistic jokes and examples and received no disciplinary consequences.

Jokes, snide remarks, insinuations, comments in class to students, laughter when women speak, and selective monitoring of female (but not male) academics by heads of departments are some of the micropolitical devices used to marginalize women in the academy, privileging the "strong" (men) and diminishing the "weak" (women) (Barnes 17). In society and the university, jokes can conceal power, hate, and privilege. Deep prejudice against women can hide behind sexual or so-called complimentary jokes. Sexual jokes can conceal the masculine and patriarchal, systemic, and structural celebration of the rape of women and other gender nonconforming bodies (Gqola, *Rape* 40). Matambo endorsed and legitimized the use of force on female students by male students if they were "out of their league" or refused their advances. This endorsement confirms Chagonda's (2001) position that the lecturer-student relationship is an essential aspect of academic life that must be analyzed when discussing masculinities in higher learning (60).

This sexism is not a trend limited to this particular university. In Zimbabwe in 2021, a fact-finding mission "brought to the fore the high levels of sexual abuse prevalent in both private and state tertiary institutions perpetrated by male lecturers" (Tsamba). As a male student, I was not privy to how the women in the classroom felt, nor was I aware of what they would discuss about these moments. My positionality limited my access to this knowledge. As a man who benefited from male privilege, I did not consider these issues at the time.

Sex for Grades and the Lecture Room as a "Female Fear Factory"

Globally, there has been an increase in sexual harassment in higher-education institutions, as shown by the *Sex for Grades: Undercover Inside Nigerian and Ghanaian Universities* documentary by the British Broadcasting Corporation (BBC). In this documentary, lecturers demanded that students be intimate with them to receive what is known as "Sexually Transmitted Distinctions" (Zimbabwe Gender Commission, 2019). A female student from a Zimbabwean state university stated, "I went to a male lecturer with an assignment, which I felt was underscored. The lecturer said it could be re-marked on the condition that I go to bed with him" (Mawere, *A Comparative Study* 116). Such cases are numerous, and students *did* file complaints against Matambo for soliciting sexual favors in exchange for marks. He was never punished.

The fear of failing disproportionately impacts female students and is why Pumla Gqola conceptualizes the university as a *Female Fear Factory*

(2021). In the case of male lecturers who use grades to get female students to sleep with them, the fear of failing is a guillotine hanging over the female students' heads. Sex that takes place under these circumstances is not consensual. Instead, the student's consent represents coerced compliance since she cannot say "no" to the relationship without facing negative consequences (de Coopération Universitaire). Due to the power differentials between lecturer and student, they cannot give meaningful consent (Mawere, *A Comparative Study* 122–23).

According to Chagonda, "the masculinity of male lecturers may, in some instances, take the form of having affairs with their female students to show their machismo" (60). In another incident at my university, a male lecturer, Dr. Zino, made it public knowledge to the class that he would give the female students he liked a hard time. Zino mentioned that if female students were failing, they should arrange to see him privately, as this could be a sign that he likes them. He would say in Shona: *Hazvizivikanwe, kazhinji kufoira kufarirwa semu USA* (You never know, sometimes failing means you are a likable USA).

Previous research on sexual harassment in Zimbabwean universities has highlighted similar events. Daniel Mawere (*A Comparative Study*, 2019) was informed that "Male lecturers do ask female students out. They even brag and say if you want to pass my module, then you can have sex with me" (119). Sitheni Ndlovu recounts a University of Zimbabwe experience during which one lecturer in the arts, who had a reputation for threatening female students who turned down his advances, said to one of his targets, "Girl, your future depends entirely upon what I decide, and you shall regret why you ever made the decision" (73). Because this woman had turned down his sexual advances, she had to withdraw from lectures to protect herself (Ndlovu). Zindi (1994) posits that in almost every institution of higher education in Zimbabwe, a significant number of male lecturers sexually harass female students (177). Of the 2,756 participants who filled out Zindi's research survey, 64 percent answered yes to the question "Has anybody been sexually harassed?" (181).

Our Conduct as Male Students

We male students were also complicit in this rape culture. These discourses and attitudes do not end in the lecture room but trickle down to the halls of residence and to the densely packed off-campus suburb where male and female students rent rooms. Contact with male peers in the university campus is unavoidable, as large numbers of women must constantly interact with men privately or publicly, in the lecture room or during consultations (Mawere, *Peer Sexual Harassment* 9–10).

Living in that suburb, I witnessed male students catcalling at female students. During one incident earlier in the semester, a popular second-year female student walked from her room to campus in a skirt. As she walked through the main road toward the taxi rank, male students stared and jeered while standing on the roadside or peeping through their windows. By the time she got to campus, these students had publicized the incident. They shouted misogynistic comments such as, *Ha chimwana icho chinoda kudyiwa chete, zvii zvaakapfeka?* (That child needs to be eaten, what is she is wearing?). In the Zimbabwean university, language is one of the dominant forms through which males affirm their masculinities (Chagonda 52). In this example, the male students infantilized the woman (calling her a "child") to justify a desire to put her in place by "eating" her, which is code for raping her.

In Mawere's study at two Zimbabwean state universities, two female participants shared the details of their sexual harassment in public:

> I was walking alone on campus. As I passed through a group of male students, they started making sexual comments about my appearance. One of them remarked "You have very big breasts. One day I will suck them."

> I got whistled to by a number of male students on university grounds. Furthermore, sexual related comments were made to me.

(Participants in Mawere, *Peer Sexual Harassment*, 11)

The sexualization of Black women has a history in the hypersexualization of the Black female body, which intersects with its racialization. Gqola (*Rape* 40) reveals how in South African colonies such as the Cape, slavocratic society created the stereotype of Black women's hypersexuality to authorize and justify the institutionalized rape of women. Sexual labor was central to the colonial project, the dual sex/gender system, the sexual division of space and labor, and the normalization of rape (Gqola, *Rape*; Abrahams 2003; Tamale 2011; McClintock 1995). Catcalling reinforces a "corrective"/"curative" rape discourse that women need to be "eaten" (raped) to realize the dangers of what they are wearing. This form of victim blaming suggests that the female victim asks for it. Likewise, the aggressive comment about the female student's breasts implies that the very fact of her body invites the man's sexual advances. Its violence evokes Bumiler's argument that even without sexual penetration, a woman can "feel raped"[4] (82). At the state university I attended, if the victim wanted to report the male students, there were no policies to deal with such cases at the time.

Chagonda made a similar observation during his study at the University of Zimbabwe. In his paper, he described how "Male university students sometimes make sexist comments such as '*USA uri chocolate pamubhedha*' (USA, you are like chocolate in bed), '*Paita gumbo apa!*' (Nice legs here) or '*ndinoda kuku cutter*' (1 want to cut you, meaning, I want to have sex with you)" (Chagonda 53), the last example using violent penetrative language. In both cases, a female student's exposure of her legs seems reason enough to provoke a male student to declare his intention to sleep with her. Violent language that undresses women also proclaims discursive entitlement to the female body. Since most female students are exposed to this phenomenon regularly, the campus is no haven for them (Mawere, *Peer Sexual Harassment*, 8).

Talking about It

Years later, I am now lecturing at a South African university. I carry the burden of knowing that I once witnessed the sexual harassment of women in the class and did nothing about it. I failed to call out my male students and colleagues when they deployed the language of rape culture. What informs my practice as a lecturer today is the admission that as a heterosexual and masculine-presenting person, I was part of the problem. This is not only a problem confined to the Zimbabwean state university but is a global trend across universities. For example, in South Africa, during the #Endrapeculture protests of April 2016, protesters accused university management of perpetuating rape culture through policies reinforcing victim-blaming and protecting perpetrators of sexual assault (Orth et al. 191). This signals the importance of university policies that enforce language that is acceptable and unacceptable in university spaces. Language can also be added to the university's faculty manuals to discourage normalized discourse like victim blaming and to promote responsibility. The notion of rape as a culture has made me aware of the multiple behaviors that precede rape.

I found critical diversity literacy (CDL) helpful in understanding my complicity in the domination of women through language in the university. One part of Steyn's (2015) CDL asks those in power to recognize how their position of power affects those in vulnerable situations (381). This means that as a man with agency over my personal decisions, how I interact with and treat women, and my failure to act justly, influences how women will experience the university. Using reflective approaches such as CDL, we men must address gender-based violence and femicide (GBVF) by eradicating rape language and culture on university campuses. This involves accepting our responsibility for the oppression of women and calling each other out. Collectively as men, Black or white, we decide how we act within the privileges of our gender. The colonial wound is no adequate scapegoat for the ongoing violence women experience every day.

Notes

1. UBA is an acronym for University Bachelors' Association, which is adopted as slang for a "male university student."
2. USA is an acronym for University Spinsters' Association, which is adopted as slang for a "female university student." The use of the term *spinsters* to refer to women is misogynist and derogatory.
3. All names (outside academic references) are pseudonyms.
4. A limitation of this study is that I did not interview female students.

Works Cited

Alexander, Bryant Keith. "Skin Flint (or, the Garbage Man's Kid): A Generative Autobiographical Performance Based on Tami Spry's Tattoo Stories." *Text and Performance Quarterly*, vol. 20, no. 1, 2000, pp. 97–114.

Bainbridge, Roxanne. "Autoethnography in Indigenous Research Contexts: The Value of Inner Knowing." *Journal of Australian Indigenous Issues*, vol. 10, no. 2, 2007, pp. 54–64.

Barnes, Teresa. "Politics of the Mind and Body: Gender and Institutional Culture in African Universities." *Feminist Africa*, vol. 8, no. 1, 2007, pp. 8–25.

Bureau de Coopération Universitaire. *Sexual Harassment and Violence in the University Context: Report from the Task Force on Policies and Procedures Pertaining to Sexual Harassment and Violence (GT-PHS).* 2016.

Chagonda, Tapiwa. *Masculinities and Resident Male Students at the University of Zimbabwe: Gender and Democracy Issues.* University of Zimbabwe Affirmative Action Project (UZAAP), 2001.

Gaidzanwa, Rudo B. "Alienation, Gender and Institutional Culture at the University of Zimbabwe." *Feminist Africa: Rethinking Universities*, vol. 8, no. 1, 2007, pp. 60–82.

Gqola, Pumla Dineo. *Female Fear Factory: Gender and Patriarchy under Racial Capitalism.* Melinda Ferguson Books, 2021.

———. *Rape: A South African Nightmare.* Jacana Media, 2015.

Mawere, Daniel. *A Comparative Study of Zimbabwe State Universities' Responsiveness to the Implementation of Sexual Harassment Policies.* PhD diss., University of South Africa, 2019.

———. *Peer Sexual Harassment in Zimbabwe State Universities: A Qualitative Exploratory Study.* International Journal of Research and Innovation in Social Science (IJRISS), 2021.

Ndlovu, Sitheni V. *Femininities amongst Resident Female Students at the University of Zimbabwe.* University of Zimbabwe Affirmative Action Project (UZAAP), 2001.

Neumann, Mark. "Collecting Ourselves at the End of the Century." *Composing Ethnography: Alternative Forms of Qualitative Writing*, vol. 1, 1996, pp. 172–98.

Orth, Z., et al. " 'What Does the University Have to Do with It?': Perceptions of Rape Culture on Campus and the Role of University Authorities." *South African Journal of Higher Education*, vol. 34, no. 2, May 2020. https://doi.org/10.20853/34-2-3620.

Spry, Tami. "Performing Autoethnography: An Embodied Methodological Praxis." *Qualitative Inquiry*, vol. 7, no. 6, 2001, pp. 706–32.

Tsamba, Stephen. "Zimbabwe: MPs Shocked by High Sexual Abuse Cases in Varsities, Colleges." *New Zimbabwe*, 9 Nov. 2021. *AllAfrica*, https://allafrica.com/stories/202111090112.html.

Vries, Gilmore De. "Pictures: MSU First Year Student Turns Lecturers' Heads with Beautiful Body." *Savanna News*, 15 Sep. 2020, https://savannanews.com/pictures-msu-first-year-student-turns-lecturers-heads-with-beautiful-body/.

"Zimbabwe Gender Commission Delivers Public Lecture on 'Sexual Harassment.' " *MSU Gender Institute*, 17 Oct. 2019, https://ww5.msu.ac.zw/gi/2019/10/17/zimbabwe-gender-commission-delivers-public-lecture-on-sexual-harassment/.

Zindi, Fred. "Sexual Harassment in Zimbabwe's Institutions of Higher Education." *Zambezia*, vol. 21, no. 2, 1994, pp. 177–86.

19

Tracking Sexual Predators across Academic Institutions

Benefits and Limits of Informal Complaints and Recommendations for Change

ANONYMOUS

James Armstrong (one of his many aliases) sees himself as a deity, untouchable. I remember him standing knee deep in the lake, arms out-stretched like the majestic Christ the Redeemer statue in Rio. At the time, I wondered what he was thinking in that omnipotent pose. Now I can see that so many of his actions fit smoothly into the behavior patterns of narcissistic personality disorder (NPD), specifically covert narcissism (also called vulnerable narcissism), which includes preoccupation with grandiosity, success, power, brilliance, beauty, or ideal love, layered over introversion, insecurity, self-consciousness, and sensitivity (see *DSM-V*, 646–49). Callousness, manipulativeness, interpersonal exploitation, and envy also characterize NPD (Bach et al.). More recently, I thought of him while watching a tall, inflatable tube figure in the parking lot next to a pop-up fireworks truck. I could not hear the blower rhythmically inflating the red nylon, but the bright figure mesmerized me with its erect, pompous puffing and quick deflation in a foppish dance that was simultaneously a desperate flailing. This hollow tube man was just like James.

Since James physically assaulted me, eight women have privately shared with me their stories of harassment, betrayal, abuse, violence, or worse, at the hands of James. I was not the first and not the last. Not long ago, a graduate student who was living with him contacted me for help, desperate to escape. Meanwhile, James continues as a tenured full professor in senior leadership roles and acts as a grievance officer for his university's Faculty Association. He challenged and overturned decisions regarding his tenure as well as promotion to full professor, and his university has enabled him to keep filed complaints, mediations, and other rulings hidden. I recognize, too, that what I know is only part of the full picture.

Years ago, a colleague connected me with a reporter who was hoping to do a story on James. His name had surfaced because there was a public investigation into nondisclosure agreements at his university and a graduate student had signed one involving James over a decade ago. The reporter asked me to pass his contact information on so that women who had stories about James could phone or email him. The other women's stories have confirmed to me that the abuse I experienced was part of a clear pattern of abuse with impunity. If James had been dealt significant consequences in any of his cases, he might not be continuing to harm, or have continued access to unsuspecting students and colleagues.

Though many years separate me from my relationship with James, like the other women who chose not to speak to the reporter, I am wary of engaging with anything related to him. I'm writing this chapter anonymously because I have seen James's cunning ability to manipulate people and situations and I still do not feel safe from him. Sharing my experiences of his abuse and harassment to protect my workspace from him has brought me victim blaming, professional discrediting, and distancing by my colleagues. I have been told it is unprofessional and rude to share that he hit me because "people don't know what to do with that information."

But while anonymous, this personal account provides political, theoretical, and professional context for needed systemic change. *Anonymous* does not mean "untrue." Real names are unnecessary, as my experiences of trauma, assault, abuse, and harassment are not unique but rather widespread and persistent in academia (Jessup-Anger et al.). The recommendations I make for changes to reporting pathways, policies, and procedures thus broadly apply to academia.

My Story of an Abusive Personal Relationship with a Colleague

James came back into my life at a time that was opportune for him. We had been in the same graduate program almost two decades before, so reconnecting felt nostalgic. I was doing well professionally, but was exhausted and it was a vulnerable time for me. He was the seemingly perfect antidote to all woes; he had a full-time faculty income, was elected to national positions, and was an established, award-winning scholar. We had common recreational interests and already knew one another. He also had a way with words, convincingly expressing his love in letters and poetry over several years. We spent almost one-third of each year together in person and communicated daily, as we did not live near each other. I believed what he texted—what he said he ate for dinner, how the Christmas turkey he made was too bland. I never suspected that the sunset pictures I recognized as sent from his home were taken on a different day or sent from another city. He fabricated events by sending sustained text updates over time, documenting things that I later learned did not happen. I later saw endearing texts and photos he sent to another woman from trips we were on together, where he twisted reality. He did a launch of our new book, picking up the delivered books at my parents' home and even taking flowers for my mother, while using the trip as a vacation with a girlfriend. I learned the true reason for his aversion to social media and photographs only after I learned of his duplicitous life.

While we were in a relationship, he convinced me and our community of academic friends that he was separated and raising his children as a dedicated single dad. Meanwhile, he was pretending to be a committed partner in three families. Last year, I learned that a woman in a two-year relationship with him surprised him with a visit and found that the basement rental where she thought he lived was not his home. She was directed upstairs to where he lived with another partner and her children. I imagine that readers must be wondering how all of us—intelligent, accomplished women—could be so fully deceived, but the fact that we were duped provides insight into the kind of elaborate and sophisticated scheming James is capable of. His violence arose when his facades were threatened. Our relationship ended when he gave me a concussion.

How Academia Harbors Abuse

When James hit me hard in the face and said I ought to learn to watch my mouth, I was in shock. I was asking him for the truth, to make sense of the lies and the multiple relationships he was in. I did not even think about going to the police because we were in a different country and were leaving for the airport within a few hours. Once home, I still did not consider reporting him. The absolute shock of his violence and then of discovering the extent of his deception was traumatic. In the months after the concussion, I learned he had carefully fabricated everything our relationship had been based on.

I was not able to stay away from him because, though we were employed by different institutions, our academic work overlapped: we both held leadership roles on the executive board of a national association. I felt very unsafe and fearful of seeing him in our Zoom meetings. I did not want him to see me or hear my voice. I did not want to see or hear him. I approached the copresidents of the association and shared my situation. They were sympathetic and offered to support me if I needed to turn off my camera or leave a meeting. While this is a loving and common response, this type of support sides with the perpetrator.[1] The association does not have a code of conduct, so the copresidents have no authority to remove someone from the meetings or the executive board, even if the person harms another member. They were also afraid he might sue or otherwise harm them, so they said nothing to him.

On Zoom, James would purposely engage with me; in group email threads, he praised me. Twice he submitted to the journal I edit. All this unwanted contact was intentional covert harassment. I wanted nothing to do with him, which he knew. While publicly praising someone and submitting to a journal are innocuous actions, to James these were calculated attempts to subjugate me—to force me, the editor-in-chief, to read and edit his work and pretend that nothing untoward had even happened.

I filed a complaint report through my university's Office of Human Rights. The director from this office recorded my story, put it in print for me to review and edit, and then sent it to James's Sexual Violence Office as an informal complaint. Since I am not an employee of James's institution, my report could not be officially investigated in that office. My report was then sent to his university's Fair Treatment Office (FTO), which deals with staff and faculty complaints and is not under the jurisdiction of the University Faculty Council. I again retold my story and worked with the FTO advocate to create the terms of a mediation document. That document, bound by a multiyear term, prohibited him from attending certain conferences, Zoom-bombing my presentations, applying to certain leadership association positions while I was on the executive board, and submitting to the journal I edit.

When the FTO mediation document was presented to James, he declined to participate on the advice of his Faculty Association, since people not at that university are outside the scope of FTO policy. The advocate relayed to me that James said he had conferred with the Faculty Association president and was advised that he did not have to engage with mediation. The advocate informed James that if he did not engage, I would escalate the informal complaint to a formal complaint, which would make the complaint known to his faculty dean. James immediately modified the mediation document, deleting a bullet point on sharing the document with his dean, and signed the agreement.

The FTO advocate was crucial for me in this process. If James had continued to ignore me and the mediation process, I would have likely dropped out of the complaint process since filing a formal complaint would have required much more commitment, energy, and fortitude—far more than I or most survivors can manage. And yet, it is only with a formal complaint that any form of justice or behavioral consequences can take place. The informal complaint solely seeks to mediate shared contact. I contacted the faculty dean about my informal complaint separately, as I wanted them to know about it and was advised that university policy did not contain any restriction on disclosure of information. As with all disclosures in my experience, listeners are sympathetic, but no one reprimands the abuser or acts on the information. This is because there are no policies in place for actions to occur in response to informal complaints, or because people are fearful themselves, don't know how to respond, or don't want to get involved. Even supervisors cannot act without an official investigation.

The process, from the time James assaulted me to when the document of safety was signed, took twenty-two months. During that period, I had to tell my story in detail numerous times, which was retraumatizing. Except for the FTO, the offices and organizations were unable to provide safety for me because of their operating policies. Furthermore, the FTO's informal complaint mediation only creates a boundary for safe space—it does not address the behaviors or actions leading to the complaint. It has been several years since the concussion and mediation experience, yet the damage and grief are slow to heal. The fear of what James might do covertly and what he can do overtly when the mediation time runs out remains unsettling.

The Benefits and Limitations of Informal Resolutions

The faster informal complaint process can be beneficial to the complainant because it protects the complainant from protracted immersion in the traumatic events and from further exposure to the perpetrator. In the formal resolution route, the complainant is required to provide a detailed retelling of the events, find witnesses, gather evidence, and be involved in an investigation. The respondent is then given an opportunity to provide a written response and the respondent again has an opportunity to reply. The investigator compiles information through multiple interviews with both parties and witnesses. Just the thought of going through this process, especially of reading and responding to any of James's words and excuses, is unfathomable to me now, so doing something like this years ago would have been impossible. Through the informal resolutions route, the focus is not on the past (what happened), but on the future (the creation of a protected space).

At the same time, an informal resolution process can also benefit the abuser in that no investigation is carried out, and the respondent's supervisors do not find out about the complaint from the reporting office. Although deans can be informed about informal complaints (when contacted directly by complainants), usually no actions are taken because there is no investigation proving that wrongdoing occurred.

Mediation documents can be very valuable, as they can be used by associations and organizations with or without code-of-conduct policies to protect the vulnerable party. The document James signed significantly changed my life in positive ways. With a mediation document, one who has been harmed can, for example, insist on removal of a respondent-attendee in a conference setting. Ideally, all academic associations and organizations would have clear codes of conduct, membership rules, or bylaws worded to protect their membership and which enable them to carry out their mandates and missions. Where protective policies and bylaws are not in place, the signed mediation document provides leaders the authority to keep members safe from aggressors.

Recommendations for Inclusive Policy Changes

In the last decade, many more faculty members and students have begun collaborating across campuses, with grant agencies increasingly promoting funding for university partnerships. New policies that protect student and faculty collaborators across universities need to be created. Schools can begin making their spaces safer by developing more inclusive and transparent operating processes and policies for reporting and investigating harassment. While the privacy of all involved parties must be respected, institutions also need to find ways of sharing information about abusive behavior more effectively, both on and off campus, so that habitual perpetrators of abuse against faculty and students across institutions can be identified and stopped.

Academic associations need to:

- Develop membership agreements that stipulate the parameters of membership and removal from online and in-person meetings.

- Create code of conduct agreements.

Universities need to:

- Lengthen or establish open time limits for reporting incidents. Victims may take a long time to come forward because of the trauma and fear caused by the perpetrator.

- Treat all complaints seriously, whether formal or informal.

- Use key questions to generate a written narrative and audio recording of a complaint, then use this narrative to move through the complaint process, which will reduce retraumatizing the victim and encourage reporting.

- Assign each complainant an advocate who will assist them in seeking justice.

- Have policies and bylaws vetted by experts in sexual harassment law and policy, especially those who are familiar with the ways perpetrators manipulate language and evade policies and procedures.

- Enforce workplace violence policies. A pattern of complaints, whether informal or formal, warrants investigation. A professor who behaves in ways that harm people is a risk to the university community and should not continue to have open access to students.

- At reappointment, tenure, and promotion review, committees should be provided with a summary outcome of any mediated or investigated reports about candidates, so they are informed of the potential risk posed by perpetrators being considered for these honors.

Sexual Harassment as Rape Culture

Instruments such as the Sexual Experiences Survey (SES) conceive of rape at the extreme end of a gender-stereotypical continuum of seductive behaviors that include coercion and harassment (Koss & Oros). These frameworks contextualize gendered harassment and abuse, like rape and other sexual violence, as patterns of accumulating behaviors that are not random or exceptional but part of a normalized and gendered system of power differentials. When viewed in these terms, it is not surprising that James was involved with a graduate student who signed a nondisclosure agreement, that numerous complaints were filed against him, and that he routinely harasses, is violent, and operates in repeating patterns.

What can seem surprising is that, while awareness of gender-related misconduct on postsecondary campuses has risen over the last forty years (Jessup-Anger et al.), incidences remain widespread. Further ethics-oriented scholarship on gendered abuse as it manifests across academia in all its guises is needed. By using victims' experiences and feedback to revise policies for reporting and disclosing complaints across academic institutions and associations, we can better protect victims and reduce unintended protections for perpetrators.

Note

1. For another example of "protecting" a victim in a way that removes them while maintaining the perpetrator's right to remain present, see "To Make a Fuss" in this volume (editors' note).

Works Cited

Bach, Bo, et al. "The ICD-11 Classification of Personality Disorders: A European Perspective on Challenges and Opportunities." *Borderline Personality Disorder and Emotion Dysregulation*, vol. 9, no. 12, 2022. https://doi.org/10.1186/s40479-022-00182-0.

Diagnostic and Statistical Manual of Mental Disorders (5th ed). DSM-5. "*Personality Disorders*." American Psychiatric Association, pp. 646–49.

Jessup-Anger, Jody, et al. "History of Sexual Violence in Higher Education." *New Directions for Student Services*, vol. 161, 2018, pp. 9–19. https://doi-org.ezproxy.lakeheadu.ca/10.1002/ss.20249.

Koss, Mary P., and C. Oros. "Sexual Experiences Survey: A Research Instrument Investigating Sexual Aggression and Victimization." *Journal of Consulting and Clinical Psychology*, vol. 50, no. 3, 1982, pp. 455–57.

20

The LIEG's Complaint Collective

Reclaiming Academic Voices

Lidia M. V. Possas and M. Emilia Barbosa

This chapter documents the pressing issues faced by the collective members of an international research nucleus, the Interdisciplinary Laboratory of Gender Studies (LIEG), linked to the São Paulo State University (UNESP), Brazil,[1] which was founded as a "collective of female researchers." Composed of faculty, graduate, and postgraduate students, we are against all forms of gender violence and rape culture, and we confront abusive behaviors in academia together. We employ ethnography as an anthropological method (Caria 12; Carvalho 29) that combines deliberate actions of intervention in each field of analysis. This approach allows us to gather evidence, including materials, imagery, and especially the behaviors we experience in everyday life, better illustrating where gender relations emerge at each moment in their hierarchies and intentional exclusions (Ginzburg 170–71). This constructivist methodology has allowed us to observe the hierarchical and hostile functioning of our academic spaces: acts of resistance that are often silenced in the halls are meanwhile written on the walls and the doors of women's bathrooms.

Having individually witnessed many instances of gendered violence, abuses, and discrimination in academia, and having been victims ourselves, we narrate, historicize, and contextualize our collective's efforts to get organized, resist, and fight, and in the process become a "complaint collective." Being individual members of institutional committees and commissions dedicated to listening to complaints and to deciding procedures, we came together with our students and colleagues to advance their causes in and outside the institution, and we have dedicated several extension courses (highly sought-out electives) to the study and analysis of our cases. Here, we tell our collective story as we create our collective support system, learn about the "institutional mechanics" and the politics of complaining, actively become "feminist ears," engage collectively in the labor of complaining with tears, groans, and moans in the mixture, and ultimately produce more information and gain more wisdom about what has been happening to us all (Ahmed 21). We are transforming our collective anger, frustration, and loss into a comprehensive project that documents and collects our experience at this moment, fighting this fight together until—paraphrasing Leila Whitley, Tiffany Page, Alice Corble, Heidi Hasbrouck, Chryssa Sdrolia, and others at the end of Sara Ahmed's book, *Complaint!* (273)—we too interrupt the abuses and move something!

Formation of LIEG and Its Complaint Collective

The LIEG, the Interdisciplinary Laboratory of Gender Studies, was created in 2010 at the UNESP/Marilia campus to understand how and why the inclusion of new subjects (students as women, homosexuals, Afro descendants) was being the target of tensions and conflicting relationships in the academic hierarchy.[2] Since its onset, the LIEG has provoked debates about the existing gender violence and the presence of rape culture on our campuses, working side-by-side with undergraduate and graduate students. We started with many questions, such as why, once complaints are filed and undergo the transit of bureaucratic processes in accordance with each academic institution's established policies, are they not resolved satisfactorily, generating fair responses? Why does the establishment assume an oppressive bureaucratic function instead of positively influencing the lives and careers of those individuals deeply affected by such processes? Why does the process result in complainants' disbelief in a fair process and positive outcomes? From the start of the formal complaint process to its end, from the archiving and statistical data collection to the unsatisfactory resolution, what happens in between? Why are such processes so removed from current inclusivity and diversity efforts in academia?

Since 2017, the LIEG has been developing research with funding from CNPq–National Council for Scientific and Technological Development, Ministry of Education [Conselho Nacional de Desenvolvimento Científico e Tecnológico, Ministério da Educação]. Some of the titles in our collection include, for instance, "Survival(s) and Gender Violence in the Academic Space: Advances, Ambiguities and Perspectives" (2016–2020) and "Violence and Diversity at the University: Legitimizing the Place of Speech and Facing Forms of Harassment and Discrimination" (2020–2023).[3] Meanwhile, the LIEG-UNESP research clusters, together with the student collectives at UNESP university units, proposed study activities including conversation circles, meetings, and debates at locations that include Marília and Bauru. These activities covered topics such as gender violence and discrimination in academia and organized resistance to campus-experienced abuses and ran for multiple years starting in 2017; some remain ongoing.

As of 2019, we have become a "grievance collective" as theorized by Sara Ahmed in *Complaint!* (2021). This occurred because academics with complaints seldom consulted the University Ombudsmen Offices [Ouvidorias Universitárias]—public bodies intended to serve academic communities—because they lacked faith in the Offices. Further contributing to student and faculty belief in the irrelevance of the Offices was the fact that institutional positions were dominated by white male professors, who didn't see a need for these Offices to exist.

Particularly since the onset of the global pandemic in 2020 and following successive reports of sexual harassment, violence, abuse, and discrimination at UNESP, Brazil, and at other Brazilian, Latin American, and US higher education institutions, the LIEG decided to organize a policy of "reception" and "confrontation," in accordance with current regulations. With the support of the new UNESP-Central Ombudsmen Offices and grounded in the aforementioned research projects that aimed at reporting, historicizing, and contextualizing the efforts of the student collectives, our research collective became an organization of resistances and fights against gender abuse in academia, by denouncing the institutional reproduction of patriarchal, heteronormative, and misogynistic relationships. To that end, we started documenting ours and others' stories, collecting all forms of denunciations, whether oral or written reports, social media and whatever signs that circulated to that effect, including the writing on the walls and doors of women's bathrooms. This mobilization gained strength with the support of the Board of the Faculty of Philosophy and

Sciences of UNESP (FFC) [Direção da FFC (Faculdade de Filosofia e Ciências da UNESP) (Gestão 2020–2024)] and, mainly, that of the Central Ombudsmen Offices, which, based on solid research data, encouraged discussions of gender violence within the university's governing bodies, thus gradually pressuring for the implementation of better norms, in turn creating support committees for all UNESP units.

Our action as LIEG gained recognition and credibility with the students, particularly those organized in existing student collectives who started to encourage discussions in their courses, in the Tutorial Education Programs (PET) [Programas de Educação Tutorial/PET], and at local academic events. The LIEG/UNESP became involved with the admission program for incoming students/UNESP [Programação de Recebimento aos Ingressantes at FFC], after the 2018, 2019, and 2020 entrance examinations [Vestibular (Exame de Acesso à Universidade)] by publicizing its academic mission, as well as functioning as a means for students to get information and access to the local ombudsman website. These interventions proved to be vital for incoming students, many of whom suffered from abusive behaviors. Therefore, in 2020 we created *The Guide to Combat HARASS-MENT—sexist/sexual/gender identity/expression/sexual orientation,*[4] which was published online that year, but unfortunately was not distributed in print because classes were suspended due to COVID-19. We began distributing copies of the *Guide* in 2023 and are very happy to report that we are currently at its third edition. It has proven to be an important and popular tool at our institutions.

From 2020 to 2021, LIEG operated remotely, increasing the number of participants in our semester activities and including guests from other universities, who engaged with us within a decolonial approach and joined in our theoretical-methodological discussions. Use of remote technology allowed us to feature national, Latin American, North American, and English researchers and guest speakers in unprecedented ways. During this period of social isolation, so tragic for so many, and at the height of the pandemic-related mortalities in our country and worldwide, we were fortunate to have the opportunity to talk with Sara Ahmed about her recent book *Complaint!* During the same period of seclusion, the local ombudsmen offices at UNESP received a significant number of complaints of harassment perpetrated by a white male professor, which mobilized the students and involved the recently created Gender Secretariat of the Academic Directorate for Students (DA) [Secretaria de Gênero do Diretório

Académico dos Estudantes]. The victimized female students reported to the Course Coordination [Coordenação de Curso de Ciências Sociais] that they had been intimidated online by the same professor in one of the evaluation meetings of the Social Sciences Course [Curso de Ciências Sociais da FFC].

The local ombudsman office forwarded the complaints to the FFC Board of Directors [Direção da FFC] who, immediately after listening to the Legal Advice Team (UNESP) [Assessoria Jurídica/UNESP], installed an Internal Administrative Commission [Comissão Administrativa Interna]. The results of those hearings, which were unsatisfying to all of those involved, teachers and students, led to the creation of an administrative process [Processo Administrativo] with members from other UNESP units. At that time, faculty who supported the accused teacher, in a meeting of the Department of Political and Economic Sciences [Departamento de Ciências Políticas e Econômicas], issued a manifesto defending their accused colleague, thus involving the Teachers Association (ADUNESP) [Associação dos Docentes da FFC/UNESP/ADUNESP]. The latter reiterated its opposition to harassment in general, but at the same time declared their support for the abusive white male professor who, in accordance with the institution's legal guidelines, had been suspended from his academic activities for sixty days.

The academic community rose in an unprecedented uproar and began to debate the matter through its internal bodies and at its coordinating committees, but without the pertinent information that the case required. The DA's gender secretariat [A Secretaria de Gênero do DA (Directório Acadêmico Estudantil da FFC)] spoke out against the denouncing movement and the actions taken collectively against the accused professor, through a letter to the students explaining what happened from their point of view. As a result, our collective, the LIEG/UNESP, began to be identified as the instigator of the complaints, mainly when the Course Completion Works (TCC)[5] [Trabalhos de Conclusão de Curso/TCC] began to be publicized on our networks: website, Facebook, and Instagram—"Cultura e Gênero." Like many before us, we knew it was time to respond in a constructive, research-informed, and collective basis to this call for action, for we felt that our own livelihoods as academics were under threat. And in that spirit, from the onset of these events, the LIEG committed to researching gender violence and other forms of discrimination in academia as one of our central lines of inquiry.

Research and Activism of the LIEG

In June 2022, a doctoral student defended her dissertation, *Decolonizing the Look: Visual and Subjective Representations in Student Collectives against Gender Violence*[6] (Godinho 2022), which represented for the LIEG a relevant theoretical and methodological analysis of the action and resistance of student collectives in the main universities in São Paulo: UNESP, USP [Universidade de São Paulo], and UNICAMP [Universidade Estadual de Campinas] Furthermore, our collective's research showed how many of the cases of harassment and rape in the universities of São Paulo were reported in the main printed and online newspapers. Since 2013, São Paulo's universities had been the target of investigations by the Legislative Assembly of the State of São Paulo/ALESP [Assembleia Legislativa do Estado de São Paulo/ALESP], (through the installation of Inquiry Commissions [Comissões de Sindicância]), the first in 2014, in the face of the numerous manifestos and student reports against the violence suffered on campus, and the second in 2021, which focused on instances in which the three universities and their students called attention to the respective deans and their Ombudsmen Offices. These facts, with concrete data, show how prevalent abusive behaviors at the universities are and that they have existed since these institutions were created (USP 1934, UNICAMP 1966, UNESP 1974), but often invisibly. The UES Paulistas, aware of their failure to acknowledge abusive behaviors taking place at their institutions, have since 2021 stated their attentiveness to the statistics presented to the public and committed to create Protocols of Immediate Action and of Coordination of Reception and Confrontation with Educational Actions [Protocolos de Ação Imediata e de Coordenações de Acolhimento e Enfrentamento com Ações Educativas].

Our collective's research projects have been developed internally and approved institutionally; thus, we have kept in touch with the experiences of our national and international partners, mainly in Latin America, sponsored by the LIEG/UNESP. During our Semiannual Activities (2020 to 2022), we published a "Dossier 1: Gender Violence in the University," which immediately motivated more participants to collaborate with our articles and research endeavors. In response, we created a Publications Committee, led by several LIEG PhDs, who revised and submitted six articles, based on the research experiences of each academic author, responding to a call for papers from the Brazilian academic journal of the *Instituto de Políticas Públicas de Marília, IPPMar*.[7] After inviting external experts to evaluate the articles, the journal published them as an ebook in October 2022, titled *Dossier I: Special Edition: Gender Violence in the University* [*Violência de Gênero na Universidadeted*], edited by Lidia M. Possas. We also presented these findings to the UNESP community at the 5th National Meeting of the GT ANPUH Gender Studies, held at the State University of Montes Claros (UEMC), on 24 and 25 November 2022. This publication has received more than five hundred positive online responses as of the time of our writing, July 2023.[8]

The LIEG/UNESP started the 2023 academic year with positive prospects, beginning with an invitation from the Directorate/FFC in partnership with the Central Ombudsmen Offices to propose activities with students admitted through the entrance exam in 2023 to our nine undergraduate courses: archivology, librarianship, social sciences, philosophy, pedagogy, international relations, speech therapy, occupational therapy, and physiotherapy. We sent to the FFC's Annual Admission Committee [Comissão Anual de Ingressada da FFC], comprised of course coordinators and student representatives, our proposal containing the following objectives:

> The Interdisciplinary Laboratory of Gender Studies (LIEG) aims to participate in the activities of Admission 2023, at the Faculty of Philosophy and Sciences of Marília (FFC), with the aim of presenting the group, disseminating advances at UNESP regarding coping with violence and protecting victims and, finally, holding a workshop about harassment, sexual and gender violence at the university. Faced with increases in cases of racism, sexism, LGBTQIA+phobia and harassment in higher education institutions around the world, and, essentially, at UNESP, our group insists on the need to build this space for dialogue and feminist listening with newcomers. In this scenario of hostility, the objective is, at *Ingressada* [*homecoming*], to flood and strengthen the reception network created by the LIEG. In this way, social minorities—who today correspond to the numerical majority at our university—will not, once again, be in a situation of vulnerability and abandonment in the institution's spaces.

After analyzing the proposals forwarded by different groups, the Committee returned our proposal a week later with the following comment: "*Rejected, due to its ideological content.*" The unanswered question:

what were the grounds for this rejection? Why reject a proposal that would publicize the creation of important committees and processes to better welcome and support our students? These committees include the Coordinator for Affirmative Action, Diversity and Equity (created by UNESP resolution on 26 January 2022) and the Central Welcoming Committee, as one of the actions provided for in the Educational Policy to Combat Moral Harassment, Sexual Harassment, Forms of Discrimination and Prejudice in Relation to Origin, Color, Gender, Orientation Sexual, Religion Or Belief, Socio-Economic Level, Physical or Mental Body Condition within the Ambit of the São Paulo State University "Júlio de Mesquita Filho"—UNESP,[9] by UNESP ordinance number 68, of 26 July 2022. Likewise, our proposal would present to student newcomers the *Guide for the Prevention of Discrimination based on Sexism/Sexual Harassment/Identity/Gender Expression/Sexual Orientation*,[10] prepared by the Educating for Diversity Project, and which was not properly distributed in 2020, thus providing the free circulation of 150 copies of the *Guide* campus-wide. Last on our proposal was a workshop, as a reflective activity based on the questions, "What UNESP do we want?" and "What is the future of the Public University that we dream of?" providing a safe space where participants would write their answer to the questions posed, first in group discussions, and then individually. These would become a mural with collages [Painel de Colagens] to be displayed in the corridors of the FFC.

A great opportunity to welcome incoming students and integrate them into the UNESP community was lost here! It became evident that this rejection was backlash in response to denouncing allegations of harassment that began to circulate nonstop throughout the FFC's corridors, mainly through the voices and actions of senior students. The denialist stance and explicit conservative tendencies expressed by the FFC's Annual Admission Committee members demonstrate the university's hierarchical gender relations and patriarchal and misogynous discourse. The Committee's lack of foresight and judgment was further evidenced by the dissatisfaction with its endeavors of incoming students in 2023, who reported disorganized scheduling and ineffective communication in their evaluations.

We in our collective remain committed to seeking solutions and dealing with the often destructive and complex power structures that lead to largely unsatisfactory institutional grievance processes. Together, our LIEG's Complaint Collective is working to foster a space for intersection and collaboration between every scholar, researcher, student, professor, and support personnel in our sphere. We are in the process of creating our own repository of what Emanuela Borzacchiello calls " 'acts of memory' as the collection of materials that allows us to reconstruct the voices of [us all together as] victims and of the perpetrators" (347), through the analysis of our lived situations of violence, abuse, and discrimination in academia. Conducting research and documenting the specific circumstances of each individual and our collective complaint propels us to better understand how academic disciplinary processes really work and how to best fight academic abusers' impunity. Selecting, collecting, naming, systematizing, and archiving these "acts of memory" is a fundamental endeavor (362) to produce an interpretative corpus from which we can read our bodies and our spaces, historicize them, and analyze evolving acts of resistance to violence historically and in the present. Ours is a polysemic, pluri-vocal contribution made of our vital perceptions and experiences in academia against gender violence.

Notes

1. São Paulo State University/UNESP (Universidade Estadual Paulista; all translations into English from Portuguese are our own) was founded in 1976, combining fifteen isolated higher education institutes, distributed throughout several municipalities of the state of São Paulo, from the coast to the interior. In 2022, UNESP positioned itself as "one of the largest and most important Brazilian universities, with emphasis on teaching, research and extensive community services." Encompassing thirty-four units, it enrolls 53,578 students: 39,244 undergraduate and 14,334 postgraduate studies (6,496 in academic master's programs, 883 in professional master's programs, and 6,552 enrolled in doctorates). Its female representation is greater than male, according to the *Statistical Yearbook of 2021.* [*Anuário Estatístico UNESP*, 2021.] https://ape.unesp.br/anuario/pdf/Anuario_2021.pdf. Accessed Jan. 2023.

2. For more information, see www.culturaegenenro.com.br.

3. "Sobrevivência(s) e violência de gênero no espaço acadêmico: avanços, ambiguidades e perspectivas" (2016–2020) e "Violência e Diversidade na Universidade: legitimando o lugar de fala e enfrentando as formas de assédio e discriminação" (2020–2023) (*A Universidade e as relações de Gênero de Poder*).

4. UNESP—"Guide to Combat Harassment" ["Guia de Enfrentamento ao Assédio"] was the final product of the "Educating for Diversity Project" ["Projeto "Educando para a Diversidade"], 2020, a joint publication with UNESP and SANTANDER Bank, and can be found at file:///C:/Users/Usuario/Downloads/guia-prevencao-assedio-da-unesp-2022%20(6).pdf.

5. The following Course Completion TCCs were defended by students with dean's scholarships and approved by the respective examining boards: "Gender Violence in the Academic Space: An Analysis of Hazing and Parties/UNESP (1990—2017); "Gender and Representations in the Academic Space: A Look through the Press and Digital Media (2018-2019); and "Gender Violence and Race at the University: Student Resistance Movements at UNESP (2018-2020) ["Violência de Gênero no Espaço Acadêmico: uma análise dos Trotes e Festas/ UNESP (1990-2017)"]; "Gênero e Representações no Espaço Acadêmico: um olhar através da Imprensa e Mídias Digitais (2018-2019); "Violência de Gênero e Raça na Universidade: movimentos estudantis de Resistência na UNESP (2018-2020)].

6. "Descolonizando O Olhar: representações visuais e subjetivas nos Coletivos Estudantis contra a Violência de Gênero," Maria Inês Almeida Godinho, 2022.

7. Revista do IPPMar is part of the Council of Editors of Scientific Periodicals (CEPEC) and has its own editorial board, being a space for the publication of scientific research prepared by academics dedicated to the study and debate of themes related to public policies in Brazil and in the world.

8. The articles are: "Escuta feminista e a revelação de violências invisíveis: análise dos movimentos estudantis na UNESP/Marília"; "Descolonizar o olhar. Análise de imagens criadas por coletivos digitais contra a violência de gênero nas Universidades"; "A gente não vai acreditar nessa neguinha! Violência sexual, de gênero, de raça e classe na Universidade"; "Experiências Femininas na Universidade: Violência de gênero e resistência feminista"; "Todavía llevando esta carga: estado actual de la violencia de género en las universidades de EE. UU"; "Violência de Gênero: práticas do/no currículo de licenciatura em Educação Física da Universidade Federal do ACRE—BRASIL."

9. Política Educativa de Enfrentamento ao assédio moral, assédio sexual, importunação sexual, formas de discriminações e preconceitos em relação à origem, cor, gênero, orientação sexual, religião ou crença, nível sócio-econômico, condição corporal física ou psíquica no âmbito da Universidade Estadual Paulista "Júlio de Mesquita Filho"—UNESP.

10. Guia de Prevenção ao Assédio sexista/sexual/identidade/expressão de gênero/orientação sexual, file:///C:/Users/Usuario/Downloads/guia-prevencao-assedio-da-unesp-2022%20(6).pdf.

Works Cited

Ahmed, Sara. *Complaint!* Duke UP, 2021.
Almeida, Tânia Mara Campos. ZANELLO, Valeska e CRUZ, Felipe Santa. "Panoramas da Violência contra Mulheres nas Universidades Brasileiras e Latino Americanas—Apresentação." OAB Nacional Editora, 2022, pp. XIII–XXXV.

https://www.oab.org.br/publicacoes/pesquisa?termoPesquisa=panoramas. Accessed July 2023.

Amaral, Isabela Grossi e Flávia Naves. "O Enfrentamento das opressões de gênero numa universidade pública: o papel dos coletivos estudantis na ótica do feminismo decolonial." *Revista Brasileira de Estudos Organizacionais* vol. 7, no. 1, Jan.–May 2020, pp. 877–910.

Anuário Estatístico UNESP 2021. https://ape.unesp.br/anuario/pdf/Anuario_2021.pdf. Accessed Jan. 2023.

Barbosa, Maria Emilia. "Todavía llevando esta carga: estado actual de la violencia de género en las universidades de EE. UU. *Dossiê I: Violência de Gênero na Universidade. Edição Especial* vol. 8, no. 22, pp. 83–96. https://revistas.marilia.unesp.br/index.php/RIPPMAR/article/view/13780. Barreto, Beatriz Jorge."Escuta feminista e a revelação de violências invisíveis: Análise dos movimentos estudantis na UNESP/Marília." *Dossiê I: Violência de Gênero na Universidade. Edição Especial,* vol. 8, no. 22, pp. 17–28. https://revistas.marilia.unesp.br/index.php/RIPPMAR/article/view/13780.

Borzacchiello, Emanuela. "Pensando en la construcción de archivos feministas en tiempos de violencia: Elementos para el análisis." *Lecturas críticas en investigación feminista,* edited by Norma Blazquez Graf and Martha Patricia Castañeda Salgado. UNAM, México, 2016, pp. 345–70.

Caria, Telmo H. Experiência etnográfica em Ciências Sociais. *ETNOGRÁFICA,* Porto, Afrontamento, 2002, pp. 9–20.

Carvalho, José Jorge de. "O olhar etnográfico e a voz subalterna." *Horizontes. Antropológicos.,* vol. 7, no. 15, July 2015, pp. 27–38. https://www.scielo.br/j/ha/a/kNnShbTR3wLSWgCspyx8JBv/.

Gaspar, Stephanie. "Violência de gênero no espaço acadêmico: trotes e festas universitárias" *(TCC) Curso de Graduação em Ciências Sociais,* UNESP-Marília, 2018.

Ginzburb, Carlos. "Sinais, inícios de um paradigma indiciário." *Mitos, Emblemas e Sinais: Morfologia e História.* Cia. das Letras, 1999, pp. 143–275.

Godinho, Maria Inês Almeida. *Decolonizando o Olhar-Análise de Imagens Criadas por Colectivos Digitais Contra a Violência de Gênero na Universidade.* Tese de Doutoramento, UNESP, 2022.

Portal UNESP. https://www2.unesp.br/portal#!/. Accessed 18 Feb. 2021.

Possas, Lidia M. V. *Dossiê I: Violência de Gênero na Universidade: Edição Especial,* vol. 8 (2022). https://revistas.marilia.unesp.br/index.php/RIPPMAR/article/view/13780.

Possas, Lidia M. V. "A Universidade e as relações de Gênero de Poder: Os Coletivos Estudantis e as Estratégias de Sobrevivência."*GÊNERO. Identidades políticas no sec. XX,* edited by Lidia M. V. Possas, et al. Recife/PE: EDUPE, 2021, pp. 55–86.

Relatóio Final da Comissão Parlamentar de Inquérito (constituída pelo Ato No. 56, de 2014). https://www.al.sp.gov.br/comissao/cpi/?idLegislatura=17&id Comissao=13033. Accessed 11 Dec. 2020.

Romania, Giovana. "Conheça três coletivos atuantes na cidade Bauru." https://www. socialbauru.com.br/2016/06/23/conheca-tres-coletivos-atuantes-na-cidade-bauru/. Accessed 11 Dec. 2020.

Salgado, Ricardo Seiça. "A Performance da Etnografia como Método da Antropologia." *ANTROPOlógicas* 13, 2015, pp. 27–38.

21

Disrupting the Past as Prologue

Recognizing and Responding to Strategies and Tactics of Gendered Oppression

CHRISTINA GALLUP, ANNE HINDERLITER, NJOKI M. KAMAU,
ARSHIA KHAN, LU SMITH, AND ELIZABETHADA WRIGHT

In 1980, the University of Minnesota and Shyamala Rajender signed a consent decree, agreeing upon action that the University would take in response to Rajender's lawsuit against the University. In this suit, which became a class action on behalf of all faculty at the University, Rajender accused the University of sexual discrimination after she was denied a tenure-track position. In the decree, the University was "permanently enjoined from discrimination against women on the basis of sex" (Clark et al. 3). The University also agreed to take various actions to ensure such discrimination would not occur in the future. Fast-forward forty-three years and—despite this decree—the University continues to grapple with ongoing incidents of sexual discrimination.

This collaboratively written article aims to understand how a university can maintain such discriminatory practices, despite court mandates. We conclude that the increasingly reified corporate structure of the university perpetuates practices that maintain systemic oppression. After reviewing research that shows that gendered oppression appears to be getting worse, not only at the University of Minnesota but nationwide, this article identifies how the corporate structure of the university perpetuates gendered oppression by discussing a characteristic example from the Swenson School of Science and Engineering, one college at the University of Minnesota Duluth (UMD), the largest of the nonflagship campuses in the University of Minnesota system. We conclude by offering a possible solution.

The authors of this article are faculty from two different UMD colleges, Swenson as well as the College of Arts, Humanities, and Social Sciences, who identify as female but come from many different positionalities. We have all experienced gendered abuse at UMD and other institutions. One name is a pseudonym, because the risks of publishing an article such as this are significant. We do want to note, though, that although this article focuses specifically on gendered abuse, most of our conclusions also would be applicable to racial abuse—something some of our authors are well aware of. Our purpose is to identify the self-perpetuating strategy that people in power use to continually replicate that power. In other words, our goal is to get the university system off its hamster wheel, endlessly repeating the same situations that benefit the privileged, and to get back to its mission of promoting learning, research, and community.

The Problem

Like the University of Minnesota, universities across the country have faced issues of gendered discrimination and have tried to address them. One means of addressing the issues is creating measures that attempt to promote diversity. Schools regularly offer diversity training, attempting to teach and encourage behaviors that will end discrimination. However, research reveals that such practices actually exacerbate the issues, legitimizing problematic practices (Brady et al.; Kaiser et al.). Additionally, a 2019 Brookings Report illustrates that there are fewer tenured associate professors in academia than there were twenty years ago, and women comprise only 21 percent of full-time university professors, up only 5 percent from seventy-five years ago, despite the fact that the number of women receiving college degrees has tripled in that time period (Kelly). Additionally, there are innumerable factors discouraging women from entering or remaining in roles as faculty (Kelly). All in all, researchers echo each other with the observation that conditions are not improving at the nation's universities (Adedoyin).

Numerous scholars discuss the high level of dissatisfaction most female academics face, especially in the sciences, with stereotypes continually hindering women's success (Van Veelan et al., Ryan et al., Kroeper et al. discuss the structures of organization as contributing to women's dissatisfaction). The authors argue that organizations engage in counterfeit diversity: they promote themselves as diverse in their hiring practices, but those newly hired employees arrive to discover an absence of the promoted diversity. Counterfeit diversity is one of those ways that universities' pretentions of engaging in diversity exacerbate problems.

UMD is no different. In 2019, former head coach for UMD's championship women's hockey team, Shannon Miller, won a $4.5 million settlement in her lawsuit against UMD for sex discrimination and Title IX violations. The settlement occurred after a six-year battle between the university and Miller, during which numerous other athletic coaches also lodged suits against UMD. Academic units at UMD also face hostility. For example, survey data regarding the workplace environment, gathered within Swenson in 2021, illustrates a tremendous lack of satisfaction with the workplace. Most significantly, in Swenson far fewer than half of the respondents (39 percent) had "trust and confidence in the college's leadership team" (compared with the system's 56 percent), while a mere 8 percent of respondents in the Department of Math and Statistics expressed such trust (Korn Ferry).

Corporatization of the Academy

The contemporary corporatization of the university appears to be one means the university uses to resist addressing issues of gender. In 2013, Benjamin Ginsberg published *The Fall of the Faculty: The Rise of the All-Administrative University and Why It Matters*, arguing that the growing number of administrators in higher education is harming higher education, but Ginsberg was certainly not the first—or the last—to lament the corporatization of the university (Clay; Steck et al.). These studies reveal that the university appears to be far more concerned with its bottom line than with education. Focus on the students does exist, but only in that universities want to keep their "customers" happy, so the university can continue to earn tuition dollars. And, of course, universities need to deliver their product, education; however, increasingly education is only a sliver of the product promoted. Athletic centers' rock walls, food for the gourmand, luxury housing, and adventurous student activities are increasingly prioritized over learning (Llewellyn).

Additionally, universities appear to put great effort into antidiscriminatory and equity policies, often incorporating them into the university strategic plans (Anucha). Such action might seem to call into question our assertion that the strategy of corporatization allows gendered abuse to continue in the academy. And at first glance it does. Yet, we see this corporatization as very much linked to the perpetuation of gendered abuse: Corporatization of the university is an example of what Michel de Certeau terms a strategy to maintain power in a particular locus. As de Certeau defines strategies, corporatization is a calculation or manipulation of power that protects what is the powerful's own and attacks what the powerful perceive as an exterior target or threat. Additionally, these powerful administrators put great effort into sustaining themselves (de Certeau 35–36).

With corporatization, administration maintains its own power, regarding the faculty and the "consumer" students as targets and threats, while resisting any attempts by either to alter this power relationship. This corporatization appears to accept many of the assumptions made by Milton Friedman in his classic essay arguing that corporations have a social responsibility to maximize their profits. Since efforts at antidiscrimination could lower those profits, administrators have a responsibility to deal with antidiscrimination without threatening the bottom line. Therefore, while the university must *appear* to promote antidiscrimination and equity efforts, most of the results are what one of our authors terms *pseudo-efforts*.

There are two main means of creating such "pseudo-efforts." One is by tasking faculty with antidiscrimination efforts via shared governance. While shared governance might appear beneficial, it has several problems. First, increasingly, universities hire contingent faculty instead of tenured or tenure-track faculty. The rationale for this hiring, which saves the university millions of dollars, is that such faculty fill sudden and irregular needs, or that these faculty have other careers in other professions and are sharing their professional knowledge with university students. However, this rationale does not hold. Numerous sources demonstrate that the majority of contingent instructors in the United States do not have careers in other fields: teaching in higher education is what they do for very long periods of time ("Background"). Not only are these faculty members' salaries significantly lower than tenured members' salaries, contingent professors are not guaranteed renewed contracts each year and contracts can be nonrenewed for any reason. Thus, these professors will remain silent when facing discrimination. If these contingent professors are tasked with creating antidiscrimination or equity policies, they would certainly not want to offer solutions that might be too radical—and thus lose their positions.

A second problem with shared governance is that the term *shared* is a misnomer. While professors do spend much time, most often uncompensated, for their work with shared governance, their work is merely advisory. While faculty members seem to have power as chairs of various and important committees, no matter what the recommendations, what the faculty suggest, want, or demand, their input is, ultimately, merely advice. Therefore, one administrative strategy is to tax faculty members with numerous shared governance responsibilities, then the exhausted faculty has little energy for response when their recommendations are ignored. Thus, faculty chairs have primarily titular positions.

Administration's methods of addressing gender and racial diversity are also pseudo-efforts, in that they are as superficial as they are clearly visible. According to Ginsberg and others, these superficial means of addressing concerns are "administrative aggrandizements" (97) that protect administrators from criticism and enhance their own power by padding administrators' résumés with details of these ineffectual initiatives (99–104). For example, after a very public "hate" incident, UMD launched an initiative to ensure the safety and inclusion of faculty and students of color, with the university asking many faculty of color to create formal plans for the initiative. However, little to nothing came from these plans, into which these faculty members had poured enormous amounts of time.

Some might respond to our concerns by observing that just as contingent professors are untenured, and therefore very powerless, so too are most administrators. While deans, provosts, and vice presidents of academic affairs do have tenure homes, most other high- and medium-level administrators (those in finance, student affairs, human resources, etcetera) do not. However, this lack of tenure home for administrators is part of the problem. Without a tenure home, administrators spend a great deal of time maintaining their positions, running campaigns to make themselves look good, and looking for positions to advance their own careers—what Ginsberg terms *administrative squandering*. While professors are constantly scrutinized by students, administrators, and their peers with evaluations of all sorts, rarely does such scrutiny apply to administrators—and when they are evaluated, the results are far from transparent. The result of this lack of evaluation means that when administrators address antidiscrimination and equity issues, there is no evaluative process to judge the success of the efforts. Meanwhile, administrators can and do list what we term *pseudo-efforts* as accomplishments; for example, they might cite creation of plans gone awry as successes.

With the structure of corporatization, administrators are more able to put their efforts where they choose—and career advancement is one of these places (Ginsberg 65–96). These administrators' self-serving attitudes toward the university mean that when serious problems erupt from failures at antidiscrimination and equity policies, the administrators do all they can to make the problems invisible. Even administrators with tenure homes are subject to administrative squandering and self-promotion. Rarely do such administrators return to their tenured homes, for various reasons (Firnim).

With our focus here on how corporatization of the university perpetuates gendered abuse, one might wonder if women in administration are changing the landscape. While we would like to believe women can make change, too often female administrators replicate the behaviors of men in similar positions. Often, when facing women with concerns about gendered abuse, female administrators cite themselves as women who made it by enduring bad behaviors. We have heard female leaders discuss, almost reverentially, the trauma they endured. They tell other women to "toughen-up," not recognizing their own internalized trauma. Additionally, there are huge problems with administrators' supposed remedies to inequities, among them that administrators have never experienced the inequities or discriminations, or they develop amnesia about their own struggles.

The result is the five symptoms of corporate perpetuation of gendered abuse: the separation of people with similar concerns and goodwill, promotion of amnesia about recognized past bad practices, silencing of dissenting voices, labeling of remedies for gendered oppression as impossible, and performance of fatuous actions that tell the community the university is addressing the unaddressed problems. To illustrate how the strategy of corporatization promotes these symptoms of perpetuation, we present the example below, which considers a well-publicized instance of gendered abuse in UMD's Department of Mathematics and Statistics.

An Example

That the Math and Statistics Department, in the climate survey cited above, had such low confidence in the system would not be surprising to anyone familiar with the UMD campus: the most visible example of the campus's poor climate occurred when one highly praised tenured female faculty department member resigned from her position after UMD's failure to resolve a hostile climate issue. While we don't have the space to recount the charges that this faculty member and others who joined her articulated, common claims from these women were continual challenges to the women's knowledge and authority, innumerable microaggressions, and gaslighting (Erikson; King & Sonderup). We want to emphasize, however, that after investigating the complaint, the EOAA found that the climate in the department was one that "any rational person would find abusive." However, little was done to change the department, and what was done was problematic.

When the women involved continually asked what would be done, they were told the administration could do little because the EOAA had found the problem to be with the collective environment rather than with individuals. As the abuses continued, the faculty union became involved and cited numerous microaggressions performed by individuals that could warrant discipline; however, the administration stated that these microaggressions "toed the line," never crossing over to discipline-worthy action. Meanwhile, the union worked with the administration on several other cases that the union argued did not warrant discipline, but the "toeing the line" argument vanished in these cases.

Due to the nature of these administrative responses, many at UMD began to distance themselves from the women who had filed the complaint because they did not want to be similarly viewed as "troublemakers," despite the fact that many who distanced themselves had also experienced abusive treatment. The distancing increased when administration began an attempt at remedying the situation, and the attempt disastrously failed. Supposedly building on restorative justice models, the administration hired a consultant who began "circles" that each professor in the department was required to attend and where they were asked to speak "their truth." The women who had lodged the complaints were the only ones who did not participate, either because they had left the university or they had medical excuses to avoid the traumatization that hearing the abusers' "truths" would cause. Many of the remaining professors had to spend hours in what they termed wasted and emotionally abusive time, and they blamed the missing women for the fact that they had to regularly attend these "circles." Some narratives relayed in the circles suggested that the department had been just fine until the women who lodged the complaint arrived—despite enormous evidence to the contrary. Additionally, the men who had engaged in the abuse presented their truths with few, if any counternarratives: the abused women were missing, and the circles were constructed so that when someone presented a fictionalized or exaggerated "truth," no one could respond until it was their turn in the circle. With all of this, the message was very clear to most other women: talk about vituperative situations, and you will be the ones we blame.[1]

The circles finally ended because of the nearly unbearable emotional damage the process was wreaking on everyone. The administration, however, did not see the circles as a failure. Instead, administrators applauded themselves. In a message to the college, an administrator spoke of the successes the administration had had, taking credit for things faculty members had done and citing numerous vacuous actions as evidence of administrative success.

And during all this discussion, the administration never mentioned many other past and present examples of gendered abuse at UMD. The rationale for the silence in the present situations was the need for confidentiality; for past situations, such as the Rajender and Miller suits, no rationale seemed to be needed. Amnesia ensured that not a peep was heard. In these examples, it becomes clear that confidentiality without a balance of transparency becomes a weapon. For example, research shows that confidentiality of wages contributes to the wage gap (Kim). So, too, confidentiality with no transparency in hostile environments leads to abuse.

We have numerous other UMD examples of the administration "circling the wagons" to maintain the corporate power of the university when challenged with charges of gendered abuse. And continually, the examples illustrate the university's claims that remedies to the problems are impossible, its separation of people with similar concerns, its promotion of amnesia, its silencing of dissenting voices, and its performance of fatuous actions that suggest the university is addressing unaddressed problems.

Power-Sharing and Design-Thinking

What can be done to rectify this steamrolling of both the gendered abuse and the victims? How can we stop avoiding the problem, as has been done for so many years? We haven't the room to detail full solutions and argue for their merit, though we do want to suggest one possibility: developing new systems of academic management that involve power-sharing and design-thinking. Such power-sharing enables what de Certeau terms *tactics*. Tactics are the opposing attacks offered by the "other," by those without a locus of power (36–37). Tactics rely on relentless pushes, continual challenges, spontaneity, and play.

Design-thinking is a kind of tactic; it is a methodological, nonlinear approach to solving complex and poorly defined problems. It takes a humanistic approach, putting the designers' need to empathize as the first of six stages. Encouraging creativity, design-thinking addresses each problem individually, using a process of creating prototypes, testing, and implementing solutions ("6 Stages"). It is designed to be inclusive, involving the people affected by potential solutions in the process of formulating and testing those solutions, in an iterative process with peer review at each stage of optimization. The embedded process of peer review—something very familiar to faculty members but less familiar to administrators—ensures that funding goes to projects vetted and tested by those who will be affected by the proposed solution.

It is crucial that power-sharing be partnered with this methodology, so it does not become yet another task given to professors to assuage them and their concerns. Such an approach also does not remove professors and put them in administrative positions, giving them fiduciary responsibility to the university instead of academic responsibility to their students and their research. People who plan these designs must have the power to implement them.

We must work together and never cease in pointing out the hypocrisies and injustices, and the fact that the corporatization of the university keeps us on a hamster wheel that benefits the corporate entity, but not what we seek to promote: learning, research, and community.

Note

1. Yet another example of DARVO (editors' note).

Works Cited

"6 Stages in the Design Thinking Process." *Design Garden*, 15 October 2021. https://talentgarden.org/en/design/6-stages-in-the-design-thinking-process/#:~:

text=In%20its%20most%20recent%20and%20known%20formulation%20
the,expectations%206%20Implement%20%E2%80%93%20actually%20
develop%20and%20launch.

"Background Facts on Contingent Faculty Positions." *American Society of University Professors*, n.d. https://www.aaup.org/issues/contingency/background-facts.

Brady, Laura M., et al. "It's Fair for Us." *Journal of Experimental Social Psychology*, vol. 57, 2015, pp. 100–110. https://doi.org/10.1016/j.jesp.2014.11.010.

Clark, Veve, et al. *Antifeminism in the Academy*. Routledge, 1996.

Clay, Rebecca. "The Corporation of Higher Education" *American Psychological Society*, vol. 39, no. 11, 2008. https://www.apa.org/monitor/2008/12/higher-ed#::text=The%20rise%20of%20consumerism%2C%20a,and%20seeking%20profit%2Dmaking%20opportunities.

De Certeau, Michel. *The Practice of Everyday Life*. University of California Press, 2011.

Erickson, Andee. "I Just Want to Feel Safe," *Duluth News Tribune*. 9 April 2021. https://www.duluthnewstribune.com/news/i-just-want-women-to-be-safe-women-who-resigned-from-umd-math-department-speak-out-about-sexism.

Firmin, Michael. "Transitioning from Administration to Faculty," 2008. Digital Commons@Cedarville, https://digitalcommons.cedarville.edu/cgi/viewcontent.cgi?article=1093&context=psychology_publications.

Friedman, Milton. "The Social Responsibility of Business Is to Increase Its Profits." *New York Times*, 13 September 1970, section SM, pp. 17.

Kaiser, Cheryl, et al. "Presumed Fair." *Journal of Personality and Social Psychology*, vol. 104, no. 3, 2013, pp. 504–19. Doi: 10.1037/a0030838. Epub, 19 Nov. 2012.

Kelly, Bridget Turner. "Though More Women Are on College Campuses, Climbing the Professor Ladder Remains a Challenge." 29 March 2019. Brookings. https://www.brookings.edu/blog/brown-center-chalkboard/2019/03/29/though-more-women-are-on-college-campuses-climbing-the-professor-ladder-remains-a-challenge/

Kim, Marlene. "Pay Secrecy and the Gender Wage Gap in the United States." *Industrial Relations*, vol. 43, no. 4, 2015, pp. 648–67. https://doi.org/10.1111/irel.12109.

King, Michael, and Elianna Sonderup. "Swenson Instructor, Students, Speak Out against STEM Sexism." *The Bark*, 14 April 2021. https://www.thebarkumd.com/news/2021/4/14/swenson-instructor-students-speak-out-against-stem-sexism.

Korn Ferry. "SCSE Math and Stats Engagement Survey," UMD Swenson College of Science and Engineering." PowerPoint presented at UMD 2021.

Kroeper, Kathryn M. "Counterfeit Diversity," *Journal of Personality and Social Psychology*, 2020. https://dx.doi.org/10.1037/pspi0000348.

Llewellyn, Kelsey. "Top 10 Most Luxurious Colleges." *College Magazine*, 13 July 2018. https://www.collegemagazine.com/top-ten-most-luxurious-colleges/.

Rajender v. University of Minnesota Consent Decree. US Court, District of Minnesota, 4th District. Civil No. 4-73-435, May 1980.

Ryan, M. K., et al. (2008). "Opting Out or Pushed Off the Edge?" *Social and Personality Compass*, vol. 2, 2008, pp. 266–79. http://doi: 10.1111/j.1751-9004.2007.00007.

Steck, Henry, et al. "Corporatization of the University," *Annals of the American Academy of Political and Social Science*, vol. 585, no. 1, 2003. https://doi.org/10.1177/0002716202238567.

Van Veelan, Ruth, et al. "Double Trouble," *Frontiers in Psychology*, vol. 10, 2019. https://doi.org/10.3389/fpsyg.2019.00150.

22

Feminist Secretaries

Silence, Authenticity, and Resistance in the Academy

Francine Banner, Pamela Aronson, Kathleen Darcy,
Maureen Linker, Jean-Carlos Lopez, and Lisa A. Martin

This chapter is a collective reflection by six faculty members at the University of Michigan–Dearborn who, since 2019, have been researching gender-based misconduct at the University of Michigan (UM). As we have been asking faculty and staff about workplace sexual harassment and gender discrimination, numerous accusations of misconduct by trusted authority figures at our university have come to light. These revelations have led to protests, public firings, and a multi-million-dollar settlement. They fostered an environment characterized by betrayal, uncertainty, and lack of trust. While our employer purported to promote a culture of respect, the people leading antiharassment efforts were themselves violating the policies they created.

Sara Ahmed invites us to join the feminist project of recording "complaint biographies" with the objective of creating a "complaint collective," a shared resource of not only what is spoken within institutions but also silences, times when complaints go unstated, or are not heard, ignored, or obstructed (*Complaint!* 285). In describing those entrusted with hearing and processing workplace complaints, Ahmed uses the word *secretary*, meaning "keeper of secrets" (294). She describes how secretaries can stall complaints by failing to move them forward, but also can be "saboteurs" who intimately know the institution and can apply that knowledge to subvert its processes (294). The term *secretary* reflects a gendered and racial division of labor; it is not the most privileged who are doing the heavy lifting in terms of creating safe and inclusive institutional cultures (294).

The reflections below highlight our position as secretaries—secret keepers—within the institution. Our research team is interdisciplinary, comprised of scholars in women's and gender studies, sociology, public health, philosophy, criminal justice, counseling, and law, and we are diverse in terms of gender, race, ethnicity, and sexual orientation. Two of us are untenured; three hold administrative appointments. Our reflections highlight how each of us has navigated the research process and our own careers, mindful that as feminist researchers we are situated as both part of, and in opposition to, the institution.

Being part of a complaint collective means not only documenting outcomes but showing the labor of what we do (Ahmed, *Complaint!* 278–79). The writing process for this chapter was iterative, attempting to consider the power relations inherent in our positions, incorporate our different lived experiences, and honor our personal intellectual autobiographies (Stanley & Wise 23). As a group, we exchanged stories of personal experiences. We then drew on our diverse disciplinary training to identify three themes in these narratives: silence, authenticity, and resistance. Our discussion of the first two themes is presented as a conversation among the authors. In addressing the final theme, resistance, we combine our reflections into one voice that explores the tensions inherent in being a feminist activist within the academy.

Silence

> The work of getting a complaint out . . . requires finding ways to enable what has been contained to spread. What is represented as an organic process is often dependent on political work. . . . The riskier it is to speak out, the more inventive we need to become.
>
> —Ahmed, *Complaint!*, 296

Lisa: In my work on abortion stigma, I spent years talking with providers about issues of safety and disclosure management—the mental and emotional gymnastics many abortion providers go through every time someone asks what they do for a living. I use the term *dangertalk* to refer to the self-censoring of authentic experiences that feels dangerous to a movement that providers support and love—with the understanding that the movement expects and sometimes demands such self-silencing (Martin et al.). Learning about these experiences has led me to reflect on times when I chose silence and times when silence was chosen for me.

Katie: I've heard survivors describe feeling empowered by breaking silence (for example, through litigation). This is especially powerful when people have been historically disempowered. In particular, survivors who have experienced sexual assault while incarcerated mention the silences that surround the abuse—ranging from those in power who turn a blind eye to peers who don't want to risk their own safety or see abuse as inevitable (Kubiak et al.).

Pam: As a researcher, I seek to bring these silences to light—to give space and to not make assumptions about what silence means. This approach gives power and claims power. Yet silence is sometimes used as a weapon against those who seek social change. I have seen projects that expose institutional inequalities pushed aside and those who speak out diminished by those in power. These instances make me question who gets to speak and under what conditions they are able to do so.

Maureen: In the academic workplace I see silence that harms and silence that helps. An example of silence that harms: A student employee reported to a staff member that they were made to feel unsafe by a faculty member. The staff member intervened on the student's behalf and met with the department chair. The chair, knowing that a case was already underway against the faculty member, took the report to higher ups but could not say more, since an investigation was going on. The student heard nothing back. They had no choice but to continue to engage with the faculty member. No one looped back as the case proceeded without them. A year and a half later the student found out the faculty member had "resigned."

Katie: I've seen silence wielded as a tool. If abuse is reported, despite policies to the contrary, administrators may purposely never update the survivor on the outcome of an internal investigation in hopes the issue will just drop. This is a denial of "informational justice": an aspect of organizational justice that is often overlooked in the research, but that survivors have no trouble identifying (Colquitt). These are not isolated cases; they are procedural decisions.

Francine: Policies around Title IX, COVID-19, and the Civil Rights Act inspire the creation of "cultures of documentation," which signal compliance with the law (Edelman 28; Ahmed xix). Eventually, the policies themselves become evidence that fairness and due process exist; when something goes wrong, we ask whether there was a policy in place instead of questioning whether that policy actually worked.

Jean Carlos: From a counseling perspective, I understand silence as an intervention that may help or harm, depending on how it is employed. Silence may be seen as opening the space for others to speak. However, we need to remain cognizant that the construction of contexts where those ranked lower in the hierarchy can freely speak *up* to power requires more than just space. It necessitates intentional engagement; otherwise it remains a mere facade.

Lisa: After we returned to campus during COVID-19, a student complained to university administration about a professor in my department who was encouraging mask wearing. As the department chair, I generally handle student complaints. However, in this case, the administrator spoke with the student, contacted the university's office of general counsel, and decided that the professor was in the wrong—all before speaking with me. What the administrator did not know, and failed to investigate, was that this student was asserting privilege over a faculty of color. This faculty member had been exposed to repeated attempts to undermine their status in the classroom, with students treating the faculty member with disdain and questioning their credentials and ability to teach. Although my dean and I were both livid, we decided that it was a better approach to quietly support the faculty member and resolve the situation and not amplify negative issues connected to this faculty member's name. On one hand, it was good that the issue was settled quickly and in a manner that did not cause reputational harm. On the other, when the institution continues to overlook the impact of complaints on faculty of color, isn't an intervention necessary for change to happen? This administrator to this day has no idea the amount of harm they inflicted, the hours of conversation, work, and, ultimately, resources that went to address her overstep.

Francine: This reminds me of Ahmed's identification of how frustration can be understood as a feminist record, and how documenting frustration is a feminist practice (*Complaint!* 7).

Maureen: I do have an example of silence that helped: when a new employee was hired, a senior staff member, a trusted person in the institution, began to act as a mentor to the new, younger employee. To the new employee, the senior staff member's assumption that he would mentor her felt predatory. The presumption of closeness seemed hostile, because the administrator didn't take steps to earn the new employee's trust or ask for her consent. The new employee disclosed what was going on to a different senior staff member but did not formally report it, because she did not want to be seen as "sensitive," and she wanted to build a case by gathering more information from coworkers. Eventually, staying silent in the short term wound up creating conditions that enabled the employee to gather relevant evidence. The senior staff member "retired early." There is never simply silence or nonsilence. Conversations, reporting, documenting, evidence gathering, dismissing, taking seriously, are all happening in different rooms. A lot of what I have seen in terms of the question of silence/harm/help has to do with assessing on a scale of "Can this person learn to do better?" on one end and "Needs to be fired," on the other.

Authenticity

> Trying to address an institutional problem often means inhabiting the institution all the more. . . . You learn about processes, procedures, policies, you point out what they fail to do, pointing to, pointing out; you fill in more and more forms, forms become norms, files become futures, filing cabinets, graves.
>
> —Ahmed, *Complaint!* 275–76

Pam: Although as a second-generation college professor I am an insider in many ways, I was almost locked out because of gender inequalities. I worked in temporary positions for seven years, through pregnancies, childbirth, nursing, raising children, following my husband's job opportunities, and living through my own career uncertainties. How could I as a woman, mother, and feminist get stuck in a "greedy institution" (Coser 4) that required so much of my energy, time, and devotion when family was important, too? To spend time with my kids, I turned down three tenure-track jobs to work as an underpaid temp with a hyped-up fancy title. When my husband's Army Reserve unit was mobilized during the Iraq War during my son's second week of life, gender inequalities in parenting also mobilized me (Aronson). When I was on a self-negotiated family leave, I revised an article during my son's infancy. The article, published by the skin of my teeth in a highly ranked journal, rescued me from staying an institutional outsider.

Jean-Carlos: I do not see reconciliation as a genuine option for BIPOC, particularly within predominantly White institutions. While the outward performance of the system may not be intentionally dismissive, discriminatory or prejudiced, an impasse remains. Inherently, even with an active desire for belonging (that is, engaging in a tenure process), I am uncertain there is a reciprocal effort being made by the institution to create the structures BIPOC faculty members need to succeed, to be welcomed in every room, and to know there is a seat at the table for us. In turn, the responsibility to oppose remains, for me, at the forefront even if such opposition results in my inability to become/perform/act as an embedded member of the institution.

Francine: I have come to understand that violence is continually being inflicted within and by institutions, even when individuals working within them have the best of intentions. Research shows that the longer a person is ingrained in an institutional setting, the more invested they will be in replicating and reinforcing institutional norms, even potentially harmful ones (Parsons & Priola). Ahmed talks about this as "institutional polishing." As academics achieve more security of position, we "tend to become more conservative and more willing to . . . play by the rules, make the institution look good" (Ahmed, "You Pose . . .").

Lisa: Fiona MacKay asks, "How do academic feminists experience being simultaneously the embodiment of institutional authority (to manage, regulate, quantify, monetize, and audit) as *managers*, as well as a source of oppositional knowledge as feminists? . . . What are the compromises or ambivalences required to work from the inside as a 'tempered radical' in the neoliberal university?" (75). For me, the compromise has been to normalize overwork and obscure the labor around my efforts to help the ease of entry of marginalized groups and knowledges into the academy, decolonize the curriculum, make low-profile service work typically undertaken by women faculty of color visible and counted, and advocate for standards of quality that reflect equality and inclusion in promotion, tenure, and merit review.

Pam: Patricia Hill Collins's "outsider within" framing, in which "marginality provides a distinctive angle of vision on the theories put forth by such intellectual communities," is relevant for thinking about the roles of feminist academics in the institution (12). Collins stresses the importance of creating a "viable culture of resistance" instead of turning "inward" and internalizing oppression (12). My own lived experiences have created my sense of opposition to institutional norms surrounding gender, race, and class inequalities; homosocial reproduction; and overwork. It is for these reasons that I have resisted becoming an administrator, even as people have encouraged me to do so. Ironically, my resistance has created more labor for me in the form of serving on leadership committees, mentoring students, and other women faculty, and researching inequalities.

Francine: I see my own career as a compilation of small resistances. I have declined some opportunities that might have advanced my status but would not reflect my personal values. I have tried not to be an active participant in oppression, but I have not been a whistleblower either. As I have moved from being a faculty member to being a department chair, I think a lot about how I can participate in repairing harm. I appreciate Danielle Sered's focus on shifting from a punitive model of justice to an accountability model that looks for ways we can identify and measure incremental change. I might not have control over the ultimate decision-making, but are there ways that I can hold institutional feet to the fire? What steps can I take to hold myself accountable in my research and workplace practices?

Lisa: As I move into academic leadership, my commitment to resistance from within the institution has meant that I have less time for scholarship, more time spent on the mundane. I can't predict that I'll successfully change the institution from within. What I hope is that through my leadership the institutional perspective shifts, and I can contribute policy and practices that make a difference—greater retention of diverse faculty and embedding antiracist and antisexist principles into the curriculum. I will certainly suffer criticism from friends and colleagues who see me as being absorbed by the institution—embodying it, rather than criticizing. But the impact of the environment on individuals is reciprocal in nature: while it may influence me, I am also influencing it.

Katie: I've been reflecting on my positionality and can see how my legal training has shaped my perspective on change. On the one hand, I understand why an organization might act in ways that prioritize preserving the brand, reducing liability, and promoting earning potential based on legal duties. However, I'm troubled that this outweighs other priorities. To reconceive reports of discrimination or sexual violence as having inherent value will take a major shift away from viewing them as litigation fodder and toward protecting the members that make up the organization. Without *people*, organizations would cease to exist, but somehow that fact has become lost.

Jean-Carlos: In order to climb up in the academic hierarchy you must show your willingness to uphold and serve the institution (not the self), but demonstrating this loyalty sits in direct opposition to a feminist performance. In order to prove devotion to the institution, one must compromise one's feminist values. While I do believe it is possible to negotiate rather than compromise these values, I would argue such negotiation estimates for net gains and losses within the system/stage where such performances take place. In other words, while one may hold feminist values, these may not necessarily be outwardly performed in lieu of the outward performance of deference to the institution, an act we are aware will enable upward movement.

Maureen: I have seen leaders who talk a good game but fail to see problems right in front of their noses. Or they see them and don't deal with them because "bad behavior" is a lot less pressing than shrinking enrollments, a nation divided over the worth of higher education, and a growing union movement. When the two spheres of influence—administrator and activist scholar—interact in the lived experience of feminist administrators, it can be overwhelming and isolating. I think the best days are when you can keep a certain set of values directly in sight and prioritize questions like: "How do I center the most vulnerable voices?"; "How do I minimize stress and mentally unhealthy conditions for the people working hardest (and for the least amount) in the organization?"; "How can I make space to learn more about those I hear from least?"

Jean-Carlos: I do wholeheartedly believe that transformation from the inside is possible. However, I do not believe transformation can occur from a singular variable but rather requires a combination of multiple internal forces marching along, in opposition to the established norms.

Resistance

> Complaints in pointing back can also point forward, to those who come after, who can receive something from you because of what you tried to do, even though you did not get through, even though all you seemed to do was scratch the surface.

> —Ahmed, *Complaint!*, pp. 299–300

UM's motto, "The leaders and best," comes from the university's fight song, "Hail to the Victors," written in 1898 after a football victory. In

2021, Michigan's football season culminated in a Big Ten championship win. As the team advanced, survivors of abuse by Dr. Robert Anderson, a former director of health services who allegedly sexually abused hundreds of student athletes, camped out on the president's lawn, handing out pins reading, "Hail to the Victims." That season encapsulated the tensions we feel as feminist academics at an institution that is set up to inspire not just compliance but devotion.

We are embedded within the institution, and we understand that through our labor we support, perpetuate, and socially reproduce it. As such, our research can never fully represent a way of "speaking out." Yet, we are simultaneously breaking norms as our research projects reveal previously unspoken traumas. For many of our research participants, it is the first time they have been involved in the process of having difficult, intentional conversations around gender-based misconduct and questioning their own roles as survivors and perpetrators.

When in focus groups we ask questions about one type of discrimination or harassment, the floodgates open, and we hear stories about so many other issues—ageism, homophobia, ableism, body shaming. Our study participants use many metaphors about speaking that are linked to the culture of the #MeToo movement, such as "speaking out," "giving voice," and "bringing experiences to light." These descriptions are contrasted with those of darkness, hiding, secrets, and silence. Ahmed writes, "Some of the words used to describe the complaint experience . . . are the same words used to describe intersectionality," which Kimberlé Crenshaw calls "a collision of traffic coming from many different directions. . . . You cannot always tell who or what determines the crash" (Ahmed, *Complaint!*, p. 24; Crenshaw, p. 129). We look for complex networks of connection that enabled the abuse. Feminist research has the potential to reveal these interconnections.

In our careers, we experience this same collision between upholding our values, creating social change, and working both within and against the institution. Personal values often conflict with institutional objectives. We are required to continually evaluate others: students, colleagues, staff, and administrators. Evaluating the work of students and colleagues prioritizes gatekeeping, criticism, and critique over supporting and championing. The higher up we move within the institution, the more beholden we become to the brand. Excavating secrets and honoring them, in terms of content and culture, is critical. There is a joy in this work in terms of the community and humanity it generates, even while the stories with which we are entrusted can be traumatic and traumatizing.

Feminist research—not just our team's research project, but more generally—has the potential to expose connections we did not see before between structure and behavior. Over the past few decades, societal understandings of violence, harm, and injury have expanded. Many people today identify violence not just as physical and interpersonal but emotional and structural. It used to be that the identification of a perpetrator was the end of the story. Now it is the beginning.

Institutions are not keenly interested in redesigning the social order, as doing so necessarily produces vulnerability and discomfort. However, organizational cultures are not static. The development of institutional memory and practice is a continual process in which members, including us, engage. Our research is an attempt to include and amplify more voices, even if such a decision creates uneven, loud, or undesirable noise. As feminist secretaries we continually strategize as to how to present new knowledge in a way that can be understood by and is useful to the organization, for example, contributing our data to the development of training and diversity efforts or seeking out high-profile research grants. Capital remains the motor that keeps the system running smoothly. We engage the language of neoliberalism to convince the institution to engage with new knowledge in a way that produces change. At the same time, we attempt to be role models for others: to give voice to marginalized people, to push for changes from the inside, and to uphold feminist values in the work we do. We nurture our feminist networks, having people inside and outside of the institution to check in with and help identify opportunities where we can push for change.

We hope we are capable of transformation from the inside, although we question if there is a possibility of separation. Can we be *of* the institution, not *be* the institution? Our experiences have shown us that what might look like silence from the outside is not always silence. We strategically make ourselves heard through constant pressure, like a thorn. We will continue to try to navigate these tensions, expose silences, and elevate voices in our role as feminist secretaries in the hope that we are effecting lasting and radical change.

Works Cited

Ahmed, Sara. *Complaint!* Duke UP, 2021.

———. "You Pose a Problem: A Conversation with Sara Ahmed" by Maya Binyam. *The Paris Review*, 14 January, 2022. https://www.theparisreview.org/blog/2022/01/14/you-pose-a-problem-a-conversation-with-sara-ahmed/.

Aronson, Pamela. "'Iraq Is a Small Purple Planet': Feminist Mothering during Wartime." *Journal of the Association for Research on Mothering*, vol. 8, no's. 1 and 2, Summer, 2016, pp. 157–70.

Collins, Patricia Hill. *Black Feminist Thought: Knowledge, Consciousness, and the Politics of Empowerment*. Routledge, 1991.

Colquitt, Jason A. "On the Dimensionality of Organizational Justice: A Construct Validation of a Measure." *Journal of Applied Psychology*, vol. 86, no. 3, 2001, pp. 386–400.

Coser, Lewis A. *Greedy Institutions: Patterns of Undivided Commitment*. The Free Press, 1974.

Crenshaw, Kimberlé. "Demarginalizing the Intersection of Race and Sex: A Black Feminist Critique of Antidiscrimination Doctrine, Feminist Theory and Antiracist Politics." *University of Chicago Legal Forum*, vol. 1989, no. 1, article 8, pp. 139-67.

Edelman, Lauren B. *Working Law: Courts, Corporations, and Symbolic Civil Rights*. U of Chicago P, 2016.

Kubiak, Sheryl, et al. "Processes and Practices Associated with Reporting and Investigation of Sexual Misconduct within Prison: A Novel Case Study Constructed Through Litigation Documents." *Criminal Justice Policy Review*, vol. 31, no. 2, 2020, pp. 182–205.

MacKay, Fiona. "Dilemmas of an Academic Feminist as Manager in the Neoliberal Academy: Negotiating Institutional Authority, Oppositional Knowledge and Change." *Political Studies Review*, vol. 19, no. 1, 2020, pp. 75–95.

Parsons, Elizabeth and Vincenza Priola. "Agents for Change and Changed Agents: The Micro-politics of Change and Feminism in the Academy." *Gender, Work, and Organization*, vol. 20, no. 5, 2013, pp. 580–98.

Sered, Danielle. *Until We Reckon*. The New Press, 2021.

Stanley, Liz and Sue Wise. "Method, Methodology, and Epistemology in Feminist Research Processes." *Feminist Praxis: Research, Theory and Epistemology in Feminist Sociology*, edited by Liz Stanley, Routledge, 1990, pp. 20–60.

23

It Is Better to Speak

A Complaint Collective

Lori Wright, Neisha Ginae Wiley,
Elizabeth VanWassenhove, Brandelyn Tosolt,
Rae Loftis, and Meg L. Hensley

Complaint activism might describe a stance or a style, a willingness to fight back, to fight for more, whatever the costs, whether or not you get through. Not getting through does not mean not getting somewhere. This also means that getting somewhere is not always about getting through. Complaint activism is a way of thinking about what we get from complaint even when we do not get through. To complain is also to create a record. Remember: you have to record what you do not want to reproduce. If you record what you do not want to reproduce, that record exists even if what is reproduced is still reproduced.

—Sara Ahmed, *Complaint!*

We are complainers, proudly, fearfully, exhaustedly so.

We did not set out to be complainers.

We had lived our lives performing niceness in an attempt to avoid being accused of being complainers.

Not complaining was killing us.

Our bodies ached. Our emotions flared. Our rage drove our decisions. Our tears could not fall.

Complaining saved us. Harmed us.

The story we share in this article, a specific incident of gendered abuse in the academy, was first documented in a collaborative dissertation written by five women and supervised by a sixth woman at a midsize public university as a part of the requirements for a doctorate in educational leadership. The group included cisgender women who identified as straight and queer, Black and White, and Christian and atheist, among other social identities. In this collaborative dissertation, we used critical autoethnography to chart our two-year journey toward building feminist sisterhood between Black women and White women. Central to this journey and our process was describing the ways we enacted feminist leadership in the academy. The story below is a story of enacting feminist leadership through complaint activism (Ahmed *Complaint!*), pushing against the institutional silencing that is done to women who report abuse.

Becoming a Collective

During our process of writing this collaborative dissertation, relational lines were blurred between us as early and established scholars, doctoral students, faculty, and colleagues, a line-blurring made more complicated by our uncovering of feminisms in action and in relationship. One example of the blurred lines that developed through our collaboration was Brandelyn's role as the chair of the dissertation. The dissertation emerged from a class that Brandelyn taught; in that class, she was a facilitator of learning and also a colearner (hooks). That relationship continued to evolve and Brandelyn occupied a space of tension. Institutionally and hierarchically, she was in the position to approve or reject the contributions made by the five dissertation authors. Relationally, she was a participant in consciousness raising and a coconspirator (Love) for much of the dissertation, including the story that is the focus of this article. The institutional barricade separating five scholars and one professor/dissertation chair served as an additional form of institutional silencing in our story.

Naming Abuse

Like Sara Ahmed's, our story is "part of a much longer and more complicated story, a story of a person, a story of an institution, a story of relationships between persons and institutions" (Ahmed *Complaint!* 9). One of our documented practices for building feminist sisterhood as women across difference was to share our anger and rage in solidarity at the oppression we experienced as individuals and as a collective. We discovered through our shared readings, consciousness-raising conversations, and collaborative writing that each of us had experiences (new and old) of abuse. As Sara Ahmed reminds us, "Feminism [is] how we survive the consequences of what we come up against by offering new ways of understanding what we come up against" (*Living a Feminist Life*, 22). We recognize(d)[1] that, while our persons and experiences are distinct, we all have experiences of being unheard, silenced, harmed, violated, taken advantage of, and impacted by lenses of intersecting bias within and outside the walls of our institutions. We had varying responses to those abuses, but for each of us, we were initially frozen by a variety of factors that prevented us from reporting our respective abuses. Some of us experienced strong emotions of shame, fear, blame, self-doubt, and guilt. Our inaction was informed by past experiences in which we were disbelieved, leading to a lack of trust in reporting systems and a lack of belief that justice was possible. Very tangible constraints, such as fear of losing one's job; family, time, and energy limitations; and the potential loss of both privacy and relationships with others also kept us quiet. Too many targets of abuse experience these consequences, thus these fears were and are very real. As we processed these experiences while building and within feminist sisterhood, we recognized that our fear and the consequences were all part of the same patriarchal systems. We recognized that feminism gave us a choice to report or not report and an understanding of why we would choose to report or not report. Learning about, through, and within feminism gave us new language and context to understand our experiences of abuse—within and outside of the academy—while also emboldening us as individuals and as a collective of six women to speak up and challenge abuse when we experienced and/or witnessed it. In feminist sisterhood and in this time, we were informed by Audre Lorde's words in "Litany for Survival."

> . . . and when we speak we are afraid
> our words will not be heard
> nor welcomed
> but when we are silent
> we are still afraid

> So it is better to speak
> remembering
> we were never meant to survive.

Whether we spoke or didn't speak, fear was inevitable. With both fear of significant consequences and fear of not being heard or believed, we decided, "it is better to speak."

It was not individual courage or choice alone that moved us each to reporting our respective abuses. When we talked about our situations with trusted others, we were affirmed in our need to report. When we saw others being abused in similar ways to how we'd been abused, we were moved to report. When those with whom we were in relationship reported their abuse, we were moved to report our own abuse. Our fear of someone else experiencing what we'd experienced moved us to report. In each of these instances, we reported our abuses, even while knowing that the likelihood of a just outcome was low and that, as Lorde writes, "we were never meant to survive." We chose to suspend our disbelief and hope for justice this time.

In reporting our abuse, none of the fears or constraints dissipated. We continued to feel terrified, sometimes determined, even as we also felt some measure of relief and power in breaking our silences. We could feel the adrenaline surging through our bodies. At the same time, we felt judged and invalidated, sometimes angry and betrayed. We experienced episodes of denial and self-doubt.

After reporting, we experienced a wide range of emotions. We felt exhausted, anxious, and sad. We simultaneously felt proud, energized, accomplished, and righteous. We hoped that there would be accountability. While we felt less burdened, the shift was unexpectedly anticlimactic and we felt disappointed. We felt jaded and that nothing would actually change, that the risk we took was not worth it. Most of all, we felt done.

Our journey toward feminism is inextricable from our story(ies) of gendered abuse in the academy. We could not have moved forward with this particular complaint alone; for us, because of our circumstances, trauma responses, and because of the minimal power we held individually within the institution, we needed a method of collective action. Sara Ahmed states, "A collective can be what you need for violence to be *witnessed* by others. A collective can be what you need to *withstand* this violence" (*Complaint!* 281). As we reflect on the abuses we have reported, we notice that with just a few exceptions, our reporting experiences have been informed by the support and solidarity of complaint supporters (Ahmed *Complaint!*), by the power of the collective.

The collective to which we refer goes beyond those who directly experience abuse. "Complaint activists can thus also be understood as *complaint supporters*; you not only work with each other, but in working together, in pooling your resources, you are also more able to give advice and practical support to those who are making complaints" (Ahmed *Complaint!* 285). If given the choice, we would choose reporting experiences with the solidarity and support of others over reporting experiences in isolation from others. You may be someone who, like each of us, has experienced abuse inside and beyond the academy. You may be someone who, as Ahmed suggests, is a complaint activist without having been the target of the abuse. We invite you—the reader—into the complaint collective. We welcome everyone who reads this, everyone who has a story they can tell, into our complaint collective.

A Monument

> Complaint activism is not simply about using formal complaints procedures to press against institutions, although it involves that. It is also about taking complaints out, making complaints across different sites: the walls, the committees, the classrooms, the dissertations. Complaints can be expressed queerly, coming out all over the place.
> Complaints can be sneaky as well as leaky.
>
> —Ahmed, *Complaint!*

While the specifics of the abuses each of the authors of this paper have dealt with are different, the helplessness and anger we have each experienced during the abuse, but most maddeningly, in attempting to seek justice, are the same. In turn, what we've each experienced individually is the same story with different characters and settings. Similarly, the story that appears below is a specific story. While you cannot read it, if you have experienced and reported gendered abuse during your life, you already know, intimately, deeply and painfully, what lies beneath the black lines. The mostly redacted text below is a monument to the all-too-familiar dismissal and silencing of folx when they report sexual harassment and to the power we (re)claimed in the process.

The redaction of the text serves three purposes. The first is practical. We were advised by legal consultants to remove any identifying information of the people involved. Though aliases could have been used to anonymize the harmer, the intimacy of the overall dissertation could have compromised the story's anonymity and further harmed the authors. The authors weighed the consequences of defying the legal advice and including the story anyway; it was a brilliant example of enacting feminist leadership that had only become possible through the journey charted in the dissertation. Brandelyn suggested the use of blackout poetry (a form of poetry made by redacting most of the words on a page and leaving behind only the words that form the poem). Using blackout poetry would allow us to tell the full, unaltered story, while also protecting the authors from further harm. This choice is undoubtedly familiar to anyone who has practiced complaint. Thus, the redacted text serves its second purpose: to challenge the silencing suggested by our legal advisers and upheld by institutional authorities, by including the story, unaltered and fully truthful. Finally, the third purpose of the redacted story is that, in redacting it, we also transform it into everyone's story.

REDACTED STORY

We

were

afraid, and

we

did it anyway.

This story is still ongoing.

Note

1. We specifically reject the chronological distinction between past and present, as we know that our understanding of anything is necessarily always evolving.

Works Cited

Ahmed, Sara. *Complaint!* Duke UP, 2021.
———. *Living a Feminist Life*. Duke UP, 2017.
hooks, bell. *Teaching to Transgress: Education as the Practice of Freedom*. Routledge, 1994.
Lorde, Audre. "A Litany for Survival." *The Collected Poems of Audre Lorde*. W. W. Norton, 1997, p. 255.
Love, Bettina L. *We Want to Do More Than Survive: Abolitionist Teaching and the Pursuit of Educational Freedom*. Beacon, 2019.

Afterword

"Heard as a Broken Record"

Sara Ahmed

A book can be a collection of complaints. A book can be a complaint collective. In their introduction to *Broken Record*, Mary K. Holland, Carrie Rohman, and Carlyn Ferrari offer a hope that it "will operate as its own complaint collective, by bringing together the complaints of a diverse group of people, and by providing a platform for the voices of these complaint collectives whose work had already begun." Reading through this collection, this collective, I was reminded why sharing our stories of complaint matters even when, or perhaps because, we have shared these stories many times before. When you make a complaint, you are usually asked to explain what happened that led you to complain—and you might have to keep giving that explanation over and over again to the different people tasked by your organization to receive complaints. A complaint can then also be an accumulation of stories we have to keep telling. As an anonymous contributor to this book describes, "During that period, I had to tell my story in detail numerous times, which was retraumatizing."

When we use the institution's own forms to address gendered abuse, the institution becomes the addressee. It is not surprising, then, that making a formal complaint can feel like talking to a brick wall. It makes such a difference to *change the structure of address*, to address our stories to those who recognize what we are going through because of what they have been through. This does not mean we will suddenly feel freed by the story. I sympathize with Sarah Cheshire when she writes, "Quite frankly, I'm tired of telling my story. I'm tired of watching the stories of other survivors get voyeuristically consumed and exploited for outside gain, only for abusive men to retain their power at the end of the day. I'm tired of being called *brave* while fighting tooth and nail for the resources necessary to survive and heal." That we have to keep telling the story can be a sign of how little has changed.

Even when we are tired of telling our stories of complaint, sharing them can be how we avoid being stuck with them. One academic wrote to me, "I want my complaint to go somewhere other than round and round in my head." When our complaints go round and round in our heads, it is a lot of movement not to get very far. We need to give complaints somewhere else to go. I call the action of giving complaints somewhere else to go "becoming a feminist ear."

It can be a relief to be on the receiving end, to listen to other people's complaints. More than a relief: a handle. Some responses to my book *Complaint!* (2021) have brought home to me why hearing about other people's complaints helps us to handle our own. These responses are in part why I am now writing *A Complainer's Handbook* (I think of a handbook as a hand as well as a handle). One person wrote, "[It] makes me (and probably a gazillion other people, sadly) feel as if you've been listening at my door/reading my texts/being copied on the email I sent, gosh, just this morning, to say, 'Uh, the guy I've been reporting for the past six years is still at it, surprise.'" It can help to know that our complaints are not so singular. Otherwise, it is hard not to feel that we are the problem, that the same things keep happening because we are making them happen. Another person wrote to me, "I thought that I had had a unique experience. It's so therapeutic to know what I experienced is real—that it actually happens to other people . . . that it wasn't just in my head. But! it's also infuriating that my experience is generalizable and it feels—I'm not sure what the right word is—disillusioned as hell that I'd never heard about this happening to other people." It helps to know that the problems you are having are not mental, "just in my head." That's how reality can be therapy.

Even when it helps to know that other people share our experiences of complaint, it can still be hard to hear. And we might end up disillusioned, or *more* disillusioned, with institutions when we hear about all the complaints we had not heard about. That we *didn't know* the continuity of other people's complaints with our own is why we need to share our stories. After all, complaints are mostly made behind closed doors. The expression "behind closed doors" can refer to the actual doors that might need to be closed before someone can share information in confidence. It can also be used to signal how information is kept secret from a public. Becoming a feminist ear means putting our ear to the door. That's how we end up *overhearing* so much ("as if you have been listening at my door"), bringing out what mostly works by being inaudible. And, that is why the collective labor of *Broken Record*, so painstaking, is also so precious, *for what it brings out*.

Labor is a lead. Complaints, however laborious, can lead us to other people, to make new connections. I think of a conversation I had with an early-career academic. She was returning from long-term sick leave. She was not given the time she needed to return to work, so she could do her work. She told me that if she hadn't complained she "wouldn't have realized that I was not the only one." She added, "It was quite amazing actually to find that in my department there were more than a handful of staff who were there complaining about the same people about the same issues but all of us were doing it not in silence but in an atomized way, so that none of us knew actually that we were all having similar problems and were making similar complaints."

When we use words like *atomize* to describe the complaint process, we resist that process. Although complaints procedures are often isolating, designed to make us smaller by keeping us apart, the very labor of complaint, the requirement to speak to different people from different offices or units, is how we identify similarities in our experiences: *similar complaints, similar problems*. When a complaint leads us to become conscious of the institutional effort to separate us from others, that consciousness is achieved because the efforts fail. As Lidia M. V. Possas and M. Emilia Barbosa note, we form complaint collectives when those in power do not "see the need for them to exist." Complaint collectives, once formed, provide evidence of their necessity.

And when such collectives are formed, there is so much more we can do. I joined a collective created by students back in 2013. They had begun working together much earlier, to address the problem of sexual harassment in their department. The students had already tried to hold the institution to account. They had combined their knowledge and experience to give the institution an account of itself, an account of what had been going on and why it was wrong. The institution did not recognize their account as a complaint, claiming that it needed to come *from* named individuals and be *about* named individuals before they could take action.

It was because of how harassment had been institutionalized that students did not want to give complaints in that form. To name themselves would be to make themselves vulnerable to retaliation, to name an individual as perpetrator would make the problem individual not institutional. The violence that complaints are made to address can be repeated in the requirement to give them a certain form. We pushed for those require-ments to be loosened. And when they were, many more students came forward to testify in the inquiries.

Students created that collective. They led the way. That is why I invited the students I worked with—Leila Whitley, Tiffany Page, Alice Corble, Chryssa Sdrolia, and Heidi Hasbrouck—as well as others who needed to remain anonymous, to write one of the conclusions of *Complaint!* I did not want to tell their story. It was their story to tell. As they describe in their contribution, "These complaints often did not sound like us: we had such a narrow channel in which to describe what happened to us, what it meant, and what it did" (268). To make the complaints, to hold the institution to account, meant being channeled in a certain direction by the institution. Holland, Rohman, and Ferrari's description of institutional routes for complaint as "choking channels" is exact.

Perhaps the more chance you have of getting a complaint through, the less the complaint sounds like you. Still, the complaint was *theirs*. As they write, "there is no one story of how our collective came together" (260). They show how their collective came into existence slowly, but also how they were a collective "long before we realized it" (260). Each per-son has their own story, a collective is how you bring them together. By coming together, those actions acquired a different meaning, "We never stopped talking to each other about what was happening. Over the years we collected each other's stories" (263). To collect stories was also to look after each other. They write that "collectivity was a way to share the costs of complaint" (266), and that "care was always prioritized over complaint work" (267). Bringing our complaints together is such an important act because we lessen the burden when we share it. When there are more people doing the work, each person carries less weight.

But the weight can still be wearing. To complain within an institu-tion about the institution—its role in enabling gendered and sexualized abuses of power—is to come up against the institution. The students, by combining their resources, "moved something" (273). I learned from them how moving something can mean to move so much and how it can take so much. As we have been hearing throughout *Broken Record* too, what comes back when you complain can be a repetition of the violence that led you to complain. A collective can be what you need for violence to be *witnessed* by others. A collective can be what you need to *withstand* this violence. The more force applied to stop a complaint from being made, *the more we need more*, more people, more complainers, to witness and withstand that force.

The more we need more is key to what I mean by "complaint as feminist pedagogy," my handle for the project. It is not simply that we see more by seeing together (though that is true). Nor is it simply that we create a more accurate portrait of institutions by bringing out what they obscure (although that is also true). It is that, as Holland, Rohman, and Ferrari describe in their introduction, we "theorize resistance and change out of our own experience." In the process of trying to redress problems, we come up with new terms and concepts to explain what we are doing. A concept is often understood as something abstract, what we drag away from a concrete situation through mental labor. In *Living a Feminist Life* (2017), thinking about Audre Lorde's work, I described concepts as *sweaty*, created by physical as well as mental labor, from the effort to make sense of a world that does not give us room or from the effort to make more room for ourselves.

Many of the terms and concepts I've introduced in recent work have come from listening to other people talk about the work of complaint. This is certainly the case for the term "complaint collective," *a sweaty term for sweaty work*. When we were working as a collective, we did not call ourselves a "complaint collective." That term came to me as I was listening to another student talk about how she worked as a member of a group. Hearing from other collectives is how I learned something about our own. That term, which came *from* other feminists, goes out *to* other feminists, as a way of communicating something about our shared struggles. Another term that arrived in a similar way is "complaint activism." That was the term that came to mind as a student was reflecting on her experience of complaining about disability discrimination. She said, "That's the nutshell of my complaint experiences: the things I have found not helpful are long complaint processes, writing letters and asking nicely and doing things for no pay. I don't do that anymore." I responded, "It almost sounds like you have a style of 'complaint activism,' is that how you would describe it?" She answered, "Yes, it is how I would I describe it."

Once I had the term *complaint activism*, it helped me to hear something in other people's stories that I might not have otherwise heard. There are reasons the word *activism* might not be the first word we think of in relation to complaint. Activism sounds powerful—the work of refusing, intervening, protesting, marching, combining our forces, our energies. Activism sounds hopeful—you work harder for change when you believe it is possible as well as necessary. The term *complaint activism* helped me realize how complaints are politicizing, not so much because of what they do, but because of what they don't do. Many of the stories shared in *Complaint!*, and also in *Broken Record*, seem to be about pushing very hard not to get very far. You might imagine that to complain would be to be left rather despondent and discouraged. That might certainly be true for some people. It was not true for me. Leaving my institution and listening to those who complained in theirs gave me a sharper sense of the point and purpose of the work. I left fighting. I am left fighting. It was also not true for others including many of the contributors of this book, with their fighting words and "poisonous pens," to evoke the contribution by Alison Vogelaar. We can hear the intimacy of exhaustion and fight in the contribution "It Is Better to Speak," by Lori Wright, Neisha Wiley, Elizabeth VanWassenhove, Brandelyn Tosolt, Rachel Loftis, and Megan Hensley. They write, "We are complainers, proudly, fearfully, exhaustedly so. We did not set out to be complainers." To be complainers, even if that is what we set out to be, is how we repurpose our exhaustion. We are willing to chip away at the walls of institutions, to be there, in the wear and the tear, for as long as it takes.

Of course, to do this kind of institutional work, wearing work, weary work, has consequences. When we keep pointing out problems, we become problems. In *Complaint!*, I suggested that we are "heard as a broken record, stuck on the same point." In *The Feminist Killjoy Handbook*, I turned that sore point into a **killjoy truth**, written in bold, a hard-worn wisdom. **We have to keep saying it because they keep doing it.** When we are heard as repeating ourselves, what is not being addressed is what we are speaking of, what they keep doing, what keeps happening, the same patterns, the structures. Many years ago, a diversity practitioner based in the UK had described her job as a "banging a head in the wall job." A job description as a wall description. I heard so much history in that wall, history as repetition. It is not just that the same things keep happening *but that we encounter the same things when we try to stop them from happening.*

When the wall keeps its place, it is you that gets sore. What happens to the wall? All you seem to have done is scratched the surface. Scratching gives you a sense of the limits of what you can accomplish. When

I think of limits, I think back to why I resigned—leaving not just my post but my profession. After three years, we could not even get a public acknowledgment that the inquiries into sexual harassment had happened let alone a discussion of why they had happened. It was like they had not happened, which was, I rather imagine, the effect they were looking for. *Silence was the wall.* I shared my reasons for resigning on my feminist killjoy blog because I could not resign in silence if I was resigning to protesting silence. And I became a feminist killjoy all over again. The university quickly launched a public relations campaign: "We take sexual harassment very seriously and take action against those found to be acting in ways incompatible with our strong values relating to equality, diversity and inclusion." If any of this had been even remotely true, I would not have had to resign.

I expected this reaction. What was unexpected was the reaction of some feminist colleagues. One colleague told me my action was "against the interest of many long-standing feminist colleagues who have worked to ensure a happy and stimulating environment." We need to learn from how the disclosure of sexual harassment can be treated as compromising not just the institution's happiness but feminist happiness. She also called my action "unprofessional." I have been calling myself an unprofessional feminist ever since!

Becoming professional is about being willing to keep the institution's secrets, to treat complaints as dust or damage, to be wiped away, or dealt with in house. In house, the master's house. Audre Lorde told us this would happen. She said that those who are resourced only by the master's house would find those who try to dismantle it, or those who even question what he does in there, "threatening" (1984, 112). We need to know that silence is not just something enforced by management or marketing departments, silence can be performed as institutional loyalty, even feminist loyalty, silence to protect important people, silence to protect resources, silence to protect reputation, silence as promotion, how you maximize your chances of going further or getting more from the institution. **What you are told you need to do to go further or faster in a system reproduces the system.** I have written this sentence in bold because it's another **killjoy truth**.

It is hard to challenge power because of how it works. If you say no, you end up with nowhere to go. If you say yes, you are more likely to progress. I think of a conversation I had with a woman of color. She had experienced bullying and harassment in her department. She told me how she was not supported by a senior white feminist professor who was head of another department. She said, "It's easy to be radical on paper but in reality, it's quite different. Her politics were to do with advancing her career and nothing to do with changing the landscape for women." Maybe the door is open to some of us on condition we shut it behind us. Shutting the door can be about stopping other people from getting in, or not supporting them so they can get in. Shutting the door is how violence remains unseen.

That's why there are so many doors in stories of complaint. It is not just that complaints happen behind doors but that when you complain, doors are shut. I think of one student who complained about harassment and bullying by the most senior professor in her department. She was warned, "Be careful—he is an important man." She did not heed the warning. This student had hoped to go on to do a PhD. But she said, "that door is closed." No becomes a door. When no is a door, the violence remains behind closed doors. It takes a political movement to open these doors. We are that movement.

Making a complaint public can be how we open a door. I noted earlier that when I shared my reasons for resigning in public, my action was treated by the institution and some colleagues as damaging. That was not the most important consequence. I began to receive messages from many different people all over the world telling me about what happened when they complained. I heard from other people who had left their posts and professions as a result of a complaint. One story coming out leads to more stories coming out. Just create a small opening, and so much will come out of those institutional closets we sometimes call filing cabinets. That's why the work of feminist secretaries matters so much, those who try to transform institutions from the inside, becoming "thorns" in the side, as Francine Banner, Pamela Aronson, Kathleen Darcy, Maureen Linker, Jean-Carlos Lopez, and Lisa Martin describe. The word *secretary* derives from *secrets*; the secretary is a keeper of secrets. Feminist secretaries can use their knowledge of what is in the file to get it out.

Let me share one such story from my research. The student who inspired the term *complaint activist* was not getting anywhere with her complaint. She had a particularly difficult meeting; a meeting when she felt that wall coming down. After the meeting, a file suddenly appeared: "A load of documents turned up on the students' union fax machine, and we don't know where they came from. They were historical documents about students who had to leave." The documents included a handwritten letter to a human rights charity by a former student who had cancer and who was trying to get the university to let her finish her degree part-time. She speculated that the file "came from someone in admin who cared about it for some personal reason, like they are disabled, their kid is disabled, and decided to carry [out] their own little bit of direct action." A secretary as saboteur, giving support to the student they were probably instructed not to give, by refusing to keep the institution's secrets.

Why did it matter, what did it do, for that file to be pulled out? Reading about past complaints helped the student know she was not alone. That the documents included a handwritten letter made the connection even more personal; she was given companions. She became part of a complaint collective. And so, we learn: complaint collectives do not always assemble in the same time and place. Complaint collectives are a way of thinking about the history of feminist activism, how we can inherit past actions, including those we learn about and those we don't.

To complain is to *lift the lid*, to let other complaints, earlier complaints, out. Who knows what (or who) might yet come out. There are many different ways that complaints end up in containers. We too, can become containers. I remember an informal conversation I had with a woman professor who said she put experiences of misogyny and heterosexism in a file she called "don't go there." Sometimes, we file away what is hardest to handle. That file is full: we don't go there because of where we have been. So, the task then is to find ways to express our complaints, to get them out of ourselves, as well as out of institutions. To get them *out* is to get them *to* others.

Sometimes, we have to be inventive, to find other ways to express our complaints so they can be released from their containers, as the final chapter of this book with its use of blackout poetry shows. Creativity is another connection. I sometimes use a picture of messy lines to describe what a complaint looks like from the complainer's point of view. It is a mess. The more you don't get through, the more you have to do. But think of this. Each line might be a conversation, one that you had to have, a conversation that can open a door, just a little, just enough, so that someone else can hear something, can enter somewhere. Each line might be time, the time it takes to get somewhere, time as a queer line, going round and about as how you find things out. Each line might be a path, the places you go, the unlit rooms, the shadows, the doorways, a line as a leap, who you find on your way there. Each line might take you back, a line as a loop, going over what is not over, how you hear of others who complained before. Each line can be thrown forward, a line as a lead, throwing something out that can be picked up by others, who can do something because of what you tried to do, even when you did not get through, even when you just scratch the surface. Those scratches that seem to convey the limits of what we can accomplish can be what we leave behind. What we leave behind, others may yet find.

The message is hopeful and hard. Yes: there is still so much work to do. Yes: we have to keep saying it because they keep doing it. Yes: the need to repeat ourselves can be tiring, frustrating. That is why we need to *say it more* and for *more to say it*. Making the same points is how we share the labor. I am grateful for this book. And for that labor.

Works Cited

Ahmed, Sara. *Living a Feminist Life*. Duke UP, 2017.
———. *Complaint!* Duke UP, 2021.
Lorde, Audre. *Sister Outsider: Essays and Speeches*. Crossing Press, 1984.
Whitley, Leila, et al., "Collective Conclusions," in *Complaint!*, Duke UP, pp. 261–73.

Acknowledgments

Mary: *Broken Record* is the direct result of many powerful feminist acts, large and small. First, my thanks to my friend and colleague, Vicki Tromanhauser, who recognized the research interests and life experiences I share with Carrie and connected us through a fateful Zoom meeting, sparking the idea for this book. Carlyn took a risk in joining the project, despite having good reasons not to—some of which she documents in her chapter in this book—for which I am enormously grateful. Her knowledge and perspective have shaped the project in crucial ways, making it stronger and wiser than it would have otherwise been. I am so thankful for all I have learned from both of my coeditors, and for the camaraderie of our "coven" through the various challenges of this incredibly moving project, and through all that happened alongside it. Thanks as well to SUNY New Paltz for the semester of sabbatical leave that created the moment of calm in my otherwise overfull professional life, in which the idea of a project like this could even arise.

Carrie: I would like to acknowledge a profound debt of gratitude to Benjamin Hagen, who collaborated to support my 2021 keynote address on gendered abuse in academia at the 30th Annual International Conference on Virginia Woolf, which he organized. Without his courageous work—and introductions that followed through the generosity of Vicki Tromanhauser—this volume would have never emerged. Mary's courageous ask, should we do this together? and Carlyn's courageous yes, to being an editor, brought forth a project that I could not have considered without them. Working alongside both of them has been extremely clarifying and sustaining; their insights, hard work, compassion, and determination helped elevate this project, which was always going to be painful, to something that was also transformative. Our contributors' bravery, vulnerability, acute clarity, and hope for change is humbling and inspiring. Reading and supporting their work made me realize even more poignantly how much *has to change* in our broken profession. I would also like to thank colleagues and friends who have been supportive throughout my own ongoing experiences of gendered abuse in academia. None of it has been easy, but being seen and heard helps one endure: thank you Amanda Anderson, Katie Arnold, Steven Belletto, Robert Blunt, Karen Carcia, Paul Cefalu, Rose Charles, Devon Clifton, Peter Adkins, Kristin Czarnecki, Prince Cunningham, Erica Delsandro, Kristin Garbarino, Dale Gilmore and Gera Summerford, David Herman, Catherine Hollis, Rebekah Pite, Lauren Kindle, Erin Kingsley, Amanda Melhem, Megan Quigley, Nandini Sikand, Jennifer Talarico, Jim Toia, Tom Tyler, Lee Upton and Eric Ziolkowski, Rodney Weems and Kathleen Weems, and Cary Wolfe. Finally, to my husband, Ernie, and our son, Gavin—you are the most impacted witnesses of my experiences in academia. On some level, you share those experiences. Your unwavering acceptance, love, and support have kept me going, and I am beyond grateful.

Carlyn: I'm grateful to my coeditors for their collaboration, generosity, and empathy. *Broken Record* is one of the most taxing projects I have been a part of, but working alongside Mary and Carrie was refreshing, inspiring, and a reminder that academic spaces don't have to be soul-crushing and isolating. When I received the invitation from Mary to participate in this project, my instinct was to decline. I did not want to offer my pain for consumption—again. I revisited past traumas and wounds to write my essay, and it was excruciating. But I realized that this project was not just about me. Our contributors had stories they wanted and needed to tell, and I'm incredibly grateful to them for trusting us with their stories and for writing with such vulnerability, honesty, and insight. It is because of them that I agreed to do this project. I end my essay in this volume on an ambivalent note, hoping that one day the pain—*the blood*—I share will be enough. I want to extend this sentiment and say I hope our contributors' essays are *more than enough* to take abuse in academia seriously. With this wish in mind, I extend my gratitude to anyone reading this book with the desire to not only bear witness to these narratives but also contribute to the *structural change* that academic institutions so desperately need. I'm grateful for the invitation I received to coedit this book, but I don't want to do this again. I don't want anyone to do it again. Make it stop.

All: The three of us are deeply grateful to our contributors, whose fortitude in telling their stories we admire as much as we value the wisdom with which they examine their experiences. Working together as a massive collective has been an enormous honor. Their suffering drives us to continue our work; their resilience inspires us to keep our heads up as we do. Thanks to Erica Delsandro for being an early reader of the Introduction, and many thanks to Rebecca Colesworthy at SUNY Press, who recognized the value of this project and delivered it to the world.

Finally, we give our profound thanks to Sara Ahmed, whose feminist activism and writing inform and inspire every bit of the work in this volume, and whose tremendous generosity in writing for the book evidences her fierce commitment to "living a feminist life."

Contributors

Sara Ahmed is an independent queer feminist scholar of color. Her work is concerned with how power is experienced and challenged in everyday life and institutional cultures. She has just published her first trade book, *The Feminist Killjoy Handbook* with Seal Press (2023). Previous books (all published by Duke UP) include *Complaint!* (2021), *What's The Use? On the Uses of Use* (2019), *Living a Feminist Life* (2017), *Willful Subjects* (2014), *On Being Included: Racism and Diversity in Institutional Life* (2012), *The Promise of Happiness* (2010), and *Queer Phenomenology: Objects, Orientations, Others* (2006). She is currently writing *A Complainer's Handbook: A Guide to Building Less Hostile Institutions*, and has begun a new project on common sense. She blogs at feministkilljoy.com. You can find her on Twitter @SaraNAhmed and Instagram @SaraNoAhmed.

The **Anonymous author of "Survival Analysis"** is a research scientist with twenty years of experience in program and personnel management, fieldwork, data analysis, and mentorship.

The **Anonymous author of "Tall Poppy in the English Field"** is a retired English professor.

The **Anonymous author of "To Make a Fuss"** is an associate professor in humanities and social sciences at a Canadian University. Her main areas of teaching and research fall within South Asian religious traditions, history, and literature.

The **Anonymous author of "Tracking Sexual Predators across Academic Institutions"** is a full professor in the Faculty of Education. Her professional interests include community-engaged, interdisciplinary research, learning, and teaching. She has won international awards for her books and scholarship, as well as for her teaching and innovations.

Francine Banner, Pamela Aronson, Kathleen Darcy, Maureen Linker, Jean-Carlos Lopez, and Lisa A. Martin are current and former faculty and administrators at the University of Michigan–Dearborn. The authors bring an interdisciplinary perspective to their work drawn from sociology, philosophy, criminal justice, women's and gender studies, and public health.

Individually and together, the researchers have authored more than sixty publications that have appeared in academic journals such as *Gender & Society*, *Philosophy and Social Criticism*, *The American Journal of Public Health*, and the *Yale Journal of Law & Feminism*. The authors have presented their work as a research team at national and international conferences and have published the results of their research in *Feminist Criminology*.

M. Emilia Barbosa is assistant professor of Spanish and Latin American Studies in the Department of Arts, Languages, and Philosophy at Missouri University of Science and Technology. She teaches Spanish, Latin American Studies, literature, gender, critical theory, and cinema. Her research interests are in the cultural production of the Americas in Spanish and Portuguese, exploring themes of gender and violence in theater/performance, poetry/spoken word, photography and film, testimony, and multimedia cultural/artistic exhibitions.

Carolyn Carpan is working as a faculty engagement librarian at the University of Alberta Library in Edmonton, Canada. Her current assignments include working with faculty and students in business, education, and law.

Nicole Carr's scholarship focuses primarily on Black maternity, Black feminisms, and the ways in which Black women negotiate their own unique subjectivities vis-à-vis white supremacy. She is currently at work on her first book, *Black Feminist Mothering in the 21ˢᵗ Century Literature: I Am Not Your Mammy*.

Sarah Cheshire is a poet, essayist, hybrid writer, and college English instructor based in Alabama. Her work can be found in *Scalawag*, *River Teeth*, *Creative Nonfiction*, and *Brevity*, among other publications. Author of the award-winning chapbook *Unravelings* (2017), she is an outspoken advocate against sexual misconduct in academia and beyond—and for better support structures for survivors.

Dr. **(Karen) Irene Countryman-Roswurm** is the executive director of the Center for Combating Human Trafficking (CCHT), Institute for Transformative Emancipation (ITE). Grounded in her own lived experiences and direct-practice expertise, Dr. Roswurm is a transformational leader who has committed her life to contemplative, emancipatory efforts that promote kaleidoscopic prosperity for individuals facing various forms of vulnerability, marginalization, and injustice. To learn more about Dr. Roswurm's advocacy and CCHT services, visit https://combatinghuman-trafficking.com/dr-irene-countryman-roswurm/ or https://combatinghu-mantrafficking.com/.

Darlene Demandante has been teaching philosophy for more than ten years. In 2020, she coedited a special issue of *Kritike: An Online Journal of Philosophy* on "Women and Philosophy: An Initial Move Towards a More Inclusive Practice of Philosophy in the Philippine Context." This pioneering collection brought together the writings of Filipina philosophers, illuminating their scholarship as well as their struggles, and resistance against the obstacles hindering women philosophers' progress in the Philippines.

Carlyn Ena Ferrari is an assistant professor of African American literature and affiliate faculty in Women, Gender, Sexuality Studies and African and African American Studies at Seattle University. Her essay " 'You Need to Leave Now, Ma'am' " was published in *The Chronicle of Higher Education* in September 2020. She is the author of *Do Not Separate Her from Her Garden: Anne Spencer's Ecopoetics* (2022). Her essays have appeared in *College Language Association Journal*, *The Chronicle of Higher Education*, *Black Perspectives*, *Consequence Forum*, and *Religion Dispatches*. She hails from the San Francisco Bay Area, and holds a PhD in Afro-American Studies from the University of Massachusetts–Amherst. Outside of academia, she lives for Janet Jackson and Prince. She is a writer and a thinker at heart, so you can find her lost in thought and meditating on the brilliance of Rhythm Nation and Paisley Park.

Christina Gallup, Anne Hinderliter, Njoki M. Kamau, Arshia Khan, Lu Smith, and Elizabethada Wright teach at the University of Minnesota–Duluth in either Swenson School of Science and Engineering or the College of Arts, Humanities, and Social Sciences. They do research and publish on a variety of subjects within the sciences, arts, humanities, and social sciences.

Mary K. Holland is professor of English and affiliate of Women's, Gender, and Sexuality Studies at the State University of New York, New Paltz, where she teaches contemporary literature, theory, and women's writing. She coedited *#MeToo and Literary Studies: Reading, Writing, and Teaching about Sexual Violence and Rape Culture* (2021) and is the author of *The Moral Worlds of Contemporary Realism* and *Succeeding Postmodernism: Language and Humanism in Contemporary American Literature* (2020, 2013). She has published articles and book chapters and given keynote speeches domestically and abroad on a wide array of contemporary writers, and has spoken about and directed teaching workshops on sexual violence at universities across the country. Currently she is coediting *The Oxford Handbook of Postmodernisms*.

Souhir Zekri Masson holds a PhD in English Studies from the University of Strathclyde in Glasgow (Scotland), and is currently assistant professor at the Higher Institute of Applied Humanities of Tunis. Her main research areas include life writing theory, Marina Warner's fiction, gender studies, and spatial theory. In addition to articles focusing on these fields both in Tunisian and foreign journals, her dissertation was published in 2019 as *Mapping Metabiographical Heartlands in Marina Warner's Fiction*.

Raphaella Elaine Miranda teaches at the University of the Philippines, Baguio. Her ongoing graduate research explores the limitations of Theodor Adorno's critical materialism. Concurrently, she writes on critical social theory, feminist philosophy, and philosophy of education.

Rachel Noorda is director of Publishing and associate professor at Portland State University. She grew up in Highland, Utah, and is an alumna of Brigham Young University. Dr. Noorda teaches and researches twenty-first-century book studies, particularly on topics of entrepreneurship, marketing, small business, national identity, and international publishing. With this expertise, she is a series editor for the Business of Publishing strand at Cambridge University Press.

Aimee Parkison is the author of eight books and has taught writing at the college level for over two decades. Recognized for her writing about women and her revisionist approach to narrative, Parkison has taught creative writing at a number of universities. She serves on the FC2 Board of Directors. Her fiction has won numerous fellowships and awards. She currently teaches in the Creative Writing Program at Oklahoma State University.

Nancy Pathak is currently teaching as an adjunct assistant professor at Lady Sri Ram College for women, Delhi University. Without tenure, she is still in a precarious situation in terms of her employment and financial security there. Although her current workplace is wonderful and has ensured her dignity and academic freedom as a gendered minority, she still struggles with the patriarchy and bias in the larger university system.

Lidia M. V. Possas is postgraduate professor in Social Sciences: Identity, Memory and Culture; post-doctorate at the Archivo Provincial de la Memoria in Córdoba/Argentina. She also coordinates Research Group/CNPq–Cultura & Gênero: História, Gênero e Cultura and Interdisciplinary Laboratory of Gender Studies/LIEG-UNESP (http://www.culturaegenero.com.br). She is the author of *Mulheres, Trens e Trilhos: Modernidade no Sertão Paulista* (2001), *O Enigma da Viuvez: Experiências e Sensibilidades—Anos de Chumbo/AL* (2019), and *Dossier I—Violência de Gênero na Universidade* (2022).

Carrie Rohman is professor of English at Lafayette College, working in environmental humanities, animal studies, modernism, gender studies, aesthetics, and performance. Her 2020 essay in the #MeToo and Modernism cluster in *Modernism/modernity* considers gendered and racialized silencing in current academic culture. In 2021 her keynote address at the International Conference on Virginia Woolf directly examined gendered abuse in academia. Coupled with a 2022 companion piece in *Modernism/modernity*, the keynote helped open up discussions about abuse and mobbing in academia. Rohman has published widely in such journals as *Deleuze Studies, Hypatia, American Literature, Comparative Critical Studies, Modern Fiction Studies, Criticism, Mosaic*, and in a number of edited volumes. She is author of the monographs *Choreographies of the Living: Bioaesthetics in Literature, Art, and Performance* (2018) and *Stalking the Subject: Modernism and the Animal* (2009) and is coeditor with Kristin Czarnecki of *Virginia Woolf and the Natural World* (2011). She is on the editorial board of the Palgrave Studies in Animals and Literature series.

Rifat Siddiqui is a third-year PhD student in the Harry W. Bass Jr. School of Arts, Humanities, and Technology at the University of Texas at Dallas. She is a 2019 Bangladeshi Fulbright scholar who completed her MA in Women's and Gender Studies from the University of Northern Iowa. She served as a lecturer in the Department of English at Jagannath University, Bangladesh, before moving to UTD.

Kudzaiishe Peter Vanyoro is a Wits Centre for Diversity Studies (WiCDS) researcher and programs manager at the University of the Witwatersrand in Johannesburg, South Africa. His research and praxis interests are critical diversity studies, diversity and inclusion, gender, sexuality, media(tion), representation, and cultural studies. He has published sixteen peer-reviewed articles and has thirteen undergoing review. He has delivered diversity keynotes locally and internationally. He is also a DEI facilitator. Queer African Studies Association (QASA) and South African Sociological Association (SASA) have recognized his work.

Alison E. Vogelaar, PhD, is an independent researcher, communication consultant and newsletter editor with the Academic Parity Movement. Her research and teaching focus on social movements, activism, and environmentalism from a communication perspective. She is the coauthor of *Reimagining Labor for a Sustainable Future* (2023) and "Care in the Time of COVID-19: Accounting for Academic Care Labor" (2024). She was a member of the faculty of Communication and Media Studies at a liberal arts university in Europe from 2008 to 2021.

Shannon Walsh is a filmmaker and writer. She has directed six feature documentaries on topics ranging from labor rights to grief and climate change, which have been screened around the world. She has also published in a wide range of research areas, including *The Documentary Filmmaker's Intuition* in 2024. She was a Guggenheim Fellow in 2020, and was awarded the Governor General's Award in Visual and Media Art in 2023.

Lori Wright, Neisha Ginae Wiley, Elizabeth VanWassenhove, Brandelyn Tosolt, Rae Loftis, and Meg L. Hensley (authors of "It Is Better to Speak"): Lori, Neisha, Elizabeth, Rae, and Meg met as students in the EdD in Educational Leadership program at Northern Kentucky University. Together, the five authored a collaborative autoethnographic dissertation, which grew out of the course in which they met. The course and their dissertation were supervised by Brandelyn Tosolt (the sixth author). Collectively, they have published in *WSQ: Women's Studies Quarterly* and presented at the International Leadership Association's Women and Leadership Conference. They continue to enact feminist leadership in their student-facing and administrative roles in which they work to dismantle barriers to access and support for learners belonging to oppressed groups such as first-generation, Black and Brown, disabled, and gender-minoritized. Each continues to exercise their *feminist killjoy* muscle, causing what they intend to be *good trouble* across Ohio and Kentucky.

Index

Oria, Shelly, 20n20
Orth, Z., et al., 171

Packer-Williams, Catherine and
  Wendy Williams, 153
Parsons, Elizabeth and Vincenza
  Priola, 214
Pasricha, Josephine Acosta, 109
patriarchy, 9, 10, 13, 16, 46, 107
Perkins, Lori, 20n20
Pittman, Chavella T., 19n3
Polley, Sarah, 163
Possas, Lidia M. V., 191
Pyke, Karen, 137

queer discrimination, activism,
  resistance, 10–11, 45, 121–127,
  222, 239

race, racism, 6–7, 9, 10, 15, 19n5,
  21n30, 34, 80–86, 114–115, 130,
  134–135, 153, 191, 210, 215
rape, 6, 42, 190
rape culture, 165–172, 182, 185–186
Renlund, Dale, 45
Reyes, Victoria, 6, 9, 16, 17, 19n3, 19n4
Rich, Adrienne, 46
Robillard, Amy E., 4, 9, 19n3, 19n5
Rohman, Carrie, 19n6, 21n30
Roos, Patricia A., 19n3
Rosenthal, M. N., et al., 34
Rubenstein, Michael, 123
Rubin, Janice, et al., 114, 116
Russell, Diana E. H., 42
Ryan, M. K., et al., 199

Saba, Fatima, 107
safe space, 13, 95–101, 179, 192
Salsberg, E., et al., 135
Sandberg, Sheryl, 71
Savigny, Heather, 49, 50

Scott, Hannah S., 70
Sered, Danielle, 215
Serisier, Tanya, 6
Settles, Isis H., et al., 19n3
sexual abuse, sexual violence, 5–7, 16,
  91, 114, 167–169, 178, 182, 215
sexual harassment, 5, 7, 10–11, 14–15,
  41, 43, 53, 56, 57–59, 64–66,
  75, 113, 116, 125–127, 144–147,
  166–171, 181–182, 187, 192, 209,
  225, 233, 237
silencing, 15, 16, 21n29, 21n30, 45,
  48, 103, 106, 109, 110, 134–135,
  202, 204, 211, 222, 225, 226
Simpson, Audra, 159
Spry, Tami, 165
Stanley, Liz and Sue Wise, 210
Steck, Henry, et al., 199
Stengers, Isabelle and Vinciane
  Despret, 3
Sweet, Paige L., 122

tenure, tenure process, 3–4, 63–64,
  67, 73–74, 79, 121, 131–132,
  135, 154, 176, 181, 197, 200–202,
  213–214
threats, verbal and physical, 10, 40,
  41, 48, 53, 56, 70, 71, 73, 75, 118,
  124, 133, 134, 146, 169
Title IX, 9, 12, 43, 66, 135, 136, 145,
  199, 212
Towl, Graham J. and Tammi Walker,
  20n18
trauma, traumatic, PTSD, 12, 16, 18,
  20n13, 62, 67, 75, 81, 85, 89, 90,
  127, 129, 134, 139, 151, 159, 163,
  176, 178, 180, 181, 202, 217, 224,
  242
Tsamba, Stephen, 168
Tsuno, Kanami, et al., 75
Turner, Caroline Sotello Viernes, 19n3

www.ingramcontent.com/pod-product-compliance
Lightning Source LLC
Chambersburg PA
CBHW030355270326
41926CB00009B/1123